The Road to Reno

The Road to Reno

A HISTORY OF DIVORCE IN THE UNITED STATES

by NELSON MANFRED BLAKE

GREENWOOD PRESS, PUBLISHERS
WESTPORT, CONNECTICUT

© NELSON M. BLAKE 1962

Second Printing 1962

A Greenwood Archival Edition—reprint editions of classic works in their respective fields, printed in extremely limited quantities, and manufactured to the most stringent specifications.

Originally published in 1962 by Macmillan Company, New York

Reprinted in 1977 by Greenwood Press
A division of Congressional Information Service, Inc.
88 Post Road West, Westport, Connecticut 06881

Library of Congress Catalog Card Number 77-11070

ISBN 0-8371-9797-X

Printed in the United States of America

10 9 8 7 6 5 4 3 2

TO *Jim*

Preface

My father practiced law for many years in a small Massachusetts city. Like most of his colleagues, he neither invited divorce cases nor avoided them when they came his way. Certainly it never seemed to offend his good Methodist conscience to handle such business. I sometimes accompanied him to the county courthouse and watched him try cases. To my youthful eyes, the divorce trials seemed as calm, serious, and dignified as any others. I was brought up, therefore, to regard divorce as a normal legal remedy available to clients who found themselves in unfortunate family situations.

When I moved to New York State, I was impressed by the different atmosphere surrounding divorce. It was not that divorce was less common. At least in the social circles in which I found myself, divorced persons were as frequently encountered in New York as in Massachusetts. But over the landscape of divorce a cloud of embarrassing ambiguity seemed to hang. The idea that any particular divorce had been honestly obtained under New York's conservative law seemed highly unlikely. Just as during Prohibition, one speculated on how the host had obtained the liquor he was serving, so one found himself mildly curious as to how his divorced friend had managed to circumvent the law.

Curious about a situation in which the law seemed to have so little foundation in the actual mores of the population, I looked for a book that would give me the history of divorce in New York. When I found no such work available, I began to gather material for a book of my own. This relatively modest project grew into something larger when I discovered that one could not understand the evolution of the New York law without relating it to the general history of divorce in America. But no adequate history of American divorce appears to have been published since 1904, when George E. Howard's able three-volume *History of Matrimonial Institutions* appeared.

Why has so little been written on the history of American divorce? For one thing, the subject tends to fall between the conventional disciplines. Historians have usually left it to lawyers and sociologists, who have been more interested in the legal complexities and social implications of the contemporary situation than in its historical background. Even more discouraging is the fact that divorce has usually been a state problem rather than a national one. To study the evolution of American divorce has therefore seemed to involve the formidable task of tracing developments in fifty different jurisdictions.

I have tried to avoid these pitfalls as best I could. To discuss every divorce law in every state would confuse rather than clarify my story. So I have concentrated on the main trends, giving particular emphasis to the changing climate of opinion. I have traced developments in New York State in greater detail than those elsewhere, not only because curiosity about the New York law impelled my inquiry in the first place, but because New York conservatism has been the principal factor in creating Reno and other marts specializing in "quickie" divorce.

Many people have helped me in my investigation. Syracuse University granted me a one-semester leave from my teaching responsibilities. Senator Janet Hill Gordon, former Assemblywoman Jane Todd, former Assemblyman I. Arnold Ross, and the Reverend Theodore L. Conklin of the New York State Council of Churches gave generously of their time and allowed me to use material from their files. The following colleagues and friends have read my manuscript, either in full or in part: Dean and Mrs. Ralph E. Kharas, Professor William Park Hotchkiss, and Professor William J. Lloyd. My wife has typed the entire manuscript and shared in the chores of editing. To all these good people and to an unnamed score of helpful librarians, I express my grateful appreciation, while reserving for myself sole responsibility for any errors.

                                                                                    N. M. B.

Syracuse, N.Y.
April 14, 1961

Contents

The Road to Reno

CHAPTER 1

The Land of Make-Believe

On May 12, 1959, Eddie Fisher accompanied by his lawyer and one witness disappeared behind the closed doors of a Las Vegas, Nevada, courtroom. Twelve minutes later the group emerged and revealed to eager reporters the not unexpected news that Eddie had been granted a divorce from his wife, Debbie Reynolds. Except for confiding that he had never been in a courtroom before in his life and had never been so nervous, the young singer was uncommunicative. Judge Zenoff, who had granted the decree, assured the newspapermen that Eddie had "ten times as much evidence as he needed to prove himself a resident of Nevada." The testimony, said the judge, was sealed and would never be revealed, but Eddie's charges against Mrs. Fisher were "more than adequate to qualify him for a divorce in the state of Nevada." Proof that Eddie was really a resident had been provided by Nat Brandwine, an orchestra leader, who testified that he had seen Fisher in Las Vegas on each of the preceding forty-four days—as indeed he must have since they were both appearing at the Tropicana night club.[1]

At sundown, three hours after Eddie's divorce, a Cadillac limousine drove up to Las Vegas's Temple Beth Shalom, and Elizabeth Taylor stepped out. Making her way through excited teen-agers grabbing at her dress for souvenirs, Miss Taylor entered the temple,

where she became the second Mrs. Eddie Fisher. One of the guests
—appropriately enough—was Judge Zenoff. The next day Eddie
and Liz were reported to be at the Waldorf-Astoria in New York
City as the first stop on a honeymoon that would soon take them to
Europe.[2]

To millions of Americans who escaped the drabness of their own
lives by participating vicariously in the romances of screen stars and
television celebrities, this was the latest chapter in a real-life drama
which had begun three and one-half years earlier with the marriage
of Eddie Fisher to Debbie Reynolds at Grossinger's, the famous
Catskill resort in New York State.[3] The public had been delighted.
Pert and vivacious, but appearing at the same time to be fresh and
innocent, Debbie had been one of the most popular young movie
actresses. In the curly-headed, boyish Eddie, then enjoying fabulous
success as a night-club singer and record star, she seemed to have
found an ideal mate. Some time later when television viewers were
given an opportunity to visit the young couple in their Hollywood
home through Edward R. Murrow's Person-to-Person program, the
impression of idyllic happiness was confirmed. They seemed like two
charming and precocious children playing house, and this illusion
was more confirmed than destroyed when in due time Debbie gave
birth to two children.

Those who read the movie magazines were well aware that the
Fishers' closest Hollywood friends were the Mike Todds. Mike was a
colorful producer of spectacular movies, and his wife, Elizabeth Taylor, was famous not only as a talented actress but as one of the
world's most beautiful women. "Liz" was reputed to have had a
somewhat tempestuous personal life—she had been married and
divorced twice before, once to Nicky Hilton, playboy son of the
hotel magnate, and once to Michael Wilding, the English actor—
but in the rough and dynamic Todd she was supposed to have
found true happiness at last. All the greater tragedy, therefore, when
Mike's private plane crashed into the New Mexico wastelands in
March, 1958. Sympathizing millions were touched by the news that
Eddie and Debbie had rushed to the side of the grief-stricken Liz
and taken three children into their home during the mourning period. It also seemed highly fitting that Eddie, who had been Todd's
best friend, should accompany the widow to the funeral in Chicago.

But the adoring public was not so certain that Eddie's conduct was commendable, when inquisitive reporters discovered that he was still comforting the Widow Todd five months later—and at Grossinger's, of all places. While Eddie and Liz were enjoying several days of vacation in the Catskills, Debbie was reported to have gone to the Los Angeles airport to meet her husband only to find that he wasn't aboard the New York plane. After all this publicity, it came as no surprise when Eddie did at length return to his Hollywood dream house that he left a short time later, giving to the encamped reporters what seemed to be a classic understatement: "We're having a misunderstanding. We hope to work it out." [4]

Apparently this misunderstanding could not be worked out. On September 10, the couple announced that they had agreed to a legal separation.[5] On February 19, 1959, Judge Roger Pfaff in Los Angeles Superior Court awarded Debbie a divorce on grounds of extreme cruelty.[6] After this event it may seem somewhat superfluous for Eddie to have gone to the trouble of getting a decree of his own in May. The explanation, of course, is simple. Under California law, the divorce would have not become final until February, 1960. Nevada's more generous provisions permitted Eddie and Liz to fly off on their honeymoon a full nine months earlier. As a final token of her forgiving nature, Debbie cooperated by having her lawyer appear for her in the Las Vegas proceedings without contesting the case.

Such was the story of this curious triangle as the public learned it through the newspapers. The truth may well have been more complicated. Liz may not have broken up a happy marriage; there had been earlier rumors of trouble in the Fisher household. Though undeniably indiscreet, Eddie's Grossinger vacation with Liz may have been innocent. All this is irrelevant to the purpose of this book. Our only excuse for reviewing this well known episode is that the private affairs of American celebrities seem to be in the public domain anyway, and this one serves very well to illustrate most of the features that have made Nevada divorces subjects of controversy.

This case illustrates in the first place the unusually short period of residence required for Nevada divorce seekers. In proving that he had been living in the state for forty-four days, Eddie had done more than was necessary—he needed only to have sung at the Tropicana for forty-two. (If Debbie had not helped by being represented through counsel, more time would have been needed.) The facts that the Fishers had been married in the state of New York and that they had maintained their joint home in California were no bar to Judge Zenoff's accepting jurisdiction in the case, nor was the fact that the California courts had already awarded a divorce to Debbie. The secrecy of the proceedings is also notable. Defended as a means of protecting the privacy of the parties and avoiding newspaper sensationalism, Nevada procedure is such that the outsider cannot judge whether its divorces are being granted on really serious grounds or on trivialities. From what the newspapers had said about this particular case, the public was somewhat incredulous that Debbie had been guilty of cruelty or some other offense against Eddie. In the popular judgment, at least, the fault lay the other way. Other features of the Fisher case that many critics found disturbing were the speed of the proceedings, their uncontested character, and Eddie's immediate remarriage.

As counterpart to this familiar story of a Hollywood marriage tangle, let's consider the case of Sadie Brown. She is a real person —perhaps more real than Eddie Fisher because her image has never been distorted in the mirror of mass publicity—but this is not her real name. Since she has little else in the world, she may at least be allowed the privilege of anonymity. At the age of twenty-nine Sadie made a serious, but unfortunately common, mistake: she married a worthless man. Bill—as we shall call him—was a problem drinker. Like many an optimistic woman, Sadie hoped that Bill would settle down into happy domesticity. But some men have no vocation for marriage, and Bill was one of these. He was soon demonstrating the pitiful symptoms of the confirmed alcoholic: inability to hold a job, trouble with the law, and uncontrollable rages. Afraid for her own safety and that of her ten-months-old baby daughter, Sadie finally left him and went back to live with her parents. Quitting the home town, Bill took up a roving life. Only on rare occasions did a qualm of conscience impel him to send a few dollars to his wife for the support of his child.

Realistic enough to know that it was futile to attempt to compel Bill to support her, Sadie adjusted to the situation as best she could. She took a job and left her child in the care of the grandparents.

The situation had been difficult for all concerned, and would become more so as the grandparents grow older and less able to handle a growing girl who needed her mother's guidance. Sadie felt that her first marriage was shattered beyond repair. She dreamed of obtaining her freedom and marrying another man with whom she could make a real home. She would have liked to have more children, but realized that time was running out, since she was now thirty-eight.

If divorce is ever right, most people would concede that it would be justified in Sadie's case. Her first marriage had failed through no fault of her own; she wanted her freedom for an eminently moral reason, so that she might reestablish a home for the child whom she loved.

Unlucky in so much else in life, Sadie had the misfortune to be a resident of New York State. If she had lived in almost any of the other states, she would have had little trouble in getting a divorce. Bill had not given her much, but he had certainly been generous in providing grounds for the dissolution of marriage. He had been habitually intoxicated and extremely cruel; he had failed to support his family and deserted them. But all the overwhelming evidence that Sadie might produce on these points would do her no good in New York State, because she could not prove that Bill had committed adultery—the one ground that the New York divorce law allows.

What can Sadie do now? The only relief to which she is clearly entitled under New York law is a judicial separation, which will confirm her right to live her own life without fear of molestation or injury from her husband, will give her legal custody of the child, and will order the father to support them. With Bill roaming in parts more or less unknown, this remedy is of little value to Sadie, and it withholds from her what she most wants—the right to remarry.

If Sadie follows the example of thousands of other New Yorkers, she will resort to some type of make-believe. Having read about Eddie Fisher, she will of course perceive that by putting up in a Reno motel for forty-two days she too can make believe she is a resident of Nevada and sue for divorce under that state's broad law. But this road to freedom, so easy for Eddie, is almost impossible for Sadie. Her fare out and back and rent for even six weeks in the humblest of rooms plus lawyer's fees will cost more than she can afford; in her case, moreover, Nevada proceedings may be slower because of uncertainty regarding Bill's whereabouts. Needless to say, Sadie will not be paid to sing at the Tropicana while she waits!

Forced by poverty to seek her legal remedies within her home state, Sadie may still resort to make-believe. If Bill, who probably wants to get out of this marriage as much as Sadie does, will come back and cooperate, perhaps they can work something out. For the good of the cause, Bill may be induced to commit adultery. The suggestion is not quite as shocking as it sounds, because all Bill has to do is to pretend to be unfaithful in a sort of ritual or symbolic act. Some private detective may be found to make the necessary arrangements. Bill will go to a hotel room with a professional co-respondent—often a tolerably respectable young woman who does this work in her spare time, like baby-sitting. The young woman, fully clothed, will climb into bed and pull the bedclothes coyly up to her chin. Bill will remove his jacket, necktie, and shirt—and at just this moment by careful prearrangement, Sadie will come bursting into the room accompanied by her detective and another friend. In the subsequent divorce trial Sadie will tearfully tell her story to the judge or official referee, her witnesses will confirm it, Bill will not deny it, and in all probability she will get her divorce, since New York jurists are prone to make believe too.[7]

But since Sadie is fundamentally a very decent girl she may not want to follow this path. Or she may be afraid. Perjury, fraud, and collusion are formidable words, and she may well wish to have no part in such a contrived case.

Sadie may find more interesting possibilities in the annulment laws. As interpreted by New York judges, these are more lenient than those of most states in allowing marriages to be declared void because of some fraud perpetrated by one party upon the other prior to the ceremony. Even though it is now nine years since her wedding, perhaps Sadie can remember something that will prove that Bill tricked her; perhaps he represented himself as a sober, hard-working citizen and concealed the fact of his dissolute habits; perhaps they were married by a judge and Bill reneged on his promise to follow this up with a religious ceremony. Her mother and father may be able to search their memories and come up with some corroborating evidence adequate to satisfy the judge—which may not be too difficult since Bill will not appear to deny anything they say.[8] But this road to freedom obviously flirts with make-believe also. In saying that she would not have married Bill if she had not been deceived in some way, Sadie may be pretending something that is not really so. In any case the New York law encourages her to claim that the real trouble with her marriage is something that occurred before the ceremony rather than after it, whereas the sober truth is that the marriage was hopefully begun but was wrecked because of Bill's uncontrollable drinking and cruelty.

If Sadie's situation becomes too hopeless and unhappy—if she cannot afford an out-of-state divorce and cannot establish grounds for divorce or annulment within the state—she may eventually be tempted to indulge in the most pathetic of all make-believes. She may pretend to be married to some man when she really is not. He may be a deserted husband similarly boxed by the New York law. As a way out of their mutual predicament, they may go to some community where they are not known and live together as man and wife. Sadie may establish middle-class respectability by becoming a model housewife and mother; she may participate happily in neighborhood coffee klatches and bridge clubs; she may become a den mother and PTAer. She may have every domestic virtue, but without a marriage certificate her new world can fall into ruins at any moment. She may unexpectedly encounter some old acquaintance who knows the whole story; the man with whom she is living may die and all the facts may come out when his estate has to be settled. Despite these risks, however, the New York divorce law results in the establishment of many such irregular households.

Nevada with its quickie decrees represents one extreme of the American divorce spectrum; New York with its antiquated law and consequent abuses represents the other. Although the remaining forty-eight states each have their own peculiarities, the divorce laws have nevertheless tended to some rough kind of uniformity. The five most commonly recognized grounds are adultery, desertion, cruelty, felony conviction, and alcoholism. Thirty-nine of the fifty states recognize all five of these; six of the remaining eleven recognize all but one. The five most conservative states from the point of view of the usual grounds are New York, New Jersey, North Carolina, Maryland, and Virginia.

Measured by another yardstick, by the length of residence required before a plaintiff may initiate proceedings, thirty-three states occupy middle ground by requiring one year's residence. Of the eight states with longer requirements, Massachusetts with five years and Connecticut with three are the most conservative. At the other extreme are six states specifying periods of less than six months: Arkansas and Utah require three months; Wyoming, sixty days; Nevada and Idaho, six weeks; Alabama makes no specific requirement at all in cases where both parties accept the jurisdiction of the court.[9]

Why is it so easy for Eddie Fisher to get a divorce in Nevada and so difficult for Sadie Brown to get one—honestly at least—in New York? Why do these and a few other states diverge from the norm of divorce law characteristic of most of the country? The answers to these questions lie largely in the past, and it is to this little-understood phase of social and legal history that this book addresses itself.

CHAPTER 2

The Long Arm of the Past

Although present-day confusion in American marriage law results in large measure from the peculiarities of our federal system, it reflects also a disagreement about the rights and wrongs of divorce that has plagued Western society for two thousand years.

Far from being an invention of Nevada lawyers, easy divorce has roots in the remote past. Athenian husbands might put away their wives at will; Athenian wives could shed their husbands with only moderately greater difficulty. In the early Roman Republic several different types of marriage evolved. In most of these the husband enjoyed a right to divorce his wife at will as part of his general patriarchal authority. Under the strictest patrician form of marriage (*conferreatio*), divorce was very difficult, even for the husband. But long before the birth of Christ a less stringent form of marriage had become almost universal. This was based upon the principle of free contract, from which either party might obtain release without court proceedings by a simple declaration before witnesses.[1]

Stern moralists have sometimes blamed this freedom of divorce for the fall of the Empire. So long as Roman life was stable, Roman institutions stood firm, the argument runs. With the cancer of divorce came the decay and death of Roman society. Yet this explanation is obviously too simple. Freedom of divorce existed for centuries without weakening healthy Roman family life, and this freedom does not appear to have been abused until wealth and luxury had already undermined the sterner Roman virtues. Even in these later days, moreover, it would be as misleading to assume that the cynical marriage and divorce practices of the capital were duplicated throughout the provinces as to leap to the conclusion that Hollywood morals are identical with those of Kansas.

Jewish custom strongly resembled that of early Rome in recognizing the full authority of the husband and allowing him to divorce his wife at will. As codified in Deuteronomy, the traditional Mosaic law provided that if a wife found no favor in her husband's eyes because of something unseemly in her, he was to give her a bill of divorce and send her out of the house, after which she might marry another man.[2] The prevailing school of broad construction held that this power of the husband was unlimited: he could divorce his wife for any reason at all; a strict constructionist minority argued that the husband could do so only on the grounds of the wife's adultery.[3]

It was against this background of Jewish controversy that a Pharisee, according to Matthew's Gospel, challenged Jesus by asking: "Is it lawful to divorce one's wife for any cause?" The reported reply has been of momentous consequence in the history of divorce:

He answered, "Have you not read that he who made them from the beginning made them male and female, and said, 'For this reason a man shall leave his father and mother and be joined to his wife, and the two shall become one'? So they are no longer two but one. What therefore God has joined together, let not man put asunder." They said to him, "Why then did Moses command one to give a certificate of divorce, and to put her away?" He said to them, "For your hardness of heart Moses allowed you to divorce your wives, but from the beginning it was not so. And I say to you: whoever divorces his wife, except for unchastity, and marries another, commits adultery." [4]

Unfortunately for Christians trying to follow the letter of their Lord's teachings, the exact meaning of these words has been vigorously disputed by theologians and commentators, beginning with the earliest Church Fathers and continuing to the present. The passage from Matthew just quoted contains ambiguities, and these points become still more doubtful when Matthew's account is compared with those of Mark and Luke.[5] For each of the following statements some reputable ancient or modern authority could be cited:

1. Christ taught the indissolubility of marriage and forbade all divorce.
2. He allowed divorce, but only to the husband, and only for one cause, adultery.
3. He allowed divorce for adultery to both husband and wife.
4. Neither party to a divorce may marry again while his former mate is still alive. To do so is adultery.
5. The innocent party may remarry, but not the guilty.
6. Both parties may remarry, after sincere repentance.
7. Adultery means only one thing, the sexual intercourse of a married person with someone other than the husband or wife.
8. Adultery is a symbolic word, standing for any sin that violates the marriage contract.

If Paul's Epistles are consulted, the confusion is increased. Although the apostle opposes divorce in general, he appears to tolerate it in one instance. In discussing the problem of the Christian yoked to a pagan husband or wife, he approves the continuance of the union so long as the unbelieving partner consents to it. "But," adds Paul, "if the unbelieving partner desires to separate, let it be so; in such a case the brother or sister is not bound. For God has called us to peace." [6] On this so-called "Pauline privilege" the commentators have also placed their different interpretations:

1. When a non-Christian husband or wife no longer wishes to live with his Christian partner, the two may separate but the Christian may not remarry.
2. In cases of such separation the Christian is at liberty to marry again.
3. This "Pauline privilege" refers only to the relations of Christian and pagan.
4. It covers also any act of willful desertion by a wicked partner of his innocent husband or wife.

5. It covers not only desertion but any serious violation of the
   marriage contract.

So far as the Western Church was concerned, the masterful St.
Augustine cut through these ambiguities and laid the foundations
for the uncompromising doctrine to which the Roman Catholic
Church has been ever since committed. In his treatise, "The Good
of Marriage," Augustine writes: "Once, however, marriage is entered
upon in the City [that is, Church] of our God, where also from the
first union of the two human beings marriage bears a kind of sacred
bond, it can be dissolved in no way except by the death of one of
the parties." [7] And in a later passage, he explains: "The good, therefore, of marriage among all nations and all men is in the cause of
generation and in the fidelity of chastity; in the case of the people
of God, however, the good is also in the sanctity of the sacrament.
Because of this sanctity it is wrong for a woman, leaving with a divorce, to marry another man while her husband still lives, even if
she does this for the sake of having children." [8]

The word "sacrament," which St. Augustine uses somewhat
vaguely, came to have much more explicit connotations in the work
of later theologians like Peter Lombard and St. Thomas Aquinas.
Marriage was included among the seven sacraments because of its
mystic significance: it symbolized the never-ending union of Christ
with his one spotless spouse, the Church. St. Paul had written:
"Husbands, love your wives, as Christ loved the church and gave
himself up for her, that he might consecrate her, having cleansed
her by the washing of water with the word, that the church might
be presented before him in splendor, without spot or wrinkle or
any such thing, that she might be holy and without blemish. . . .
'For this reason a man shall leave his father and mother and be
joined to his wife, and the two shall become one.' This is a great
mystery, and I take it to mean Christ and the church. . . ." [9]

Holy though the married state was, Catholic doctrine held celibacy in still greater esteem. St. Paul had sounded a fateful note
when he wrote: "To the unmarried and the widows I say that it is
well for them to remain single as I do. But if they cannot exercise
self-control, they should marry. For it is better to marry than to be
aflame with passion." [10]

St. Augustine expounded upon this at length. "It is a good to marry," he wrote, "since it is a good to beget children, to be the mother of a family; but it is better not to marry, since it is better for human society itself not to have need of marriage." [11] He was not afraid to push this argument to its logical conclusion, explaining: "But I know what they murmur. 'What if,' they say, 'all men should be willing to restrain themselves from all intercourse, how would the human race survive?' Would that all men had this wish, if only in 'charity, from a pure heart and a good conscience and faith unfeigned.' Much more quickly would the City of God be filled and the end of time be hastened." [12]

In Catholic teaching the chief end of marriage was defined as the procreation of children; the secondary end was the avoidance of sin through fornication and adultery. Thus Catholic doctrine was somewhat ambivalent: on the one hand, marriage was sacred, but, on the other, the need for it was rooted in the frailty of human nature. In the subsequent history of marriage and divorce, it was a fact of no little significance that a celibate clergy was attempting to provide moral guidance and legislation for their fellow Christians who had chosen to marry.

The mere fact that the indissolubility of marriage was now proclaimed by theologians, church councils, and popes did not assure that divorce would disappear from Western society. Even after Christianity became the official religion of the Roman Empire, divorce continued to be available under the old forms. Husband and wife could separate by mutual consent, or one partner could on his own initiative declare the marriage at an end. Under Roman law, marriage continued to be an entirely private arrangement, over which neither church nor state had any coercive power. The courts were involved only insofar as the property rights of the parties were concerned, and it was in this area that the new Christian teachings had their only legal influence, as divorce for insufficient cause was now penalized by forfeiture of this or that pecuniary interest.[13]

The German tribes who invaded the Empire and finally established their own independent kingdoms brought with them folk laws under which marriage was also considered a private concern with the husband enjoying the right to put aside one wife and marry another at will. Under the influence of Roman customs the Germans later adopted the practice of divorce by mutual consent. After the Germans were converted to Christianity, the right of divorce and remarriage was somewhat restricted, yet neither popular custom nor the law was in harmony with the strict teachings of the Church.

To deter her communicants from divorcing their mates and remarrying, the Church had of course a powerful weapon in her power to withhold the sacraments from those deemed to be living in sin. Yet even within her own jurisdiction she sometimes found it necessary to compromise her principles. In a manual for English priests, prepared in the seventh century under the authority of Theodore, the Archbishop of Canterbury, divorce with the privilege of remarriage was allowed for several causes. A husband, deserted by his wife, might marry again after five years, if he received his bishop's permission. Even a pope could occasionally nod: in 726 Gregory II addressed a letter to St. Boniface, permitting a man whose infirm wife was unable to perform her conjugal duties to marry again.[14]

But from the standpoint of Catholic history, this was the hour of darkness just before the dawn. Under the pious Charlemagne and his successors, the state undertook to back up the discipline of the Church. With the spiritual arm thus supported, the bishops' courts grew steadily in power, carving out for themselves an extensive jurisdiction that included all issues arising out of marriage. The ecclesiastical, or canon, law administered in these courts was a vast miscellany deriving not only from such religious authorities as the Scriptures, the writings of the Church Fathers, the decrees of the popes, and the pronouncements of Church councils, but also from Roman law and Germanic custom. The great task of collecting the canon law and reducing it to a coherent whole culminated around 1148 in the *Decretum*, compiled by the Italian monk Gratian in a Bologna monastery.

Although divorce in the modern sense was not permitted, the canon law—somewhat to the confusion of later discussion—did retain the Latin word *divortium*. What the canonists called *divortium a vinculo* (divorce from the bonds of matrimony) is in modern parlance annulment; what they called *divortium a mensa et thoro* (divorce from bed and board) is judicial separation, or limited divorce without the privilege of remarriage. Separation from bed and board was the only remedy allowed by the canon law for causes arising after marriage. Three grounds were recognized: adultery, "spiritual adultery," and cruelty. Spiritual adultery was a somewhat vague term, but was usually interpreted to mean the heresy or apostacy of one of the parties to the marriage.[15]

Since medieval husbands like their modern counterparts sometimes wanted to get rid of their wives and marry other women, the ecclesiastical courts were under frequent pressure to grant annulments. Because of the complexities of the canon law dealing with impediments to marriage, numerous grounds for such petitions were available.

In the first place, marriage might not take place between parties who were in some way related to one another. Not only was a man forbidden to marry his own blood relatives: mother, sister, daughter, aunt, niece, first cousin, second cousin, and third cousin; but neither might he wed those related to him by affinity, that is his deceased wife's mother, sister, aunt, and cousins of various degrees. Still other impediments were created when a man had illicit sexual relations. Not only was he prohibited from marrying his guilty partner but also any of her female relatives. The matter became still more complicated through the teaching that spiritual affinities were created through baptism: a man might not marry his godmother, his godchild, the woman who had stood godmother for any of his children, or any of their female relatives.[16] It is little wonder that a husband who wanted to get rid of his wife could usually figure out some obscure relationship that vitiated the marriage.

A second line of attack was on grounds of precontract, that is, the contention that one of the parties was already legally bound to another person. This was a more puzzling issue than one might suspect, because the canon law was somewhat obscure on a most vital point: when did a marriage become a marriage? Borrowing heavily from Roman law, the canonists emphasized the idea of contract: the essential step was the exchange of mutual promises by the bride and groom. Indeed, the celebration of the marriage ceremony in the church was a somewhat late development in Christian history. At first, couples continued to exchange vows in the home; later the ceremony took place at the doors of the church. The priest's role— highly important but not essential—was to be present during the exchange of vows and to give the couple his benediction. The newly-married couple then entered the church to receive communion at a bridal mass. In the final stage of evolution, sometime after 1300, the priest's role became the vital one of pronouncing the parties man and wife, and still later the whole ceremony was moved into the church.[17]

But this assumption of ecclesiastical authority did not clarify the status of every couple. Even though the participation of a priest might be required for a *legal* marriage, that is, one assuring the legitimacy of the children and the property rights of the parties, it was not essential to a *valid* one. A man and woman might form an indissoluble union by simply exchanging promises without the presence of priest, parents, or witnesses. Canon law on this point was full of subtleties. The binding character of such clandestine vows depended in part on the intentions of the parties; it depended also on grammatical niceties: "I *will* take thee to be my wife" was a *sponsalia per verba de futuro*, a contract for future marriage from which the parties might be released; "I *do* take thee to be my wife" was, on the other hand, a *sponsalia per verba de praesenti*, or actual marriage contract, which usually bound the parties and barred them from marrying anyone else. Impetuous swains sometimes learned the differences between tenses through chastening experience.[18]

Whether or not a clandestine marriage was valid depended to some degree on whether it was followed by *copula carnalis*, or physical union. The canonists did not entirely agree on the importance to be laid on *copula carnalis*: a marriage solemnly contracted might be indissoluble even though it had never been consummated; on the other hand, a mere promise of future marriage might be transformed into an indissoluble union if it were followed by sexual intercourse. In doubtful cases, therefore, it became a point of great importance to determine whether *copula carnalis* had actually occurred—an issue to which the ecclesiastial judges addressed themselves with commendable thoroughness.[19]

Annulments might be granted on still other grounds. If one of the parties could be proved to have been impotent or insane at the time of the wedding, the marriage was invalid; if these conditions developed later, however, there was no remedy. Marriages were also invalid if force or fraud had been employed so that the element of free consent was lacking. The Pauline privilege was interpreted to permit the remarriage of a Christian deserted by an infidel spouse.[20]

Ecclesiastical marriage law was made even more complex by the practice of papal dispensations. These were necessary because of the far-ranging character of the impediments themselves. To forbid all third cousins to marry might make marriage almost impossible in certain isolated medieval villages where most of the population was to some degree related. Even more difficult would it have been for European royalty or the higher nobility to arrange marriages entirely free from some taint of consanguinity or affinity. In relaxing the ecclesiastical rules to permit particular unions, the popes were therefore acting wisely, since the whole system would have broken down if it had not been given a degree of flexibility. Nevertheless, the practice exposed the Church to recurrent accusations of selling her favors—particularly since a carefully graduated scale of fees was established, depending upon the social status of the applicant and the seriousness of the impediment. Moreover, even the fact that a dispensation had been granted did not entirely guarantee that the marriage could not be annulled. If it could be proved that the Pope had been misled or that the document was improperly drafted, the marriage might still be dissolved. There was also a possibility that in granting some particular dispensation the Pope might have exceeded his power, since some of the impediments to marriage were regarded—at least by many theologians—as so serious as to allow for no exceptions.

Ironically therefore, medieval Europe had a divorce problem, even though in theory it had no divorce. Whatever the technicalities by which the deed was accomplished, it was notorious that wealthy husbands had little difficulty in putting away their wives and marrying other women. Around 1100, St. Anselm was grieved to hear that in Ireland men exchanged wives "as publicly and freely as horses." Some ninety years later Petrus Cantor of the University of Paris lamented that "for money's sake, at our own choice, we clergy join or separate whom we will." About 1380, the Dominican Bromyard complained that "nowadays, when a wife displeases, or another woman is coveted, then a divorce is procured." In England the unknown author of the poem *Piers Plowman* wrote bitterly that a man could get rid of his wife by giving the judge a fur coat;

church lawyers, he added, "make and unmake matrimony for money." [21]

Great issues sometimes hung on these medieval annulments. While King Louis VII of France and his Queen, Eleanor of Aquitaine, were in the Holy Land on the Second Crusade, they began a quarrel that culminated in Louis's seeking an annulment three years after their return to France. In 1152, a church council dissolved the marriage on the ground that Louis and Eleanor were related in the seventh degree of consanguinity.[22] Louis's great-great-great-great grandmother had been the sister of Duke William IV of Aquitaine, from whom Eleanor was descended. So absurd was this contention, even for its day, that it was regarded as mere pretext. Gossipy chroniclers speculated on the couple's real reasons for seeking release. Had the high-spirited Eleanor been unfaithful? Was she plotting to marry another man? Was Louis disgruntled over Eleanor's failure to produce a male heir to the throne? Whatever the cause, the consequences were momentous. Within a year after the annulment, Eleanor married Henry Plantagenet, Count of Anjou, soon to become King Henry II of England—thus bringing under potential English control some of the choicest fiefs in France and creating a situation that led to many decades of war between the two countries.

The ancient documents reveal many curious matrimonial tangles. In 1426, for example, Pope Martin V granted a dispensation permitting Alexander Home and Marion Lauder, Scottish third cousins, to marry. But young love is impatient, and Alexander and Marion evidently did not wait for the slow Church machinery to operate. In 1428, a new papal dispensation was necessary, for reasons that the document itself best reveals. Without permission the couple had exchanged vows, consummated their union, and begotten children. When knowledge of this sin came to their bishop, he had annulled the marriage. But the penitents petitioned that "if they remain divorced much scandal may arise," and so the Pope granted the couple permission to remarry and legitimatized their offspring.[23]

To protect the inheritance rights of children in cases of annulment, it was often important to establish the fact that the parties had not been aware of the impediment when they contracted the marriage. In another Scottish case of 1459, the documents show that six arbiters were chosen to arrange the pleadings in just the proper form to protect the interests of the offspring. The Earl of Rothes was to swear "that he knew of late, within the year last past, and had certain knowledge of the impediment of consanguinity set forth in his libel, and that formerly he was altogether ignorant thereof, vizt., for the space of 13 years after the birth of Sir Andrew Leslie, Knight, the last of the children then alive, procreated betwixt the said Earl and his spouse." [24]

The annulment was sometimes preceded by an arrangement between the parties. A surviving agreement of 1486 declares that:

whereas the said Richard Willoughby wrongfully took away and married Jane, late the wife of John Saucheverell, against her will, as she says, she having made a pre-contract with the said William Zouche, as he and she allege, it is agreed that if the said William or Jane will sue in Court Spiritual before a competent judge against the said Richard to have a divorce according to the laws of Holy Church between him and the said Jane, Richard shall appear to show his interest in the premises and to obey the judgment without appeal.[25]

Willoughby must have put himself clearly in the wrong, because the document goes on to stipulate that his mother is to pay William Zouche and Jane damages in the amount of twenty pounds immediately and certain additional sums in the future.

Catholic marriage doctrine received its most important restatement and clarification at the Council of Trent. The resolutions adopted in 1563 were in large part devoted to condemning the heretical teachings of the Lutherans and the Calvinists. Anathema was solemnly declared upon anyone asserting that marriage was not truly and properly one of the seven sacraments, that it was not better to remain in virginity or in celibacy than to be united in matrimony, or that the indissolubility of wedlock was not a necessary consequence of its sacramental character.

The Council's most important pronouncement on the specific issue of divorce was worded thus:

If any man shall say that the Church errs when she teaches as she has taught in accordance with evangelical and apostolic doctrine, that the bond of marriage cannot be dissolved on account of the adultery of either party; or when she teaches that neither of them, even an innocent party who has not given the cause of adultery, can contract another marriage while the other party lives; or when she teaches that the husband who puts away an adulterous wife and marries another, and also the wife who puts away an adulterous husband and marries another is guilty of adultery, let him be anathema.[26]

Yet at the same time the Church clung to a wide area of discretion in the matter of annulment. The Council denied that the Church's power to establish impediments to marriage was limited to the Levitical degrees of consanguinity and affinity and pronounced anathema upon anyone who said that the Church had no power to dispense with some of these impediments or establish others of equal force to prohibit or void marriages.[27]

Despite the uncompromising character of these assertions of doctrine, the Council of Trent did admit the validity of some criticisms being made of the Church's actual practices. As one measure of reform, the Council sensibly limited the affinities created through baptism to the parties immediately participating in the ceremony.[28] As another, it limited the affinity arising out of illicit sexual intercourse to the guilty parties themselves and their relatives of the first and second degrees.[29] Most important of all, as a curb upon clandestine marriages and many of the abuses arising out of allegations of precontract, the Council made the presence of a priest and two witnesses essential to a valid marriage. Not equally necessary, but, nevertheless, sternly enjoined were such additional safeguards as the proclaiming of the banns, public celebration of the wedding in the church, and the pronouncing of the couple as man and wife by the priest.[30]

In the eleven centuries since St. Augustine's day the Church had struggled doggedly to establish the principle of the indissolubility of marriage. This effort had been more successful in theory than in practice. Despite her prohibition on absolute divorce, the Church's willful children had frequently been able to manipulate the machinery of annulment to dissolve their marriage contracts and make new ones. Yet the Church could console herself with the thought that without her efforts things would have been worse. In challenging the traditional right of the husband to cast off his wife at will, medieval Christianity had contributed to the dignity and stability of family life and given women needed protection in an age of violence.

CHAPTER 3

Impact of
the Protestant Revolt

When the Protestant reformers broke with the Roman Catholic Church, they used as one line of justification the abuses alleged to abound in Catholic handling of marriage affairs. According to these Protestant critics, priests mocked their vows by living with concubines and were in effect licensed to do so by their bishops; ecclesiastical authorities refused honest divorces but tolerated innumerable irregular connections; and church courts displayed venality in granting annulments to wealthy laymen on farfetched allegations of affinity and precontract.

The Protestants had no difficulty in identifying the evils they sought to correct, but it was a harder task to develop new theories and practices of their own. Radicals might hope to throw out the whole canon law and return to older Jewish and Roman principles, but social conservatives instinctively clung to many of the basic concepts of the canonists.

Both conservatives and radicals drew comfort from the writings of Martin Luther. The great German explicitly denied that marriage was a sacrament. Asking the question, "What is the proper procedure for us nowadays in matters of marriage and divorce?" he answered that "this should be left to the lawyers and made subject to the secular government." Marriage was "a secular and outward thing, having to do with wife and children, house and home, and with other matters that belong to the realm of the government, all of which have been completely subjected to reason." [1] On the other hand, marriage was not to be taken lightly; it was "a splendid institution and a matter of divine seriousness"; it was not only an honorable but a necessary state. "It is earnestly commanded by God that in every condition and station in life men and women, who were created for it, should be found in this estate." [2] Except for a very few, the unmarried state was an undesirable condition. For this reason, Luther condemned clerical celibacy, practicing his own teachings by marrying a former nun and begetting six children.

In commenting on Jesus' teachings on divorce, Luther explains: "Christ is not functioning here as a lawyer or a governor, to set down or prescribe any regulations for outward conduct; but He is functioning as a preacher, to instruct consciences about using the divorce law properly, rather than wickedly and capriciously, contrary to God's commandment." [3]

Luther accordingly distinguishes sharply between what the law may permit and what the Christian ought to do. The law may sensibly permit rather liberal divorce, since it is better to allow "wicked and unmanageable people" to be divorced than to let them do worse by "vexing or murdering each other or by living together in incessant hate, discord, and hostility." [4] But he goes on to admonish: "Those who want to be Christians should not be divorced, but every man should keep his own spouse, sustaining and bearing good and ill with her, even though she may have her oddities, peculiarities, and faults." This is not an absolute principle; Luther interprets the Scriptures to sanction the Christian's right to seek absolute divorce in cases of adultery or desertion, and limited divorce without the privilege of remarrying for other causes. According to Luther, the Christian ought to practice forgiveness and reconciliation wherever possible, but if the guilty party persists in his bad conduct, it is he who has dissolved the marriage and the innocent party should be completely free.

In a characteristically blunt passage, Luther extends desertion to cover the case of the husband or wife who unreasonably refuses to meet his partner's sexual needs:

One spouse may rob and withdraw himself or herself from the other and refuse to grant the conjugal due or to associate with the other. One may find a woman so stubborn and thickheaded that it means nothing to her though her husband fall into unchasteness ten times. Then it is time for the man to say: If you are not willing, another woman is; if the wife is not willing, bring on the maid. But this is only after the husband has told his wife once or twice, warned her, and let it be known to other people that her stubborn refusal may be publicly known and rebuked before the congregation. If she still does not want to comply, then dismiss her. . . .[5]

On the disputed question of whether the guilty party should be permitted to marry again, Luther is realistic. An adulterer deserves death, but since the civil authorities are not likely to be this stern, let the guilty one "flee to a distant land and there marry, if he cannot be continent."

The Swiss reformer Ulrich Zwingli went further than Luther in countenancing divorce. In the Zurich marriage ordinances of 1525, divorce is allowed for adultery, malicious desertion, and plotting against the life of the other partner to the marriage. The judges are also permitted to take into account such other possible causes as cruelty, insanity, and leprosy.[6]

John Calvin was more cautious, yet the Geneva Ecclesiastical Ordinances of 1541 allowed divorce for the two causes of adultery and malicious desertion. Calvin agreed with Luther that the adulterer ought to be put to death, but that if he was allowed to live it was better to permit him to marry again.[7]

The subsequent history of divorce in Protestant Europe is a confused one. The old ecclesiastical courts lost their authority, yet in many places clergymen kept a hand in the decision of matrimonial cases through the consistorial courts composed of both lay and ecclesiastical members. Many of these local jurisdictions were conservative: some allowed divorce only on the one ground of adultery; the majority recognized the two grounds of adultery and desertion. But the seeds of a greater liberalism had been sown, and the trend was toward broadening the grounds for divorce and bringing these cases under purely secular courts. Under the influence of eighteenth century rationalism, a few lawmakers gave up all pretense of grounding the divorce law on Biblical authority. In

Prussia under Frederick the Great, divorce was allowed to childless couples by mutual consent and to others on a variety of specific grounds.[8]

For a long time, it was uncertain just what effect the English Reformation would have on marriage and divorce law. The notorious marital tangles of Henry VIII well illustrated the ambiguities of the old canon law. The willful Tudor was first married to the Spanish princess Catherine of Aragon. Advantageous on dynastic grounds, the marriage was of dubious legality, because Catherine was the widow of Henry's brother Arthur—and had not the Mosaic law declared: "You shall not uncover the nakedness of your brother's wife?" [9] For the time being, Henry's scruples were adequately eased by the dispensation granted by Pope Julius II sanctioning the marriage. But after Catherine's six rounds of pregnancy had produced only one live child—and that a girl—the king began to doubt whether his marriage was valid after all. Learned theologians, not only in England but also on the Continent, gave their opinion that the Pope's dispensing power had not extended to so grave a transgression of the moral law. A point of consequence was whether the fifteen-year-old Arthur had consummated his marriage with the eighteen-year-old Catherine, or whether—as Catherine claimed—she had come to Henry's marriage bed a virgin.[10] Since these intimate events had occurred over twenty years before, determination of the facts was obviously difficult.

At first Pope Clement VII seemed not inhospitable to the suggestion that his predecessor's action might be declared invalid because of some technical flaw in the document. He probably would have acquiesced in the annulment except for one uncomfortable fact: he was the virtual prisoner of Catherine's nephew, the powerful Emperor Charles V. Clement's resort to delay, first by authorizing a trial in England, then by ordering the case referred to Rome, finally provoked the impatient Henry with the support of a complacent Parliament to repudiate the papal authority. Once this was done, the English clergy did not long delay in interpreting the canon law to support the king's cause. The Archbishop of Canterbury, Thomas Cranmer, who had been elevated to his high post largely because of his support of the king, solved Henry's problems, first by declaring invalid the king's marriage to Catherine of Aragon and then by upholding his union with Anne Boleyn, in ample time to give the stamp of legitimacy to the birth of the future Elizabeth I in September, 1533.

Conservative on theological issues, Henry VIII had no intention of allowing the Church of England, now set loose from Rome, to follow the leadership of Luther or Calvin. The ecclesiastical courts continued to exercise jurisdiction over matrimonial cases in accordance with existing canon law. In 1540, Parliament tried to correct annulment abuses by providing that no prohibition, "God's law except," should trouble or impeach any marriage that did not violate the Levitical degrees of relationship.[11] This closed the door to suits based upon the more exotic types of affinity, but later legislation unfortunately revived the troublesome doctrine of precontract.

Since a clarification and revision of the canon law was much needed, Henry obtained Parliamentary support for entrusting this responsibility to a committee of thirty-two theologians and lawyers under the chairmanship of Archbishop Cranmer. After many years of study the committee had largely completed its work when Henry died in 1547. Recommissioned under the youthful Edward VI, the committee finally brought in a report in 1552. A combination of circumstances—opposition in the House of Commons, the illness and death of the king, and the succession of the Catholic Mary Tudor to the throne—prevented the revised canon law from being put into effect. Nevertheless, the *Reformatio Legum Ecclesiasticarum* is a document of importance in showing the ideas of the early English reformers.

The *Reformatio Legum* departed sharply from the old canon law by abolishing separation from bed and board in favor of absolute divorce with the right of remarriage for the innocent party. The recommended grounds were adultery, desertion, cruelty, several years' absence with presumption of death, and "such violent hatred as rendered it in the highest degree improbable that the husband and wife would survive their animosities and again love one another." [12] The influence of Luther and the other continental reformers was clearly at work in the *Reformatio Legum*. Especially influential were the liberal ideas of Zwingli, which had made their way into England through the writings of Henry Bullinger, his disciple and successor at Zurich. In Bullinger's *The Christian State of Matrimonye,* translated into English in 1541, divorce is described as "permitted of god for the welth and medicine of man and for amendment in wedlock." [13] Even more advanced in his defense of divorce was Martin Bucer, German reformer of Strassburg, who became professor of divinity at Cambridge University in 1549. In a pamphlet dedicated to Edward VI, Bucer contended that the Lord "did not only permit, but also expressly and earnestly commanded his people . . . that he who could not induce his mind to love his wife with a true conjugal love, might dismiss her, that she might marry to another." [14]

Another precedent of importance was laid down in 1548, when a commission of churchmen headed by Archbishop Cranmer considered the case of Lord Northampton, brother of Queen Catherine Parr, the sixth and last wife of Henry VIII. After Lord Northampton had been granted an ecclesiastical separation from his first wife on grounds of adultery, he attempted to contract a second marriage. Cranmer's commission upheld the validity of this second union on the ground that "the former contract had been absolutely destroyed" by the first wife's infidelity. In 1552 this decision was confirmed by an act of Parliament declaring the marriage valid "by the law of God,—any decretal, canon ecclesiastical, law, or usage to the contrary notwithstanding." [15]

For the next fifty years English custom apparently tolerated the remarriage of innocent parties divorced on the ground of adultery. Although conservative moralists deplored the practice and the legal rights of second wives and their children remained dubious, something equivalent to absolute divorce appeared to be taking root. This drift was halted by the Foljambe case of 1602, when a court declared such a second marriage invalid. This decision followed the recommendations of an ecclesiastical commission headed by the conservative John Whitgift, Archbishop of Canterbury, who pronounced "in harmony with the ancient law that remarriage after judicial separation is null and void." [16] Stricter canons and statutes punishing bigamy emphasized the return to the old theory of the indissolubility of marriage.

The victory of the conservative party was bitter medicine to the Puritan faction. Although the issue of marriage and divorce was less important than questions of general church government and practice, it nevertheless continued to be a subject of fitful controversy. Some Puritans like Thomas Cartwright attacked the ecclesiastical courts and demanded that the decision of matrimonial cases should be entrusted to the civil magistrates.[17] William Perkins in the *Christian Oeconomie*, originally written in Latin in 1590 and translated into English in 1609, advocated the granting of divorces for four causes: desertion, malicious dealings, long absence, and adultery. Perkins was in advance of many writers of his day in recognizing the wife's right to divorce on an equal basis with the husband's.[18]

The Separatists, or Independents, more radical than the Puritans on many issues, took advanced ground on the matter of marriage and divorce. Marriage they regarded as a purely civil affair to be contracted by the parties in the presence of witnesses without any religious ceremony. Reverting to Old Testament authority, some Separatists taught the right of private divorce. On grounds sanctioned by the Scriptures, the husband might give his wife a bill of divorce, appealing to the civil magistrates only to confirm his action. Although English law did not sanction private divorce, it appears to have been occasionally practiced during the early seventeenth century.[19]

All this is background for John Milton's famous pamphlet *The Doctrine and Discipline of Divorce, Restored to the Good of Both Sexes from the Bondage of Canon Law and Other Mistakes*. First published in 1643, while the English Civil War was in progress, this tract was an appeal both to the Westminister Assembly of Divines and to the Long Parliament. More radical than any of his Christian predecessors, Milton broadens the grounds for divorce to include "that indisposition, unfitness, or contrariety of mind, arising from a cause in nature unchangeable, hindering and ever likely to hinder, the main benefits of conjugal society, which are solace and peace." [20] Divorce for incompatibility he considers to be especially appropriate when there are no children and both parties consent to the separation. He also strongly asserts the right of private divorce:

But the popes of Rome, perceiving the great revenue and high authority it would give them even over princes, to have the judging and deciding of such a main consequence in the life of man as was divorce, wrought so upon the superstition of those ages, as to divest them of that right, which

God from the beginning had entrusted to the husband: by which means they subjected that ancient and naturally domestic prerogative to an external and unbefitting judicature. For although differences in divorce about dowries, jointures, and the like, besides the punishing of adultery, ought not to pass without referring, if need be, to the magistrate; yet . . . the absolute and final hindering of divorce cannot belong to any civil or earthly power, against the will and consent of both parties, or of the husband alone. . . .[21]

To modern minds, Milton's argument is disturbing insofar as it exalts the husband's rights over those of his wife. Nor is the great Puritan always convincing when he resorts to hairsplitting exegesis in an attempt to marshal Scriptural authority for his thesis. Despite such defects, Milton's pamphlet contains passages of striking beauty and eloquence. Condemning the idea that "to grind in the mill of an undelighted and servile copulation must be the only forced work of a Christian marriage," Milton holds that "it is a less breach of wedlock to part with wise and quiet consent betimes, than still to foil and profane that mystery of joy and union with a polluting sadness and perpetual distemper: for it is not the outward continuing of marriage that keeps whole that covenant, but whatsoever does most according to peace and love, whether in marriage or in divorce, he it is that breaks marriage least: it being so often written, that 'Love only is the fulfilling of every commandment.' " [22]

Was Milton's fervent defense of divorce motivated by his own marriage troubles? Many students have so assumed, noting that the poet's seventeen-year-old bride Mary Powell deserted him during the summer of 1643 to return to her father's household. But other careful investigators are convinced that Milton wrote his tract before this unhappy event occurred.[23] However this may be, it is true that Milton and his young wife were not finally reconciled until two years later, and in the interval he continued to agitate the divorce question with three more pamphlets.

These later writings display all the vigor of the original tract. In *Tetrachordon* Milton considers the famous words: "What therefore God hath joined, let not man put asunder," and asks: "Shall we say that God hath joined error, fraud, unfitness, wrath, contention, perpetual loneliness, perpetual discord; whatever lust, or wine or witchery, threat or incitement, avarice or ambition hath joined together, faithful and unfaithful, Christian with anti-christian, hate with hate, or hate with love; shall we say this is God's joining? . . . In a word, if it be unlawful for man to put asunder that which God hath joined, let man take heed it be not detestable to join that by compulsion which God hath put asunder." [24]

Milton's advocacy of the right of private divorce without restriction from Church or State, was too advanced for most of his fellow Puritans. Indeed many of them denounced his writings as scandalous and wanted to suppress them. Without influence on immediate policy, the tracts had their greatest impact long after Milton's death. Nineteenth century American liberals quoted them frequently.

The Assembly of Divines, dominated by the Presbyterian or conservative wing of the Puritan movement, dealt with divorce in the Westminster Confession of 1648 in these words:

> Nothing but adultery or such wilful desertion as can no way be remedied, by the church or civil magistrate, is cause sufficient of dissolving the bond of marriage, wherein a public and orderly course of proceeding is to be observed, and the persons concerned in it not left to their own wills and discretion in their own case.[25]

By contrast with the position taken by the Independents and by Milton, this stand was decidedly conservative. Yet by Catholic and Anglican standards the Presbyterians had moved into dangerous territory by sanctioning divorce on any grounds.

In Scotland the Westminster Confession gave religious approval to practices already adopted. Scottish courts had assumed the power to grant absolute divorce soon after the break with Rome. At first adultery was the only ground, but in 1573 the Scottish parliament added that of desertion.[26] The fact that the Scottish and English laws were different led in time to legal tangles not unlike those of twentieth century America. In 1817 a writer deplored the not uncommon practice of English husbands or wives establishing domicile in Scotland by only forty days' residence and suing for divorce, often with the collusion of the other party. "But," he warned, "if the Courts of England do not recognize a decree of the Scots Consistorial Court dissolving a marriage in England, many painful and disagreeable consequences may result." [27]

In England the Presbyterian sanction of divorce was curiously devoid of practical consequences. Cromwell's Civil Marriage Act of 1653 required all weddings to be performed before justices of the peace and registered by the civil authorities, but it failed to incorporate the logical corollary of assigning divorce jurisdiction to the secular courts.[28] Evidently the Puritans were too divided on this issue to legislate effectively.

The opportunity for action was lost with the restoration of the monarachy in 1660, and for another two centuries the English law of divorce continued to be the canon law as administered by the ecclesiastical courts. In practice this was much more rigorous than it had been before the Reformation. In the words of John Cordy Jeaffreson, an authority on English marriage customs:

. . . our ancestors lived for several generations under a matrimonial law of unexampled rigour and narrowness. The gates of exit from true matrimony had all been closed, with the exception of death. Together with the artificial impediments to wedlock, the Reformation had demolished the machinery for annulling marriages on fictitious grounds. Henceforth no man could slip out of the matrimonial bondage by swearing that he was his wife's distant cousin, or had loved her sister in his youth, or had before his marriage stood godfather to one of her near spiritual kindred.[29]

The only type of divorce available was separation from bed and board, and in accordance with a canon of 1603 this remedy was not granted unless the plaintiff gave bond not to marry again during the lifetime of his former mate.[30]

Jeaffreson regards this insistence upon the indissolubility of marriage to have been, not a victory for the purity of English family life, but a moral disaster. "The profligacy of Charles the Second's court," he says, "is far more referable to the restraints on divorce, than to the revolt against Cromwellian Puritanism." [31]

Gradually a path to absolute divorce did open up, but it was available only to the rich and influential. In 1669, Parliament passed a bill permitting Lord Roos, to whom an ecclesiastical court had already granted a divorce from bed and board, to marry again. The debate on the issue was spirited, and Charles II—suspected of toying with the idea of divorcing his own wife—attended daily in the House of Lords, declaring the spectacle to be "better than going to a play." [32] The next case occurred in 1692, when the Duke of Norfolk attempted to divorce his wife on a charge of adultery. At first the House of Lords balked, probably because of the Duke's own unenviable reputation as a ladies' man, but after failing to win his case in 1692 and 1693 the persistent peer finally succeeded on a third attempt in 1700.[33] Meanwhile a third petitioner, the Earl of Macclesfield, had obtained a parliamentary divorce in 1698.[34] At first parliamentary divorce was rare: only five were granted prior to 1715. Therafter the rate picked up: from 1715 through 1775 there were 60; from 1776 through 1800, 74; from 1801 through 1850, 90.[35]

By 1800 the procedure to be followed in parliamentary divorce cases had been incorporated into standing rules. Each case was thoroughly investigated by the House of Lords, and the plaintiff's petition would not be considered unless he had first been granted a separation from bed and board on the ground of adultery by the ecclesiastical courts. He was further required in most cases to have successfully prosecuted an action for damages against his wife's lover.[36] Three trials were thus required for absolute divorce: one in the church court, one in the civil court, and one in the House of Lords.

Difficult and expensive for husbands, this path to divorce was almost impassable to wives. In a woman's case it was not enough to prove her husband's adultery: she had also to show that he had aggravated his offense by extreme cruelty or some other infamous conduct. Only three or four women were ever successful in such cases.[37] The eighteenth century point of view is amply illustrated by the famous Dr. Samuel Johnson's remarks upon the subject of adultery:

. . . Confusion of progeny constitutes the essence of the crime: and therefore a woman who breaks her marriage vows is much more criminal than a man who does it. A man, to be sure, is criminal in the sight of God: but he does not do his wife a very material injury, if he does not insult her; if, for instance, from mere wantonness of appetite, he steals privily to her chambermaid. Sir, a wife ought not greatly to resent this. I would not receive home a daughter who had run away from her husband on that account. A wife should study to reclaim her husband by more attention to please him. Sir, a man will not, once in a hundred instances, leave his wife and go to a harlot, if his wife has not been negligent of pleasing.[38]

The injustice of a situation in which the wealthy might obtain divorce but the poor could not became steadily more manifest during the nineteenth century. It was not until 1857, however—and then over the die-hard opposition of the devoutly Anglican William E. Gladstone—that Parliament finally stripped the ecclesiastical courts of their divorce jurisdiction and established a new Court for Divorce and Matrimonial Causes. The English law was still conservative, granting absolute divorce to husbands only on the ground of adultery and to wives only when their husbands' adultery was coupled with cruelty, desertion, or other offenses. Judicial separation was allowed to either husband or wife on the grounds of adultery, cruelty, or two years' desertion.[39] Further liberalization of the British law had to wait until the twentieth century.

CHAPTER 4

Divorce in
the American Colonies

When the first English settlements were planted in the New World, the English Puritans were still debating the subject of marriage and divorce. In Virginia this did not matter, because conservative Anglicanism remained dominant for several generations, but in New England the situation was altogether different.

Symbolic of new attitudes was the first marriage solemnized at Plymouth. The groom was Edward Winslow, who had lost his first wife seven weeks earlier during the colony's first terrible winter; the bride was Mrs. Susanna White, recently widowed under similar circumstances. The ceremony was thus described by William Bradford:

> May 12 [1621] was the first marriage in this place which, according to the laudable custom of the Low Countries, in which they had lived, was thought most requisite to be performed by the magistrate, as being a civil thing, upon which many questions of inheritance do depend, with other things most proper to their cognizance and consonant to the Scriptures (Ruth iv) and nowhere found in the Gospel to be laid on the ministers as a part of their office.[1]

In 1635 when the same Edward Winslow was in England on colony business, he was sharply interrogated by Archbishop Laud on the marriage question. Winslow admitted that as a magistrate he had joined several couples himself. He stoutly defended his right to do this on the ground that "marriage was a civil thing and he found nowhere in the Word of God that it was tied to the ministry." The magistrates, he explained, had had to perform the ceremony, because for a long time there had been no regular minister in the colony. "Besides," Winslow added, "it was no new thing for he had been so married himself in Holland by the magistrates in their Statt house." [2] So incensed was the Archbishop at this reply that he ordered Winslow to be locked up in the infamous Fleet prison for seventeen weeks.[3]

Civil divorce was the natural corollary to civil marriage, but this issue did not arise at Plymouth for some time. In 1661 the first case occurred when the General Court, or colonial legislature, granted a divorce to Elizabeth Burge on the ground of her husband Thomas's adultery—a crime for which he was sentenced to be severely whipped, first at Plymouth and again at Sandwich. The next case, that of William Tubbs of Scituate, is interesting, because he apparently attempted to cast off his unfaithful wife in Old Testament style by giving her a bill of divorcement written out and witnessed by his neighbors. But although do-it-yourself divorce had been strenuously defended by Milton and other English Independents, the Plymouth authorities would have none of it. They held the bill of divorcement to be invalid and fined the presumptuous witnesses. In 1668 the unhappy Tubbs finally obtained a proper divorce through the General Court. Only four other divorces were granted during the remainder of Plymouth Colony's independent existence ending in 1692.[4]

The Boston Puritans agreed with the Plymouth Separatists on the question of civil marriage. Not only did they require all marriages to be solemnized by the magistrates, but in 1647 they even forbade the preaching of a wedding sermon, because, said Governor John Winthrop, "we were not willing to bring in the English custom of ministers performing the solemnity of marriage, which sermons at such times might induce." [5] Not until 1692 did Puritan prejudice on this issue finally relax to the point that the General Court gave permission for ministers as well as justices of the peace to perform the marriage ceremony.[6]

In the earliest surviving compilation of Massachusetts laws, that of 1660, there is provision for the civil trial of divorce cases. "For the better administration of justice and easing of the Country of unnecessary charges and travaile," reads this ancient statute, it is ordered "that there be two Courts of Assistants, yearly kept at Boston, by the Governour, Deputie Governour and the rest of the Magistrates, to heare and determine all and onely actions of appeale from inferior Courts, all Causes of divorce, all Capital and criminal cases, extending to life, member or banishment. . . ." [7] It is uncertain just when this measure was originally passed, but the context indicates that it may have been as early as 1639.

The law did not say what type of divorce was to be granted or on what grounds. Probably the Court of Assistants followed its own discretion. In 1639, that body declared void the marriage of James Luxford on the excellent ground that he already had another wife. To support the victimized woman and the children born of the invalid union, Luxford was stripped of all his possessions, and he was further punished by fine, exposure in the stocks, and banishment to England. Four years later the Assistants granted a divorce to Anne Clarke, because her husband Dennis had deserted her and was living with another woman.

Some forty Massachusetts divorce cases have been discovered for the years 1639 to 1692, and there may have been more, because the records are incomplete. Most of these were decided by the Court of Assistants, but the colonial assembly did not hesitate to grant divorces on its own or to overrule the Assistants upon appeal. Ignoring English ecclesiastical law, the Massachusetts magistrates granted either absolute divorce or none at all. In addition to adultery and bigamy, they recognized such grounds as desertion, impotence, and affinity.[8]

The first period of Massachusetts history ended with the loss of the original charter in 1684; and a second began with the issuance of the second charter in 1691, intended to give greater authority to the King. But under the new dispensation civil marriage and civil divorce were immediately reinstated. The act of 1692 for "the Orderly Consummating of Marriages," allowed ministers as well as justices of the peace to perform the ceremony, laid down strict requirements for registering all marriages with the civil authorities, and specified that "all controversies concerning Marriage and Divorce shall be Heard and Determined by the Governeur and Council." [9]

Two or three years later the Cambridge Association, composed of the most influential clergymen in the colony, took up the question: "In what cases is a divorce of the Married justly to be pursued and obtained?" The divines agreed that "to judge, determine and accomplish a divorce . . . the civil magistrate is to be addressed or concerned." They then specified seven grounds upon which a marriage might be dissolved: impotence, bigamy, adultery, incest, fornication before marriage with a relative of the present husband or wife, malicious desertion, and long absence with the presumption of death. On two questions controversial among Christian theologians, the Massachusetts group took forthright positions. On one of these, they declared:

In case of a *malicious desertion* by a married person, who is obliged and invited to return, a divorce may be granted by lawful authority unto the forsaken. For the word of God is plain, "that a man is not bound in such cases" by the marriage unto one which has thus willfully violated the covenant; and tho' our Saviour forbids "a man's putting away his wife, except it be for fornication," yet he forbids not rulers to rescue an innocent person from the enthralling disadvantages of another that shall sinfully go away.

And on another oft-disputed point, they said:

A divorce being legally pursued and obtained, the innocent person that is released may proceed unto a "second marriage in the Lord:" otherwise the state of believers under the New Testament would in some of these cases be worse than what the God of heaven directed for his people under the Old.[10]

In a region where many men took to the sea in search of a livelihood, it was not uncommon for some never to return. Presumably their ships had gone down in some fierce storm with all hands lost, but occasionally a vessel foundered on some remote coast, where the shipwrecked crew survived for years until they were finally by accident discovered. Massachusetts law provided as fairly as it could for the unhappy wives, whose husbands disappeared to

an unknown fate. In a statute of 1694 prescribing the death penalty
for bigamists, an exception is made for those who marry when
husband or wife has been absent for seven years.[11] In 1698 the waiting period was reduced and the procedure to be followed was
clarified.

If any married person, Man or Woman, has lately or shall hereafter go
to Sea in a Ship or other Vessel bound from one Port to another where
the Passage is usually made in three months time, and such Ship or other
Vessel has not been or shall not be heard of within the space of Three full
Years . . . the matter being laid before the Governour and Council . . .
the man or woman whose Relation is in this manner parted from him or
her, may be esteemed single and unmarried; and upon such Declaration
thereof, and License obtained from that Board, may lawfully marry
again.[12]

Although data on Massachusetts divorces from 1692 to 1760 are
sketchy, the records for the period 1760 to 1786 are apparently complete. Scholars who have studied the manuscripts find that during
these twenty-six years the Governor and Council heard 96 cases. In
only two or three of these did they deny any relief, but in ten they
ordered separation from bed and board instead of divorce. The revival of this old canon law remedy apparently resulted from the conservatism of the magistrates in dealing with cases where the wife
complained of her husband's cruelty but did not charge him with
adultery.[13]

Unlike Massachusetts, Connecticut specified the grounds upon
which divorce might be granted. In 1667, four grounds were recognized: adultery, fraudulent contract, willful desertion for three
years "with total neglect of duty," or seven years' absence of one
party without being heard of after due inquiry had been made. For
any of these causes the Court of Assistants might issue a bill of
divorce, and the innocent party was then free to marry again.[14]
These four grounds remained in effect throughout the rest of the
colonial period, but jurisdiction in divorce cases was transferred
from the Assistants to the new Superior Court in 1711.[15]

Legislative divorce, rare in Massachusetts, was more common
in Connecticut. In 1655 the General Court gave ear to the "sad
complaint" of Goody Beckwith of Fairfield and directed a court

sitting at Stratford to give her a divorce if they found it to be true that she had been deserted by her husband Thomas. Two years later the assembly dissolved the marriage of Robert Wade of Seabrook, because of his wife Joane's "unworthy, sinfull, yea, unnatural cariage" in staying in England and "disowning fellowship" with him for "neare fifteen yeares." [16] In the case of Elizabeth Rogers, freed by the General Court in 1676, the principal grievance against the husband John seems to have been his "hettridox" opinions in renouncing "all the vissible worship of New England" and declaring the Christian Sabbath to be "a mere invention." [17] Eleven legislative divorces have been discovered for the period 1655 to 1691, but there were only two or three during the rest of the colonial period. Only in hardship cases where no relief was available under the general statute did the General Court intervene. [18]

But if the General Court gave fewer divorces during the eighteenth century, the ordinary courts gave more. Benjamin Trumbull, a Congregational minister writing in 1788, complained that about 390 Connecticut couples had been divorced in the preceding half-century. [19]

Rhode Island—ever a difficult child from the standpoint of Boston and Hartford—went its own way in divorce matters as well as in other things. Its first step was surprisingly conservative. In 1650 the General Assembly ordered that no bill of divorce shall stand legal, "butt that which is sued for, by the partie grieved"—that is no self-divorce—and not "for any other case but that of Adulterie." The General Assembly reserved to itself exclusive jurisdiction in divorce cases. Five years later the colonial legislature opened a wider exit from marriage by ordering "that in case of adulterie, a generall or towne magistrate may grant a bill of divorce against ye partie offendinge uppon ye demand of ye partie offended." In all other cases of separation or divorce, the parties were to address themselves to the assembly. In 1685 the General Assembly specified that five years' neglect or absence should be a ground for divorce, but in 1749 this period was lengthened to seven years. [20]

Legislative divorces during these early years were not uncommon. In 1655 the Rhode Island General Assembly considered three divorce cases, only one of which involved a charge of adultery. One of the others was based on desertion, and the legislature ordered Thomas

Gennings to "goe and demand his wife to live with him"; if she refused, he was to report the fact to the legislature. The other is a case whose liberal disposition would have pleased John Milton. John and Elizabeth Coggeshall, who had parted by "mutuall and voluntarie consent," were each granted permission to take new partners. But the colonial assembly was not always so generous. In 1667, Richard and Mary Pray jointly petitioned for a dissolution of their marriage, but they were allowed only a separation without right of remarriage —the only such limited divorce that has been discovered.[21]

There were two roads to divorce in Rhode Island after 1663 when the government was regularized by a royal charter. The Court of Trials, composed of the governor and the assistants, exercised divorce jurisdiction until 1747, when these cases were transferred to the Superior Court. But although legislative divorce became less common, the lawmakers never renounced their power to grant relief in exceptional cases.[22]

The last of the New England colonies, New Hampshire, followed the lead of neighboring Massachusetts in its treatment of marriage questions. Petitions for divorce were usually considered by the governor and council, but a few legislative divorces were granted after 1766.[23]

The situation in Virginia was in striking contrast to the one in New England. Not only did ministers have the right to marry from the beginning, but the Anglican parsons were given exclusive authority to do so—much to the discontent of the other denominations that eventually infiltrated the colony. According to legal theory, the Virginia colonists, like those elsewhere, took with them all the laws of the mother country that were suited to their new circumstances. Marriage and divorce, therefore, were still covered by English ecclesiastical law. This did not permit absolute divorce, but it did allow judicial separations from bed and board on two grounds, adultery and cruelty. A legal remedy, however, is of little avail, unless there is some court to handle such cases. Here the difficulty was obvious. There were no bishops in colonial America and hence no ecclesiastical courts.

By one of those paradoxes so common in legal history, a misused Virginia wife might be able to get alimony even though she could not get divorce or judicial separation. In 1691, for example, the governor and council referred the prayer "of Ruth Fulcher for separate maintenance against her husband, John Fulcher" to the justices of the county court, "who, after hearing the testimony, decided in favour of the plaintiff." In this and subsequent cases, the reasoning apparently was that every wrong ought to have some remedy, and that in aggravated cases the courts might assume the power to grant separate maintenance as a matter of equity. This was dangerous doctrine, as legal purists will recognize, but it offered the colonial judges some rationalization for awarding limited relief to litigants unable to get either absolute or limited divorces.[24]

In the other Southern colonies—Maryland, North and South Carolina, and Georgia—the situation was similar to that in Virginia. Although civil marriage was sometimes permitted, particularly in the earlier years, there was no provision made for divorce. The equity courts did, however, usually assume a power to compel an erring husband to pay for his wife's support.[25]

The Middle Colonies—New York, New Jersey, Pennsylvania, and Delaware—were middle not only in geographical location, but in many of their institutions. Neither Puritan nor Anglican, except in certain local situations, these settlements drew their population and their customs from a variety of sources.

During the period of Dutch rule New Netherlands witnessed an occasional divorce. In 1655 John Hickes of Flushing presented a petition to the colonial council alleging that his wife Hardwood Longh:

ran away from him and has been married to another man for about nine years and has procreated by him 5 or 6 children, he therefore requests that whereas his wife has broken the bonds of marriage (without his having given any occasion for it) he may be authorized and allowed to enter with some virtuous maiden or widow into the holy estate of marriage, according to political and ecclesiastical law.

Finding "that John Hickes according to divine and secular law cannot be refused his request," the council granted him "letters of divorce" and authorized him to marry "some honest maid or widow." [26]

John Hickes's case is of unusual interest, because the other side of the story, that of the allegedly adulterous wife, happens to have been preserved in the records of Rhode Island. In 1665, Horrod

Long—as the name is more plausibly spelled in this document—
presented a long complaint to certain royal commissioners then in
the colony. She asserted that she had been brought to Massachusetts
about 1637 as the unhappy thirteen-year-old bride of John Hickes.
About three years later they moved to Rhode Island, and not long
after, Horrod continued, "there happened a difference betweene
the said John Hickes and myselfe, soe that the authority that then
was under grace, saw cause to part us, and ordered I should have
the estate sent me by my mother." If Horrod's story is true, this
is the earliest known Rhode Island divorce. She goes on to relate
how Hickes defied the colony's order by running off to New Netherlands, taking most of Horrod's property with him. Left almost des-
titute, she became the common-law wife of one George Gardner,
bearing him "many children" over the next twenty years. But
George too became a problem, refusing either to support her or
leave her alone. Hence her appeal to the authorities in 1665 for
separate maintenance. The royal commissioners were touched by
her story and requested that the governor "doe justice to the poore
petitioner." But the assembly viewed the matter quite differently:
Horrod and George were each fined twenty pounds and warned in
the future not "to lead soe scandalous a life, lest they feel the ex-
treamest penalty that either is or shall be provided in such cases." [27]

New Netherlands records contain two other clear cases of divorce. In 1657, the council granted a decree to Jon Baldingh on the
ground of the adultery of his wife Abigail. In 1664, it released
Anneke Adriaens, whose husband Aert Pietersen Tack had "not
hesitated to marry another woman at Amsterdam in Holland." [28]

After the English conquest in 1664, divorces continued to be
granted for the next eleven years. The so-called Duke's Laws, under
which the colony was governed for a time, dealt with divorce only
indirectly. One clause provided that in cases of long absence where
a husband or wife had been traveling "into any forraigne Parts"
and had not been heard from in five years, "it may be justly pre-
sumed such Person is Dead and . . . the other is free to Marry." [29]
Another stipulated that in cases of adultery, "all proceedings shall
bee according to the Lawes of England, which is by divorce (if
sued), Corporal punishment or fine or imprisonment." [30]

This reference to divorce from bed and board was of dubious

meaning, because New York, no more than the other colonies, had ecclesiastical courts. But this lack did not inhibit the early English governors, who apparently felt within their powers in handling divorce cases in accordance with earlier Dutch precedents. In 1669, somebody—the records are not clear as to who—granted a divorce to William Bogardus on the ground that his wife had engaged in "carnall copulacon with a stranger." [31] That same year Governor Francis Lovelace annulled the marriage of Eleazer and Rebecca Leveridge, after "surgeons" had examined Eleazer and reported him to be impotent. The governor gravely stressed the fact that in consequence Rebecca had not received

due benevolence from ye said Eleazer according to ye true Intention of Mattrimony The great end of wch is not onely to Extinguish those fleshly desires & appetites incident to Humane nature but likewise for ye well ordering & Confirmation of the Right of meum & tuum to be devolved upon ye Posterity lawfully begotten betwixt man & wife according to ye Laws of ye Land & practise of all Christian Nations in that Case provided.[32]

The affair of Thomas Pettit in 1672 sheds more light on the way in which these early cases were handled. When Thomas accused his absent wife Sarah of "defiling the marriage bed and committing adultery with several persons," his charges were considered by the Court of Assizes, which ordered, "That whensoever ye Said Sarah shall bee found within this Government, shee shall bee committed to Prison, there to remaine untill the next Cort of Sessions or Assizes, when shee shall be prosecuted & receive punishment as the Law doth direct for the Crime of Adultery." The Court also recommended to Governor Lovelace that he grant Thomas a divorce. This the governor proceeded to do, asserting his action to be "Conformable to the Lawes of the Government as well as the practice of the civill law, & the laws of our nation of England in such cases provided." Thomas was pronounced "to bee discharged & acquitted from the Matrimonniall Contract . . . to all Intents & purposes whatsoever; for the wch this present Writing & recording thereof shall bee an absolute and Authentick Bill of Divorce." [33]

Governor Lovelace granted two more divorces in 1672, and Governor Edmond Andros still another in 1675. There were probably more, but only tantalizing clues of these have survived from the New York State Capitol fire of 1911 which badly damaged the colonial records. In addition to these awards of absolute divorce, there were two or three cases where the colonial courts granted judicial separation with separate maintenance.[34]

After 1675, the governors apparently decided that this assumption of divorce jurisdiction was of doubtful legality. There is no clear evidence of any further divorces being granted in New York for the rest of the colonial period. The only clue to the contrary is contained in a somewhat obscure item in the colonial records of 1711. In that year one Jean Cast wrote a letter to Governor Robert Hunter, concerning a trip that he had made to inspect the German Palatine settlement east of the Hudson. The Palatines, an unhappy displaced persons group, had been transported to this site by the British government to be employed in the gathering of naval stores. To the governor, Cast reported:

> I have drawn up the necessary notices for the dissolution of the two Marriages mentioned by Mr. Hayer [probably a Palatine pastor] to Your Excellency, and have presented them to Mr. Livingstone who says, he is not a Magistrate of that Country where the Palatines live, that his jurisdiction is between his Manor and Albany, that application must be made to Mr. Dirck Wessellse ten Broeck. The interested parties desiring the prosecution of these proceedings, I shall address myself accordingly, without giving any explanation for fear of displeasing the honest people, and affording greater encouragement to the wicked in their wickedness; for the good are a long time wishing for the establishment of an effective police which they do not find in the person of an absent judge.[35]

Without further data, it can only be inferred that as late as 1711 the New York governors were receiving divorce petitions which they probably handled by ordering local magistrates to investigate after giving due notice to the interested parties.

Whatever Governor Hunter did about these particular cases, it is clear that the door to divorce in New York colony was almost, if not entirely, locked. One highly intelligent leader regretted this turn of events. Writing in 1759, Cadwallader Colden, physician and colonial official, noted the fact that the governors of New York had once granted divorces but had not exercised this power since the

Revolution of 1688-1689. Nor was there any court in the colony that could give this remedy "tho' in the neighboring colonies a divorce is more easily obtained than perhaps in any other Christian country." Colden then asked:

. . . whether this may not be for the advantage of a new Country which wants people[?] It is certain that the natural increase of People in New England has been very great perhaps more than in any other of the English Colonies.[36]

The divorce history of colonial New Jersey is even more obscure than that of New York. Settled by a great variety of colonists, some of whom like the Dutch and the Puritans looked upon marriage as a dissolvable civil contract, New Jersey took at first a liberal position. Even divorces by mutual consent were recognized: one such was granted to Marmaduke and Mary Potter of Woodbridge in 1676, another to Thomas and Margaret Davies, also of Woodbridge in 1683. Probably the early governors assumed a right to grant divorces as they had in New York, but on this the record is not clear. A new precedent was established in 1772 when the colonial legislature passed an act dissolving the marriage of David and Margaret Baxter. The royal governor, William Franklin (Benjamin's natural son), signed the act, but it was eventually disallowed by the English Privy Council under circumstances presently to be discussed.[37]

In Pennsylvania our story is complicated by the troubled internal history of the proprietorship. In the earliest code, the so-called Great Law or The Body of Laws, proposed by William Penn and approved by an assembly of colonists on December 7, 1682, there is included among the penalties for adultery the statement: "And both he and the woman shall be liable to a Bill of Divorcement, if required by the grieved husband or wife, within the said term of one year after Conviction." Since no judicial machinery was provided to implement this, the injured person would presumably have to appeal to the General Assembly for his remedy.

After a period of controversy in the colony, William Penn came over to straighten out affairs at the end of the century, and in 1700 a number of new laws were passed. Three of these made some provision for divorce as part of the punishment designated for adultery,

bestiality, and bigamy. But under Penn's charter the King and Privy
Council had reserved a power of disallowance, and these three laws
were disapproved in 1705. Meanwhile, however, the Assembly had
enacted four more bills. Now authority to grant divorces was specifically entrusted to the governor or lieutenant-governor in cases of
marriages within the forbidden degrees, adultery, bigamy, and ho-
mosexuality.[38]

Whether the governors actually used this authority to grant divorces, we do not know. In any event, the General Assembly began
to take matters into its own hands in 1769. In that year it passed an
act dissolving the marriage of Curtis Grubb and Anne, his adulterous wife, and permitting him to marry again. After some hesitation
Lieutenant-Governor John Penn assented to the bill. But the Board
of Trade and Plantations considered this transaction to be new and
extraordinary in nature. Thinking it of "very great Importance that
care should be taken that the Assemblies in Your Majesty's Colonies
do not assume the exercise of powers beyond what the nature and
principles of the Constitution admit," they referred the divorce
act to a respected London barrister, Richard Jackson. The latter's
findings were cautious. Noting that British law gave validity to
both colonial and foreign marriages, he concluded that "it seems
as reasonable and as little inconvenient to give Faith to the Dissolution of that Contract under an Equivalent Sanction." Nevertheless,
he advised that the issue be referred to the consideration of the
Attorney General and the Solicitor General. These worthies made
no report, and this particular divorce act was therefore allowed to
stand.[39]

Encouraged by success, the Pennsylvania assembly passed another private divorce bill in 1772, granting a dissolution of marriage
and permission to wed again to George Keehmle, a Philadelphia
barber who charged his wife Elizabeth with adultery. But this time
the British authorities decided to put a curb upon legislative divorce
as "a power which has been rarely and recently Assumed in Your
Majesty's Colonies in America." The officials were particularly disturbed because these divorces were being enacted without any of
the safeguards that surrounded the parallel practice of the British
Parliament. "There does not appear," they complained, "to have
been any Suit instituted in any Ecclesiastical Court, nor any Verdict,

previously obtained in a Court of Common Law." Accordingly, the Board of Trade suggested that if such divorces were deemed to be either "Improper or Unconstitutional, Your Majesty may be advised to give such Directions as shall have the effect to prevent the Laws passed by the Legislature of Pensilvania becoming a Precedent and Example for the Exercise of the like powers in other Colonies." [40]

Acting promptly on this advice, the King and Privy Council disallowed the latest Pennsylvania divorce, and over the course of the next two or three years disapproved three similar colonial acts— one New Jersey divorce of 1772 mentioned above, and two New Hampshire divorce bills passed in 1771 and 1773. What embarrassments were thus caused by upsetting divorces two or three years after the event, we can only imagine.

To nail down the new policy, the British government coupled the divorce problem with another in an instruction sent out to all the royal governors on November 24, 1773:

> Whereas, We have thought fit by our orders in our Privy Council to disallow certain laws passed in some of our Colonies & Plantations in America for conferring the Privileges of Naturalization on persons being aliens, and for divorsing persons who have been legaly joined together in Holy Marriage. . . . It is our expressed will and Pleasure that you do not upon any pretence whatsoever give your assent to any Bill or Bills that may have been or shall hereafter be passed by the Council and Assembly of the Province under your Government for the naturalization of Aliens, nor for the divorce of persons joined together in Holy Marriage. . . .[41]

It would be absurd to think that Thomas Jefferson had the divorce issue in mind when he listed as the first specific grievance against George III in the Declaration of Independence that he "has refused his Assent to Laws, the most wholesome and necessary for the public good." Yet the British government's unwillingness to allow the colonial legislatures to handle this problem according to their own best judgment was probably an additional pinprick in arousing the resentment of colonial politicians against the paternalism of the British system.

CHAPTER 5

The Wine of Independence

In 1788, an anonymous Philadelphia author, disturbed by the news that an unhappy wife had taken her own life, published an *Essay on Marriage*. America had become famous for her love of liberty and hatred of tyranny of every kind. "Therefore," he said, "it is hoped, the same spirit of indulgence will extend still further—to those unhappy individuals, mixed among every class of mankind, who are frequently united together in the worst of bondage to each other, occasioned by circumstances not in their power to foresee, or prevent, at the time of their union; which should entitle them to relief from humane legislators and the rest of mankind." [1] Noting with approval the new sentiment for freeing Negro slaves, the author asked: "But where is there any relief to the miserable, hen-pecked husband, or the abused, and insulted, despised wife? . . . They are not only confined like a criminal to their punishment, but their confinement must last till death." [2] Refuting religious objections, he asked: "Doth God require this sacrifice of our happiness, or in other words, accomplishment of our destruction? or would not this supposition be more applicable to the enemy of mankind, who, they say, goes about like a roaring lion seeking whom he may devour?" [3] Liberal divorce, he argued would decrease suicides, prevent cruelty in marriage and encourage loving care, prevent fraud in courtship, save parents from irreparable sorrow at their children's unsuitable marriages, keep bachelors from avoiding marriage and practicing vice, and provide husbands for girls who could then become virtuous wives. "It would inculcate more friendly and beneficent ideas of the wisdom and goodness of Divine Providence in the disposition of human affairs, and dispose mankind more sincerely to reverence and adore the great Author of their being." [4]

Probably not many Americans were as optimistic as this over the benefits to be gained through freedom of divorce, yet almost everywhere legislators used their newly won powers to relax what they regarded as the undue rigidity of the old English law.

The changed situation was clearly evident in Pennsylvania. Before the Revolution the assembly's willingness to dissolve marriages had been curbed only by the Privy Council's power of disallowance; with that obstacle removed the lawmakers promptly began to pass private divorce bills. Between 1776 and 1785, the General Assembly granted eleven such divorces, most of them involving charges of adultery. [5]

But the Pennsylvania leaders recognized the need to transfer at least some of this business to the courts. In February, 1785, John Dickinson, president of the Supreme Executive Council, included divorce and alimony among the subjects requiring legislation. [6] He submitted the draft of a suggested bill, and the General Assembly eventually passed a divorce statute on September 19, 1785. "Whereas," the preamble asserted, "it is the design of marriage and the wish of parties entering into that state, that it should continue during their joint lives, yet where the one party is under natural or legal incapacities of faithfully discharging the matrimonial vow, or is guilty of acts and deeds inconsistent with the nature thereof, the laws of every well regulated society ought to give relief to the innocent person." Not distinguishing between annulment and divorce, the statute authorized the supreme court to dissolve marriages on four grounds: impotence, bigamy, adultery, or willful desertion for four years. Wives might gain separation from bed and board with alimony in cases where the husband was extremely cruel or was guilty of other misconduct. [7]

The Massachusetts statute or March 16, 1786, was more conservative than the Pennsylvania law. Divorces from the bonds of matrimony were to be granted only for bigamy, impotency, or adultery; divorces from bed and board might be awarded in cases of "extreme cruelty." [8] In failing to permit divorce for desertion, the new statute was less liberal than Puritan practice for more than a hundred years. Perhaps this conservatism reflected the prejudices of professional lawyers indoctrinated with the maxims of English law; perhaps it resulted from the Congregational clergy's retreat from the position taken by their seventeenth century forebears. In 1805, for example, a Congregational church council recorded its conviction that "the Lord Jesus permits no separation except for the cause of adultery." [9]

Elsewhere in New England the trend was in the opposite direction. Connecticut continued to permit divorce on the four grounds of its colonial law; New Hampshire passed a statute in 1791 granting divorce to either party on four grounds: impotency, adultery, extreme cruelty, or three years' absence, and also to wives in cases of abandonment and failure to provide for three years.[10] Vermont made provision for divorce even before it achieved statehood and in 1798 redefined the grounds as impotence, adultery, intolerable severity, three years' willful desertion, or long absence with presumption of death.[11] Rhode Island's law of the same year provided four similar grounds, and also included a broad authority to the courts to grant divorces in cases of "gross misbehaviour and wickedness in either of the parties, repugnant to and in violation of the marriage covenant." [12]

In New York and New Jersey the lawmakers proceeded more cautiously. The New York law of 1787—to be more fully discussed in the next chapter—permitted divorce on the one ground of adultery. The New Jersey statute of December 2, 1794, empowered the court of chancery to grant absolute divorce in cases where the parties were related within the degrees prohibited by law, or where either had been guilty of adultery or of "wilful, continued and obstinate desertion for the term of seven years." Separation from bed and board was the remedy provided for either party in cases of extreme cruelty.[13]

The new trans-Appalachian states made provision for divorce early in their history. Tennessee, for example, enacted its first general statute in 1799, Ohio in 1804, and Kentucky in 1809. Each granted absolute divorce on grounds of adultery and desertion, and each defined one or two additional grounds such as cruelty or imprisonment for crime.[14]

The states of the Old South were much slower to entrust divorce jurisdiction to their regular courts. With dubious wisdom they followed the English example of allowing absolute divorce only by special act of the legislature. After a slow start these legislative divorces poured out in a steady stream after 1820.

In Maryland one of the earliest cases was that of John Sewell, to whom the legislature granted a divorce in 1790 on the ground that his wife Eve had born a mulatto child—an evidence of guilt so damning that both wife and child were sold into slavery in accordance with Maryland law. In 1805, the lawmakers came to the relief of Susanna Alexander, who had married again on the "well founded report" that her first husband was dead. Two years later they released Pamela Sampson from her husband George, because she had long lived "on terms incompatible with the happiness of the conjugal union, which every day, if possible, increased owing to intoxication whch deranged his mind." On the following day the legislature granted the same relief to Catherine Dunmett, whose husband James was in "one continuous state of intoxication." [15] Twenty years later the legislature was still very much in the divorce business. "Hail, Wedded Love!" scoffed the *Cleveland Herald* in 1827, noting that the Maryland lawmakers had passed seven private divorce bills in a single day.[16] In the 1835 session the legislature voted 31 divorces, and in 1836, 36 more. Not until 1842 was full jurisdiction in such cases given to the regular Maryland courts, and not until 1851 was the Maryland legislature prohibited from passing private divorce bills.[17]

In Virginia events followed a similar course. In 1803, the legislature dissolved the marriage between Benjamin Butt, Jr., and Lydia Bright, "who is of a respectable family, and was at the time of the said marriage supposed to be unsullied in her reputation," but "not long thereafter, the said Lydia was delivered of a mulatto child, and has since publicly acknowledged that the father of the said child was a slave." [18] The legislature continued to pass about one divorce bill a session until 1808 when the number suddenly jumped to five. Sometimes the ground was stated, sometimes not. The humiliation of Henrietta, wife of Daniel Rose, is perpetuated in an act of 1806:

not only had she given birth to a mulatto child seven months after her marriage, but "there are reasons to believe that since her intermarriage she has permitted a negro slave, the supposed father of the said child, to have a carnal intercourse with her." [19] The misdeeds of one Martin Kimberland are similarly stated in a divorce bill of 1809: he had been suspected of trying to shoot his father-in-law but had been acquitted in a Virginia court, only to move on to Kentucky where he had been convicted of horse stealing and served a prison term; after that he had disappeared to parts unknown.[20]

Feeling a need to regularize its procedures, the Virginia legislature enacted a statute in 1827, authorizing the court of chancery to annul marriages that were invalid because of impotency, idiocy, or bigamy and to grant divorces from bed and board for adultery and cruelty. Still reserving to itself sole power to grant absolute divorce, the legislature stipulated that there must be a jury trial in the superior court to ascertain the facts in each case.[21] In 1848, legislative divorce was finally prohibited in Virginia, and the courts were empowered to grant absolute divorce on the ground of adultery. Five years later the law was liberalized to recognize such other causes as impotency, imprisonment, conviction for an infamous offense prior to marriage without the knowledge of the other party, being a fugitive from justice for two years, desertion for three years, or evidence that the wife had been pregnant by another man at the time of her marriage, or that she had been a prostitute.[22]

Virginia's experiment in combining judicial process with legislative divorce was anticipated by Georgia, whose constitution of 1798 permitted two-thirds of each branch of the legislature to pass acts of divorce, but specified that this might be done only after the parties had had a fair trial before the superior court and obtained a verdict authorizing a "divorce upon legal principles." [23] But what were these legal principles? On this point much confusion was destined to arise, even though the Georgia legislature had formally adopted the English common law by act of 1784.[24] Ignoring this crucial issue, the legislature passed a statute providing for jury trial of the facts but reserving for itself sole power to grant absolute divorce.[25]

After a slow start the Georgia legislature began to move briskly in the divorce business during later decades.[26] In December, 1831, twenty-four divorces were granted. By this time a concise formula for such bills had been worked out. No grounds were given, and it was merely stipulated that such and such persons "shall in future be held as separate and distinct persons, altogether unconnected by any mystic union, or civil contract, whatsoever, at any time heretofore made or entered into between them." [27] Between 1798 and 1835, the legislature passed 291 such private divorce bills.[28]

By a constitutional amendment that went into effect in 1835, the Georgia courts received sole authority to grant divorces in cases where the parties had obtained concurrent verdicts from two special juries authorizing a "divorce upon legal principles." [29] But the situation remained confused, because "the legal principles" were still undefined.

In 1847, all Georgia husbands and wives who had remarried after being divorced found themselves in serious trouble. With fine juristic logic but doubtful realism, Justice Eugenius Nisbet of the Georgia Supreme Court ruled in the case of *Head* v. *Head* that the only grounds for divorce in Georgia were those of the common law —that is of English ecclesiastical law. Marriages could be completely dissolved only for causes that invalidated the original contract, namely "pre-contract, consanguinity, affinity, and corporal infirmity." For partial divorce, or separation from bed and board, the only admissible grounds were adultery and cruelty.[30] Since Georgia legislatures and courts had been handing out divorces on other assumptions for half a century, the new decision left it highly uncertain just who was married to whom.

The Georgia legislature met the crisis manfully. In 1849 it passed an act validating all second marriages formed in consequence of divorces granted for illegal causes by the courts or the legislature. A constitutional amendment adopted that year declared that "divorces shall be final and conclusive when the parties shall have obtained the concurrent verdicts of two special juries authorized to divorce upon such legal principles as the general assembly may by law prescribe." [31] The final step in tidying up the situation was for the legislature to pass an act in 1850 defining eight grounds for absolute divorce. Some of these such as consanguinity, mental incapacity, force, or pregnancy of the woman at the time of the marriage by another man without the husband's knowledge might more properly have been considered grounds for annulment, but the others, adultery, willful desertion for three years, and imprisonment for two years for crimes involving moral turpitude involved true divorce. The Georgia statute also permitted either absolute or partial divorce, at the jury's discretion, for cruel treatment and habitual drunkenness.[32]

Before Kentucky's general divorce law was enacted, the legislature sometimes empowered the courts to act in particular cases. Eleven such conditional divorces were granted in February, 1808. Thus the Kentucky legislature declared it lawful for Richard M. Thomas to sue in the circuit court, "and if the jury . . . shall find for the plaintiff or . . . shall find in substance that the defendant hath been in a distracted situation, and that the plantiff hath made provision for her future support, and that she has been delivered of two coloured children . . . said marriage shall be totally dissolved." [33] Similarly Polly Pringle Henry is to have a divorce if a jury finds it true that her debtor husband has abandoned her without leaving enough for her support and has probably left the United States, and Parthenia Meigs is to have her freedom if it be true that her husband John used to beat her and has now deserted her for four years.[34]

Even after the general divorce act of 1809, the Kentucky legislature continued to pass private divorce bills, usually to accommodate individuals whose cases did not come clearly under the regular statute. Unlike the unadorned Georgia acts, these Kentucky bills usually stated the ground for action, thus providing a melancholy record of the marital disappointments of an earlier age. Consider, for example, this sad case:

. . . Joshua Pyle about the 27th of July, 1819, intermarried with one Lucinda Woodward under the expectation and belief that she was a virtuous and chaste woman, and . . . he was induced to said marriage by the purest and unfeigned love and attachment to her; but to his utter astonishment and confusion after his marriage rights [sic] were celebrated, he discovered that she was sometime advanced in a state of pregnancy with another man. . . .[35]

Undoubtedly the reluctance of American state legislatures to turn over exclusive divorce jurisdiction to the courts was based upon English precedents. If the British Parliament reserved for itself the final authority to grant absolute divorce, should not its American counterparts retain a similar sovereignty? Yet the evils of legislative divorce were obvious to all sober critics. Confronted by thirty or forty divorce petitions each session, the lawmakers either handled these in a casual log-rolling fashion or they attempted to act conscientiously on each particular case. To do the latter was a time-consuming process and one for which the ordinary legislative committee was poorly equipped. The best procedure was undoubtedly to follow English practice by requiring a preliminary trial in the regular courts,[36] but even this was a cumbersome business. New York State's highly respected Chancellor James Kent raised a new objection to legislative divorces by suggesting that they might not be valid outside the states where they were granted. If a New York marriage should be dissolved, "not by a regular judicial sentence, but by an act of the legislature in another state," would such a divorce be received in New York as binding? If a statute were to have the same effect in one state as in another, he reasoned, "then one state would be dictating laws for another, and a fearful clash of jurisdiction would instantly follow." [37]

The sharp division of contemporary opinion was best illustrated by events in Missouri. Despite the fact that the state had a general divorce law, each session of the legislature was confronted by a stack of petitions from unhappy husbands and wives seeking this road to freedom instead of appealing to the courts. Governor Daniel Dunklin tried to halt the practice by a sharp veto message in 1833. If Chancellor Kent was right in believing that legislative divorces were valid only in the state where they were granted, they were highly inexpedient. They were also, he argued, in violation of the Missouri constitution, which provided that "no person charged with the exercise of powers properly belonging to one of these departments shall exercise any power belonging to the others." To which branch of government, asked the governor, did the power of granting divorces properly belong? Obviously to the judiciary.[38]

Unimpressed by Dunklin's arguments, the lawmakers promptly passed the divorce bill over his veto. The battle continued throughout the session. On February 8, the governor rejected an omnibus bill divorcing thirty-seven couples, only to have the legislature overrule him.[39] For the session as a whole, the legislators granted forty-nine divorces. To only two of these, because of special circumstances, did Governor Dunklin give his approval.[40]

Why did the Missouri legislature persist in its course? Sheer love of power was probably one reason, but there was also a feeling that the ordinary law did not provide for many cases of real hardship. A partial solution, therefore, was to define additional grounds. This the lawmakers did in 1835 by providing that the courts might grant divorces in cases of habitual drunkenness and extreme cruelty. They also abolished the halfway station of divorce from bed and board and relaxed an earlier prohibition to permit the guilty party to remarry after a five-year probationary period.[41]

Even after this liberalization of the law, some representatives jealously clung to their old prerogatives. In 1839, the house engaged in a spirited debate on the question of private divorce bills. Each side in the controversy tried to commit the body to its own position, and the members proved to be very evenly divided. A resolution declaring "that the power to grant divorces is not vested in the Judiciary" was finally killed by a vote of 47 to 42.[42]

As late as 1850, American legal authorities were still regretting the frequency of legislative divorce. Without pretending to have made an exhaustive search, Henry Folsom Page, an Ohio writer on marriage law, offered an interesting miscellany of information. The Ohio legislature had granted a total of over 100 divorces; the Georgia legislature, over 300. The Pennsylvania legislature had enacted over 100 private divorce bills between 1817 and 1849; that of Illinois had dissolved 24 marriages in its 1830-1831 session; that of Delaware, 12 in the 1848-1849 session; and that of Missouri—still going strong —55 in the 1848-1849 session.[43]

In most states the granting of legislative divorce was halted sometime before the Civil War. Often the determining factor was a new state constitution, specifically prohibiting the legislature from passing such bills. Pennsylvania, for example, took such action in 1838, Kentucky in 1850, and Missouri in 1852. By 1867, at least 33 of the then 37 states had prohibited legislative divorce.[44] Here and there, nevertheless, the old practice continued. The Delaware legislature passed 63 private divorce bills at its 1889 session and 102 in 1897; the practice was finally banned by the constitution of 1897.[45]

The demise of legislative divorce was hastened by more liberal general statutes. In Pennsylvania, for example, a law of 1815 reduced from four years to two the period of desertion required for divorce and defined two new grounds: cruel and barbarous treatment by the husband endangering the life of the wife, and such indignities to the wife's person as rendered her condition intolerable, thereby forcing her to leave home. Still further grounds were later recognized: the lunacy of the wife (1843); two years' imprisonment of either party on a felony conviction, and the wife's extreme cruelty to the husband (1854).[46]

In view of Connecticut's pioneering during colonial days, her subsequent adventures with divorce are of particular interest. To such a respected authority as Judge Zephaniah Swift, writing in. 1795, Connecticut had good reason for pride. "The institution of a court for the decision of such controversies, and the limitation of their power to such cases as the public good requires to be remedied, gives the practice adopted by our laws a decided preference to the practice of all other nations, and renders our mode of granting divorces, as favourable as the other modes have been unfavourable, to the virtue and happiness of mankind." [47] Certainly it could not be said that Connecticut encouraged outsiders to avail themselves of her facilities: in 1797 the legislature amended the divorce law to require plaintiffs to reside in the state three years before instituting action, except in cases where the cause of divorce had arisen after a couple moved to the state.[48]

But not all Connecticut dignitaries were happy with the situation. In 1788, Benjamin Trumbull, pastor of the North Haven Congregational Church, published an *Appeal to the Public, Especially to the Learned with Respect to the Unlawfulness of Divorces*. The particuar case that occasioned his pamphlet involved a woman whose husband had deserted home to avoid imprisonment for debt. He had subsequently attempted to return, but the wife had spurned reconciliation, obtained a divorce, and married another man. "The pastor and brethren of this church," said Trumbull, "view *this man*, as having *committed adultery*, in marrying her, who has been put away without a warrantable cause, and *this woman* as *an adulteress*, in putting away her husband, and in becoming one flesh with another man." [49] Despite the unpopularity of combating long-established practices, Trumbull stated his strong conviction that divorces except for adultery were in violation of the law of Christ. Whether or not marriage was a civil contract was not the decisive issue, "for in what case soever God hath made a law, whether it respect a civil or any other matter, that law is binding on all to whom the knowledge of it comes. As He therefore hath given laws respecting marriage, and, in certain cases, prohibiting divorce, no legislators, or judges, can, in any such cases, have any right to make laws that a divorce shall be given, or by any public judgment to declare a dissolution of marriage." [50] He called upon the clergy "to unite in an humble petition and address to the honourable General Assembly to take these matters into their serious consideration, and to make such further provision for the preservation of conjugal chastity and fidelity, as their wisdom shall direct." [51]

About 1816, Yale's famous President Timothy Dwight condemned the divorce laws in a sermon preached before the governor and many of the legislators.[52] Dwight rejected the contention of earlier Presbyterian and Congregational divines that the Scriptures sanctioned divorce on the ground of desertion. The case of the deserted wife is a hard one, he acknowledged, but "it is incomparably better that individuals should suffer than that an Institution, which is the basis of all human good, should be shaken, or endangered." [53] Divorces had once been rare in Connecticut: "the deformity of the object was so great, the prevalence of vital Religion was so general, and the power of Conscience and of public opinion so efficacious, that few, very few comparatively, had sufficient hardihood to apply." Alas, Dwight groaned, conditions had now greatly changed:

At the present time, the progress of this evil is alarming and terrible. In this town, within five years, more than fifty divorces have been granted: at the average calculation, more than four hundred in the whole State during this period: that is, one out of every hundred married pairs. What a flaming proof is here of the baleful influence of this corruption on a people, otherwise remarkably distinguished for their intelligence, morals, and religion! [54]

Stanch Federalist that he was, President Dwight found his most terrifying examples in the twenty thousand divorces reputed to have been granted during one and one-half years of the French Revolution. This gave him a launching pad from which he could fire his supercharged peroration:

From these facts, as well as from the nature of the case, it is clearly evident, that the progress of Divorce, though different in different countries, will, in all, be dreadful beyond conception. Within a moderate period, the whole community will be thrown, by laws made in open opposition to the Laws of God, into a general prostitution. No difference exists between this prostitution, and that which customarily bears the name, except that the one is licensed, the other is unlicensed, by man. To the Eye of God, those who are polluted in each of these modes are alike, and equally impure, loathsome, abandoned wretches; and the offspring of *Sodom* and *Gomorrah*. They are divorced and undivorced, adulterers and adulteresses; of whom the Spirit of Truth hath said that not one of them *shall enter into the kingdom of God*. Over such a country, a virtuous man, if such an one be found, will search in vain, to find a virtuous wife. Wherever he wanders, nothing will meet his eye, but stalking, barefaced pollution. The realm around him has become one vast Brothel; one great province of the World of Perdition. . . .[55]

Refusing to be frightened by the fate of Sodom and Gomorrah, Connecticut continued to grant divorces under her venerable law. When change finally came, it was not in the direction that Trumbull and Dwight had demanded but toward greater liberalism. The four original grounds: adultery, fraudulent contract, three years' desertion, or long absence with presumption of death were expanded by the addition of two new ones in 1843: habitual intemperance and intolerable cruelty.[56]

Even then, the law was not broad enough to cover all deserving cases—particularly in view of the strictness of the courts in limiting "intolerable cruelty" to physical inflictions hazardous to life itself. Hitherto relatively rare, legislative divorce became common in Connecticut during the 1840's. Things came to a climax in 1849, when the house committee on divorce tried over forty cases, recommending favorable action on fourteen of them.[57] The grounds for the committee's decisions were stated with Yankee bluntness. The charges against Nancy Hall of Wallingford were neglect of duty, desertion, and placing affection on another man. "She had been seen in his lap, with her sleeves about his neck, kissing him most

affectionately—telling her husband that if he had children at home
he had better go and take care of them—she would not." [58] Polly
White of Colebrook appeared to be an industrious and worthy
woman, yet her husband Barnice "went to bed with his boots on, to
annoy her—put dead chickens in her tea pot—would put out the fire
when she was up—send her to bed wet and cold, and then make up
a fire for himself—did not provide food enough for her, etc." [59] According to Sally Beach of Litchfield, her husband Luman was an
equally difficult man. She had been forced to leave him after stick-
ing it out for forty-three years, because he "treated her cruelly, com-
pelling her to leave her bed and sleep in a cold room—had fastened
her out of doors—declared he hated her, and wished she was in 'a
place where it is so warm that it is difficult to get fresh air'—threw
a butcher's knife at her." [60]

The lawmakers tried to administer even-handed justice. Not only
did they require husbands to provide adequate alimony, but they
sometimes compelled them to pay the wives' legal expenses. Thus
the legislature ordered Abner Hunt to turn over $30 to his wife's at-
torney so that she might contest his divorce petition.[61]

Yet the more conscientiously the legislators tried to proceed, the
more they became convinced that they should turn over the whole
responsibility to the courts. On May 17, 1849, the house judiciary
committee brought in a bill giving exclusive divorce jurisdiction to
the superior court and enlarging the grounds. The issue was vigorously debated, with some members expressing fear that divorce
would be made too easy. Supporters of the bill stressed the importance of halting the expensive and time-consuming practice of legislative divorce. William W. Boardman of New Haven emphasized
the legislature's inability to chart a straight course. Sometimes the
legislature was composed of men who granted divorce for slight
causes; at other times petitioners with real grievances could find no
favor. The courts, he believed, would settle principles and adhere
to them.[62] In the end the divorce bill passed: legislative divorce was
prohibited; the superior court was given exclusive jurisdiction; and
earlier grounds were now expanded to include life imprisonment,
any infamous crime involving a violation of conjugal duty, and—
most importantly—"any such misconduct as permanently destroys

the happiness of the petitioner and defeats the purpose of the marriage relation." [63] This "general misconduct" clause obviously granted wide discretion to the courts—so wide as to cause acute distress to strict moralists, as we shall show in a later chapter.

Massachusetts divorce law continued to be more conservative than that of Connecticut, yet here too the trend was toward greater liberalism. The strict act of 1786 permitting full divorce only for impotence, bigamy, and adultery, and separation from bed and board only for cruelty was relaxed in 1811 to the extent of allowing judicial separation "whenever any husband shall utterly desert his wife, or shall grossly or wantonly and cruelly neglect or refuse to provide suitable maintenance for her." [64]

More important were the steps gradually taken to provide additional grounds for absolute divorce. In 1835, divorce was allowed to either spouse in case the other party were sentenced to seven years' imprisonment at hard labor. Three years later it was made available to those whose husbands or wives had been guilty of willful desertion for a term of five years. In 1850, still another ground was provided, "if either party shall leave the other without consent and join a religious sect or society that believes, or professes to believe, the relation between husband and wife unlawful, and there remain three years." [65] By this enactment, Massachusetts fell in step with a number of other states, where the lawmakers had seen fit to penalize the Shakers, highly unpopular because of their antimarriage doctrines.

In 1867 and 1870, the Massachusetts legislature made two very important changes in the divorce laws. In the first year, the decree *nisi*, borrowed from recent English legislation, was introduced into American jurisprudence.[66] This meant that a divorce decree became final only after a six months' waiting period—a useful device in discouraging hasty remarriage and uncovering any chicanery that might invalidate the original decree. The statute of 1870 abolished divorce from bed and board and broadened the grounds for absolute divorce to include extreme cruelty, habitual intoxication, and failure of the husband to provide.[67] In rejecting judicial separation—that canonist invention which had survived the Reformation and become rooted in the English common law—the Massachusetts legislators were acting with their eyes wide open. Reporting from the senate judiciary committee, William W. Warren of Middlesex County said:

It is believed that this form of divorce has received the condemnation of some of the most eminent jurists of England and the United States. Lord Stowell speaks of it as leaving the parties "in the undefined and dangerous characters of a wife without a husband, and a husband without a wife." Judge Swift . . . says it "places them in a situation where there is an irresistable temptation to the commission of adultery." Chancellor Kent observes that "these qualified divorces are regarded as rather hazardous to the morals of the parties." [68]

With these reforms Massachusetts created a system that many jurists considered to be excellent. In defining the grounds upon which divorce might be granted the substantive law was humane and realistic, yet in its procedural safeguards the possibility of frauds and abuses was minimized.

Perhaps because of the large New England element among the early settlers, the states of the Old Northwest tended to pass rather liberal divorce laws. Ohio's pioneer law of 1804 recognized four grounds for divorce: bigamy, willful absence for five years, adultery, and extreme cruelty. In 1822, the term of willful absence was reduced to three years and two new grounds were added: physical incompetence at the time of marriage and imprisonment for crime. In 1853, four more grounds—fraudulent contract, gross neglect of duty, habitual drunkenness, and a divorce decree in another state whereby one party had been forbidden to remarry—were added.[69]

As early as 1834, some moralists were showing concern at the growing number of divorces. Correcting some misstatements about the situation, the Cleveland Herald reported that the Ohio supreme court had found two hundred divorce cases on its docket during the 1833 circuit term; besides this, some fifty applications had been made to the legislature.[70] Seven years later the same paper commented that "Hymen's chains appear to be anything but silken in Hamilton County." The supreme court in Cincinnati had cut no less than fourteen ties in a single day; in eleven of these the wife had been the petitioner. "Such a Queen City!" scoffed the Herald.[71] In 1846, the editor praised the Ohio legislature for refusing to pass private divorce bills: "The disgraceful legislation of former sessions has thus been avoided, and an excellent precedent has been set, of referring all cases to the proper tribunals—the Courts—to which great latitude of power has already been given." [72]

Even judicial divorce had its pitfalls, as Justice Hitchcock pointed out in the case of *Harter* v. *Harter*:

Perhaps there is no statute in Ohio more abused than the statute concerning divorce and alimony. Perhaps there is no statute under which greater imposition is practiced upon the court and more injustice done to individuals. It seems to be considered, by a great portion of our community, that the marriage contract is the least obligatory of all others, and that nothing more is necessary to dissolve it than that application should be made to this court to register a decree to this effect. Not infrequently a husband, who has by cruelty driven his wife from her home, seeks to be divorced from her, charging her with wilful absence. And there are cases where the adulterous wife seeks a similar remedy, charging the husband with extreme cruelty. The hearings are generally ex parte. Witnesses are examined friendly to the applicant, and it is almost, if not utterly impossible, for the court, in most instances, to arrive at the real truth of the cause. [73]

In Illinois and Indiana divorce was reputed to be even easier to get than in Ohio.

If by 1860 the states of the Old Northwest were the most liberal in the nation in their divorce policy, South Carolina and New York were the most conservative. South Carolina's case was simple. Conservatives commented with approval on the fact that in all her long history as a colony and as a state South Carolina had never granted either a legislative or a judicial divorce. New York's case was much more complex, as we shall demonstrate in the next chapter.

CHAPTER 6

New York Holds Back

During these years when neighboring states were relaxing their divorce laws to fit a new nation's sense of justice, New York followed her own more conservative course. In recognizing only one ground for divorce, New York lawmakers demonstrated not so much a stern sense of duty as an inability to give the problem of marital law more than fitful attention. Again and again legislative committees proposed more liberal legislation; several times either the senate or the assembly approved these recommendations, but the advocates of change always failed to carry through.

New York's first general divorce law was enacted in 1787. On January 22 of that year the assembly received a petition from Isaac Gouverneur, Jr., member of a prominent New York City family, praying for a divorce on the ground of his wife's adultery.[1] This request was referred to a special committee under the chairmanship of Assemblyman Alexander Hamilton, the future Secretary of the Treasury. Three weeks later[2] the committee brought in a bill whose purpose was well stated in the preamble:

Whereas the laws at present respecting adultery are very defective and applications have in consequence been made to the Legislature, praying their interposition. And whereas it is thought more advisable for the

Legislature to make some general provision in such cases than to afford relief to individuals, upon their partial representations without a just and constitutional trial of the facts. . . .

The proposed law provided that persons charging their marital partners with adultery should petition the chancellor of the state, who might provide for a jury trial of the facts before some lower court. If the case were proved, the chancellor was empowered to dissolve the marriage. The bill provided that it should not be lawful for the party convicted of adultery "to remarry any person whatsoever" but the innocent party might make another marriage "in like manner as if the party convicted was actually dead." [3]

Hamilton's bill readily passed the assembly and the senate, but met a temporary block in the council of revision, entrusted with the veto power under the constitution of 1777. On March 19, Governor George Clinton, Chief Justice Richard Morris, and Justice John S. Hobart adopted a report, objecting to the bill "as inconsistent with the public good," because of its prohibition on the remarriage of the adulterous party, "thereby preventing every person who may be tempted to falsify the marriage promises . . . from becoming thereafter a reputable member of Society, unless by renouncing the comforts and gratification which results from a connexion between the Sexes and maintaining a degree of Preserve and Continency scarcely to be expected after such an Instance of frailty." To lock up such offenders in a "cloyster" might be an appropriate punishment, but "to suffer them to remain in Society without a possibility of remarrying, is, in a degree, to compel them, by Law to live in open violation of the Rules of Chastity and decency, and will, it is to be apprehended, have a pernicious influence on the public morals." [4]

This sensible eighteenth century point of view was rejected by the legislature, which overrode the council's veto by a vote of 38 to 16 in the assembly and 10 to 4 in the senate.[5] Not for almost a century did the lawmakers see fit to relax the troublesome ban on the remarriage of the guilty party to a divorce.[6]

In February, 1813, commissioners appointed to revise the New York laws presented a new divorce bill. The senate passed the commissioners' bill without change,[7] but the assembly insisted on practically rewriting the measure. Elisha Williams, a prominent Colum-

bia County Federalist, offered an amendment broadening the
grounds for divorce to include desertion for five years.[8] On April 5,
the Williams amendment carried the assembly by the close vote of
41 to 39,[9] but the conservatives rallied to overturn this result. Assemblyman George Huntington, a Federalist from Oneida County,
obtained a reconsideration, and on April 8 the desertion clause was
expunged by a vote of 47 to 30.[10] Analysis of this first important
showdown reveals that 28 Federalists opposed the desertion clause
while 12 favored it; the Democratic-Republicans were evenly divided
with 17 in favor and 17 opposed. (Two more opposition votes came
from members whose party affiliations are uncertain.) Geographi-
cally the vote was scattered, but the two leading cities, New York
and Albany, were unanimously opposed to the desertion clause,
while such rural counties as Dutchess, Saratoga, and Chenango were
heavily in favor.

As finally enacted on April 13, 1813, the revised divorce law retained only one ground for absolute divorce and made only slight
changes in procedure. The statute's most significant innovation was
to empower the count of chancery to grant judicial separation and
separate maintenance in cases where the husband had been guilty
of cruel and inhuman treatment, had conducted himself in such a
manner as rendered it unsafe and improper for the wife to cohabit
with him, or had abandoned her and refused to provide for her.[11] In
1824, judicial separation was made available to husbands on the
same grounds.[12]

In 1827, another general revision of the laws focused attention
on the divorce problem. On November 23, the assembly debated
a proposed amendment to add habitual drunkenness as a ground for
divorce. According to a contemporary report, the proposition was
warmly pressed, but lost. Drunkenness was also urged as a cause for
judicial separation, but without success.[13] The Domestic Relations
chapter, eventually approved December 4, 1827, continued the divorce and separation provisions of earlier statutes with only minor
procedural changes. For the first time, however, the legislature defined five grounds for annulment: a marriage was either void or
voidable whenever one of the parties was under the age of legal
consent, was guilty of bigamy, was a lunatic or idiot at the time of
the contract, had obtained consent to the marriage by force or

fraud, or was physically incapable of entering into the marriage state.[14]

Throughout these years the legislature had many requests for private divorce bills. In 1802, for example, Henry Steward of Tioga County related how he had lived with his wife Sally in "conjugal felicity" until 1799, "when it pleased Divine Providence to reduce her to a deplorable state of insanity wholly incapable of performing any of the duties of society. . . ." In addition to "the disagreeable solitary life" these circumstances compelled him to lead, Henry found himself "under peculiar embarrassment in the course of his business, having frequent occasion to receive and transfer title to land, the conveyance of which he is unable to complete." [15] But the legislature turned down his request for a divorce, as it did also that of the Reverend Noah Crane of Blooming Grove, Orange County, who petitioned for a legislative divorce in 1811 because of his wife Mary's "violence of temper and the perversity and malignity" of her disposition.[16]

Obviously the New York legislature was much more resistant to the legislative divorce virus than were the lawmaking bodies of most states. Nevertheless, a few cases presented such unusual circumstances that private bills were passed.

The petition of Elizabeth Ross of Clinton County, submitted in 1809, read like the plot of a Gothic novel. Soon after her marriage to Daniel Ross in 1785, Elizabeth's father William Gilliland, a large landowner, had given the young couple a considerable estate and had otherwise contributed to Daniel's advancement. With this help and through the joint industry of both husband and wife Daniel had made a large fortune. Elizabeth had borne five children and had always been a chaste and dutiful wife, so she claimed, but her husband had treated her with extreme injustice, barbarity, and cruelty. He had committed personal violence against her, and—to cap his crimes—falsely accused her of wholesale adultery with her own brother, her husband's brother, and still a third man. Daniel had attempted to obtain a divorce, but a jury had acquitted her of these infamous charges. Finally, according to her story, this heartless husband had left her in childbirth without any assistance, "exposed to perish," and had abandoned her and her youngest child without providing for their support. By a special act of March 24, 1809, the

legislature authorized Elizabeth to present a petition to the chancel
lor, who was to proceed in the same manner as in adultery cases. I
the allegations were found to be true, the chancellor was empowered
to pronounce the marriage dissolved; Daniel, in such an event, was
prohibited from remarrying during the lifetime of Elizabeth, but
Elizabeth might marry again as if Daniel were actually dead.[17]

But the lawmakers had not heard the last of the case. Two years
later Elizabeth Ross again laid her problems on the Albany door-
step. The chancellor had ordered a trial before a Clinton County
judge and jury, where she claimed to have proved all the facts required by "the true spirit and meaning" of the legislature's directions. However, the trial judge had decided "that the testimony so
adduced did not maintain the issue . . . according to those technical rules which he felt himself bound in his judicial capacity to apply, and thereupon ordered a nonsuit to be entered." [18]

The assembly committee, to which Elizabeth's new petition was
referred, studied the minutes of the Clinton County trial and concluded that she had proved her case. It recommended a direct legislative divorce, but the issue was complicated by a petition from Daniel
Ross praying for the right to defend himself.[19] The legislature now
became so mired in the question of procedure that Elizabeth's case
was almost lost.[20] Eventually, however, a new bill in her behalf
passed the assembly by a vote of 41 to 35 and the senate by 17 to
6.[21] As finally adopted, the act of 1811 went back to the principle
of that of 1809: the case was refered to the chancellor with power
to grant the divorce if Elizabeth proved her case. This was now reduced to a few simple issues, that Daniel Ross "hath falsely and
maliciously accused the said Elizabeth with incest with her own
brother, or that he the said Daniel hath treated Elizabeth with extreme injustice, barbarity and cruelty, and hath committed personal
violence against her the said Elizabeth." [22]

Particular cases stir the emotions to a degree that general principles never can. We should not be surprised, therefore, to discover
that the New York legislature devoted more of its time and energy
to a single private divorce bill than it ever did to any general marriage law proposal. On February 7, 1815, the petition of Eunice
Chapman was first presented to the lawmakers, and from this time
until the day when Eunice's legislative divorce was finally enacted

three years later, this woman's marital troubles were under repeated debate whenever the legislature was in session.

Married in 1804, James and Eunice Chapman lived together for seven years in the town of Durham, near Albany. Three children— a boy and two girls—resulted from their union. But the marriage became increasingly unhappy. James was a heavy drinker; Eunice was sharp-tempered and quarrelsome. In June, 1811, James deserted his family and drifted off to live for a while in New York City and later in Albany.

In October, 1812, the Chapman marital drama began a new act, when James not only got religion but got it in one of its more bizarre American forms. Much impressed by the Shakers at Watervliet, he sought to join the society, "for I felt myself unfit either to die or to live in my then present situation." [23] The Shakers would not accept him until he had put his affairs in order and made just provision for his family. James's way of meeting this requirement was to propose to Eunice that she either follow his example in joining the Shakers or that she at least take up her residence close to the Shaker community. Eunice refused both these alternatives, and a new tug of war developed over the custody of the children. James wanted to take them into the Shaker community with him; Eunice insisted upon keeping them and threatened to make trouble for both her husband and his new Shaker friends unless he made adequate financial provision for her.

The Shakers finally admitted James to their settlement, but the tussle over the children continued. In October, 1814, Chapman visited his former home while his wife was away, bundled the three children into a wagon, and spirited them off to the Shaker community. James relented to the extent of allowing Eunice to see her children, but he would not give them up. From the husband's point of view, he treated his difficult wife kindly by allowing her to live in the neighborhood, "but in return for these favors, she neglected no opportunity to abuse me and the people, to make the children unhappy, and, if possible, to create confusion and discord wherever she went." James then resorted to stern measures: he sent Eunice away and forbade her to see the children for three months. When she disobeyed this order and not only returned to Watervliet but threatened to appeal to the legislature for help, James disappeared, leaving word for Eunice that she would probably never see either him or the children again in this life.[24]

This was the shape of affairs on February 7, 1815, when Eunice Chapman first petitioned the legislature for a divorce. The assembly rejected the request by a close vote, but a substitute remedy was eventually enacted into law on April 17, 1815.[25] This provided that when husband and wife were living apart without being divorced, a supreme court judge might on application of the wife award her the custody of the children, if he thought best.[26]

But this law was of no use to Eunice because she could not find out where her husband had gone with the children. After a pathetic search she returned to Albany, where she supported herself teaching school while she sought further assistance. On February 21, 1816, she again petitioned the legislature for a divorce.[27] A select committee of the senate brought in a report abounding in sympathy for the wife and emphasizing the problems created by the Shaker doctrines. These people, the committee explained, "consider themselves a spiritual society, wholly separate from what they call the world of mankind. They hold the marriage contract to be unlawful and immoral, and place the relationship of husband and wife, and of parent and child, on a footing which absolves them from the legal, moral and religious ties and duties which have always been considered of the utmost importance to the peace and welfare of the community." Although professing to be scrupulously regardful of the rights of conscience, the committee considered it not improper "by prudential laws to guard against the mischievous consequences which experience has proved to be attendant on the exercise of the religious tenets of a particular society." To grant an unconditional divorce simply because a husband left his wife and joined the Shakers would be unwise, since "the dissolute and unprincipled" might join the society merely for this purpose. But if the Shaker converts were penalized by being treated as civilly dead, this objection would be overcome.[28]

It was too near the end of the session for further consideration of the Chapman case, but when the legislature reconvened in November, 1816, Eunice renewed her petition. James Chapman and his fellow Shakers presented memorials of remonstrance, but the senate brushed these aside to pass a bill not only dissolving the Chapman marriage but containing drastic provisions of a general character. Senator Martin Van Buren of Columbia County, the future President, endeavored to soften these anti-Shaker clauses but was voted down.[29] With some amendments the Chapman divorce bill passed both houses of the legislature in April, 1817.[30]

All this was but prelude to the exciting climax of the Chapman case. Nine months after the legislative divorce had been voted, the council of revision vetoed the bill. It was, the council declared, unfair to James Chapman, because it disqualified him without judicial examination from exercising his natural right of contracting marriage; moreover, some of the general anti-Shaker provisions were invalid, because they made the mere fact of joining the Shakers not only a cause for divorce but a bar to remarriage without previous judicial inquiry, which was "inconsistent with free exercise and enjoyment of that religious profession or worship, secured by the constitution." [31]

"We hope," said the conservative *Albany Gazette*, "this subject is now put to rest, and that the members will no longer be harassed by the pressing importunities of this fair and fascinating petitioner." [32] At first this hope seemed to be well founded. On January 29, 1818, the senate voted 14 to 12 against overriding the veto.[33] But Eunice appears to have been one of the most successful lobbyists ever to have invaded the capitol. On February 2, the senate passed a new divorce bill by a vote of 19 to 3, and two weeks later the assembly concurred.[34]

On February 27, 1818, the council of revision vetoed this newest bill. Dominated by Chancellor James Kent and other conservatives, the council was determined to stand its ground. Reviewing Eunice's case, it held that "it would be unwise and unsafe to dissolve the contract of marriage for the causes stated in that recital." If James had been guilty of abandonment and neglect, Eunice had ample redress in judicial separation. As for the children, the husband had the legal right to keep them under his exclusive guardianship and control. If this right had been abused, the mother's proper course was to appeal to the chancellor, who was the superintending guardian of the rights of all infants. In its general anti-Shaker provisions, the council of revision held that the new bill, like its predecessor, infringed upon the constitutional guarantee of religious liberty. The Shaker practices were not inconsistent with the peace and safety of the state, and, as for their belief that sexual intercourse was sinful, "the absurdity of that tenet is so plain and obvious as to provide an antidote and security against any serious danger of its prevalence."

Included among the council's objections was a sweeping condemnation of all relaxation of the divorce laws:

> Anxiously aware of the evils which threaten the dearest interests of society, by increasing the causes or facility of divorces, the Council feel it to be their solemn and indispensable duty to oppose the dissolution of the marriage contract for any other than the single cause already provided by the general law of this state. . . . While the partial evils of indissoluble matrimony are sometimes witnessed and deplored, we ought to be consoled by the reflection that the peace and character of many thousands of families are preserved by the mutual forbearance and concessions between husband and wife, which are induced by the ever impressive consideration that the voluntary tie which bound them can never be dissolved.[85]

This veto brought a new issue to the fore. Should an outdated citadel of aristocracy be allowed to thwart the will of the people's representatives? Demonstrating its independence, the senate repassed the divorce bill by a vote of 20 to 6.[86]

For three exciting days, with spectators crowding every available space, the assembly debated the case. Nathan Williams of Oneida County asserted that the very name of Eunice Chapman excited disgust. She was not "one of those modest, retiring, deserving women, for whom we should entertain a sympathy." Williams went on to warn:

> By passing this bill we shall give boldness to the female character. Those who are now apparently amicable, encouraged by the success of Eunice Chapman, would be emboldened. The vermil-tinctured hues which modesty casts upon the cheek at the least indelicate expression or action, would be chased away. They, like Eunice Chapman would leave their retirement, and by familiarity with gentlemen would soon become emboldened, and would be haunting the members—for divorces.[87]

But Eunice's conduct was warmly defended by other legislators. Simon G. Throop of Chenango County praised her as a "pattern of virtue and an ornament to her sex," whereas her husband was "a drunken wretch—an abandoned debaucher." Isaac Sargent of Washington County found Eunice's character to be without blemish. He criticized the existing laws that gave the chancellor exclusive power of granting divorces. "It is high time," he continued, "that we should *convince* the council of revision and the people that we are sent here for other purposes than to sanction their edicts. The people . . . *were looking for this.*"[38]

General Erastus Root of Delaware County, a champion of the rising democracy, struck the most telling blows in Eunice's behalf in a speech sprinkled by ribald wit. What if this divorce did open the door to thousands of similar petitions. "If these thousand applications were as just as this, he would legislate a thousand days in disposing of them." As for the argument that Eunice had an adequate remedy in judicial separation, he was opposed to "divorces in part," which he considered to be one of the worst institutions adopted by an earlier generation. The present bill he considered to be "a temple erected to chastity and domestic felicity." [39]

When the key roll call was taken, the divorce bill won by a vote of 85 to 27. "*O Tempora, O Mores!*" mourned the *Albany Gazette*[40] —a comment that so annoyed the lawmakers that they deprived the editor of his privilege of sitting on the floor of the House to report the proceedings. Accusing the legislators of interfering with freedom of the press, the indignant journalist offered his own explanation of the episode:

"*O Tempora, O Mores!*"—We understand that the cause of our being excluded from our seat, in consequence of uttering this expression, was the misapprehension of some gentlemen as to its meaning—they thinking that it was *profane language* in an *unknown tongue.*[41]

As finally passed, the divorce bill had been purged of its most objectionable anti-Shaker provisions. The first section merely dissolved the marriage of James and Eunice Chapman without depriving either party of the right to remarry. The second provided that in case a husband or wife joined the Shakers and took underage children with him, the other partner might apply for a *habeas corpus* writ to bring the question of the custody of the children before the chancel-

lor or any supreme court judge. If the child could not be found, the
judge might issue a warrant directing the sheriff or some other official
to search Shaker premises. Anyone taking a child out of the state so
that the writ of *habeas corpus* could not be executed, might be
punished by a fine not exceeding $200 or six months' imprisonment,
or both.[42]

This was the end of the Chapman case so far as the legislature
was concerned, but Eunice still had the problem of getting her children back. Learning they were with James in a Shaker village near
Enfield, New Hampshire, Eunice set out alone in the spring of 1818
to reclaim them. With the help of sympathetic townspeople she
managed to snatch her boy and hustle him back to Albany despite Shaker efforts to hide him. A year later she made a second trip
to Enfield and obtained custody of the girls after peaceful negotiations with the enemy camp.[43]

Fear that Eunice Chapman's success would open a floodgate for
similar legislation proved groundless. Although beset with frequent petitions, the legislature did not often weaken in its resolution to leave divorce to the courts. When Nathaniel Winslow applied for relief because his wife Electra had decided "that sexual
intercourse is inconsistent with holiness of heart," the lawmakers
decided that to grant a divorce on this ground "would subvert the
established policy of this State." [44] Nor were they moved to make
special provision for Louisa Crandall, who had painfully saved $80
and wanted to keep it out of the clutches of her adulterous husband:
$80, the solons ruled, was enough for Louisa to hire a lawyer and
get her divorce through the courts.[45] The legislators were impressed
by the argument that, if they once started passing private divorce
bills, they would be swamped with business. Noting that the
Missouri legislature had recently granted thirty-six divorces in a
single bill, a committee calculated that since the population of
New York was fourteen times that of Missouri the New York legislature might be confronted with five hundred petitions in a single
session.[46]

A few cases were sufficiently exceptional to receive serious consideration. In 1840, for example, an assembly committee recommended a legislative divorce for David Frost of Springfield, who was
involved in a strange marital tangle. His bride, Eveline Willis had

fled from him on her wedding night and refused to live with him, claiming "an insuperable repugnance." She had been secretly in love with another man, who had talked her into agreeing to marry Frost. The plan, so she confessed, had been that her lover would be present at the wedding and would at the proper moment substitute himself for the groom. But the faithless Lothario, no doubt glad to be rid of his gullible girl friend, had skipped out and allowed David to have the bride.[47] When the legislature failed to grant the recommended divorce at this session, the case was renewed a year later with identical results.[48]

Jacob Scramling of Mendon came closer to his goal. In 1840, his wife wandered away from home in a fit of insanity. She was tracked to the Erie Canal, in which she was believed to have drowned. Two years later Jacob remarried, only to learn that his first wife was alive. Still insane, she had arrived at her brother's house in Vermont in the company of a salt-boiler from Syracuse. She subsequently regained her reason, but refused to return to her husband. Jacob had made generous provision for her, and she and her three brothers united in petitioning the legislature to grant a divorce as the best way out of an unhappy situation. The assembly judiciary committee recommended favorable action, since this case "can hardly be quoted as a precedent for any future case that is likely to occur." [49] A private divorce bill passed the assembly in April, 1845, but was rejected by the senate.[50]

Since cases like that of Elizabeth Ross and Eunice Chapman had been highly exceptional, the abolition of legislative divorce was achieved with little trouble. Included in the bill of rights of the New York constitution of 1846 were these words: "nor shall any divorce be granted otherwise than by due judicial proceedings." [51] Although this provision ruled out any direct dissolution of marriage by the legislature, it did not prevent an occasional special bill to help some individual hop over a hurdle in the general law. In 1866, for example, the famous feminist, Dr. Mary Walker, was given an extension of the usual time limit on initiating a divorce action to cover the months that she had been absent from the state caring for sick and wounded soldiers during the Civil War.[52]

Legislators dissatisfied with the existing situation realized that their proper course was not to legislate for particular individuals but to provide additional grounds for judicial divorce. On April 18, 1840, the assembly committee on grievances strongly urged a more liberal policy. Accepting as a proper guide the principle of "the greatest happiness to the greatest number," it condemned New York divorce policy: "How inconceivably unwise is that severe policy which compels the continuance of a connection, where hatred and disgust is the predominant feeling, and where quarrels and criminations, and often personal violence and brutal outrage make up the sum of every day life." Condemning judicial separations as an invitation to immorality, the committee urged the legislature to pass a divorce bill modeled on the Rhode Island law.[53]

The 1840 bill never came to a vote, but in 1849 the advocates of a more liberal law received more encouragement. The assembly judiciary committee introduced a bill to define such additional grounds as two years' imprisonment, incurable insanity, and living five years as a member of a religious sect holding marriage to be sinful. "Where the very essence of the marriage relation is extinguished," the committee did not "consider it consistent with good morals to preserve the hollow form. Where there can be no union in sentiment, feeling and common respect, and that for good cause, the interests of public virtue cannot be subserved by the confining together in indissoluble ties, two mere bodies." [54]

The 1849 assembly was extraordinary in its political complexion: a schism among the Democrats had resulted in the election of a house in which there were 108 Whigs to only 14 Free Soil Democrats and 7 Hunkers. The dominant Whigs were sharply divided on the divorce issue: Speaker Amos K. Hadley of Troy and George I. Cornell of New York were strong advocates of liberalization; James M. Beekman of New York and Wessel S. Smith of Queens County led the opposition.[55] On March 9 the conservatives temporarily killed the bill by a 46 to 42 vote striking out the enacting clause.[56] Four days later, however, the advocates of change reopened the issue and succeeded in restoring the enacting clause by a vote of 51 to 43.[57] On this crucial division, 43 Whigs, 6 Free Soilers, and 2 Hunkers supported liberalization of the law, while 40 Whigs and 4 Free Soilers opposed it. But no further action was taken before adjournment.

The next year the divorce question was again raised when a select committee of the assembly recommended four additional grounds: willful desertion for five years, three years' imprisonment, gross habitual drunkenness, and incurable insanity.[58] Because of its desertion clause and its avoidance of the controversial Shaker issue, this was a sounder bill than that of the preceding year, but it did not come to a vote.

In 1852, the champions of change made a much stronger showing. The assembly judiciary committee brought in an extensive report reviewing the whole history of divorce. Strongly condemning the theory of the indissolubility of marriage, the committee said: "Its pernicious effects are visible in the social institutions and domestic manners of most of the countries of Catholic Europe. And a more forcible commentary can scarcely be made upon the subject under consideration than by a comparison of the manners and morals of two such countries for example, as Scotland and Holland, where not only adultery but desertion are causes of divorce with the morals and manners of Italy or Spain, where the marriage tie is indissoluble." The committee introduced a bill abolishing judicial separation and expanding the grounds for absolute divorce to cover not only cruel and inhuman treatment and willful desertion for three years, but "other cases of extreme hardship and peculiar inconvenience whenever, in the discretion of the court, substantial justice will be thereby promoted." [59] After extended debate and some amendment, the assembly passed this bill on April 9 by a vote of 66 to 38.[60] The majority favoring a more liberal law was made up of forty-two Democrats, twenty-two Whigs, and two assemblymen whose political affiliation has not been determined; the conservative minority included thirty-one Whigs and seven Democrats. The New York City delegation supported liberalization by a margin of 9 to 2. But this opportunity to bring the New York law into line with that of the other states failed when the senate adjourned without taking action on the house bill.

In 1855, the assembly judiciary committee reported a new bill authorizing divorce in cases of willful desertion and habitual drunkenness by either party. The committee even advocated a provision forbidding divorced drunkards from remarrying, "thereby creating a legal stigma which will involve the delinquent party in public disgrace the same as now in the case of adultery." This, the committee said, "will have a most salutary power in deterring people

from this most loathsome and disgusting vice." [61] But the 1855 bill
did not come to a vote, and neither did a bill reported by the
senate judiciary committee in 1856 providing for divorce in cases of
desertion and cruelty.[62]

Efforts to change the divorce law came to a climax in 1860 and
1861. On January 13, 1860, Senator Volney Richmond from the
Twelfth District (Rensselaer and Washington counties) introduced
a bill, which was favorably reported by the judiciary committee and
intermittently debated throughout February and March.[63] After
amendment from the floor the Richmond bill defined three new
grounds for divorce: desertion, cruelty, and drunkenness.[64] Exert-
ing powerful influence against the proposal were the two most
potent Republican editors of the state, Thurlow Weed of the *Albany
Evening Journal* and Horace Greeley of the *New York Tribune*. On
February 10, Weed wrote: "There are no less than four or five bills
pending in our Legislature to promote adultery by weakening the
marriage bonds. In twenty years more than fifty such efforts have
been made. In a majority of instances these general bills are pressed
to meet some particular case." [65] Four days later he asserted: "It
would be a pity to have New York open a huge matrimonial hospital
when other States are getting tired of the disgusting results which
have flowed from their lax laws on the subject of Divorce." [66] And
on March 1, Greeley added his admonishment that the legislature
should "ponder long and carefully" before it consented to "increasing the facilities of Divorce." [67]

Despite these thunderings from the right, the state senate passed
the Richmond bill on March 23 by a vote of 19 to 10.[68] Favoring
liberalization were 15 Republicans and 4 Democrats; opposing it
were 6 Republicans and 4 Democrats. Religious lines apparently
counted for little: among the bill's supporters were three New York
Democrats bearing the good Irish names of Connolly, Kelly, and
Murphy. But once again the advocates of change failed because they
could not push their bill through the other house.

The senate took up the issue again the next year, but this time
with different results. The judiciary committee reported in favor of
a liberal bill sponsored by Joseph H. Ramsey of the Fourteenth District (Delaware, Schoharie, and Schenectady counties). But the 1861
bill was killed by a 9 to 16 vote.[69] This time only 7 Republicans

and 2 Democrats voted in favor of change, while 9 Republicans and 7 Democrats were opposed. Among the senators who shifted their position were New York City's Kelly and Murphy. Connolly, however, stuck with the liberals; indeed he attempted to broaden the bill by inserting a clause that would permit either party to a divorce to marry again.

With the coming of the Civil War the divorce issue dropped into the background, and in the postwar period there was no serious move in the legislature for many decades. The proponents of change had lost their best chance when they failed to push a bill through during the hopeful years between 1840 and 1861. During this period the general tide of events had been toward humanitarian reform; after the Civil War the trend was in the opposite direction toward self-righteous conservatism.

CHAPTER 7

Divorce Debated

During the 1850's and 1860's American moralists—both professional and amateur—addressed themselves frequently to the question of divorce. Every conceivable point of view had its advocates. At one extreme were the conservatives who insisted that a valid marriage was indissoluble; at the other were the radicals who contended that the right of divorce should be completely unrestrained. And between these two any number of middle-of-the-road positions could be defined.

Many Americans deplored the necessity of divorce, yet believed that the laws must provide some escape hatch from unhappy unions. In 1825, *Niles' Register* published the following item—of doubtful authenticity as a travel note but pointing a lesson to domestic legislators:

The following inscription is written in large characters over the principal gate of the city of Agra, in Hindostan: "In the first year of the reign of king Julief, two thousand married couples were separated, by the magistrates, with their own consent. The emperor was so indignant, on learning these particulars, that he abolished the privilege of divorce. In the course of the following year, the number of marriages in Agra was less than before by three thousand; the number of adulteries was greater by seven thousand; three hundred women were burned alive for poisoning their husbands; seventy-five men were burned for the murder of their wives; and the quantity of furniture broken and destroyed, in the interior of private families, amounted to the value of three millions of rupees. The emperor re-established the privilege of divorce.[1]

American divorce law in all its bewildering local ramifications received its first thoughtful analysis in 1851, when Joel Prentiss Bishop published his two-volume *Commentaries on the Law of Marriage and Divorce*. Although an unsparing critic of legislative divorce and an advocate of strict procedures, Bishop had no criticism to make of divorce itself. He admired Connecticut for its forthright policy. "Notwithstanding this liberty of divorce, or in consequence of it," he wrote, "there is in our Union no State wherein domestic felicity and purity, unblemished morals, and matrimonial concord and virtue, more abound than in Connecticut, always justly termed 'the land of steady habits.' " [2]

Not to permit divorce at all, Bishop believed, was dangerous folly. On this point he poured scorn on South Carolina:

So it has become necessary to regulate by statute how large a proportion a married man may give of his property to his concubine—superfluous legislation, which would never have been thought of, had not concubinage been common. . . . But in this State . . . we have a condition of things peculiar, explained by Nott, J., from the bench of its highest tribunal as follows: "In this country," he said, "where divorces are not allowed for any cause whatsoever, we sometimes see men of excellent characters unfortunate in their marriages, and virtuous women abandoned or driven away houseless by their husbands, *who would be doomed to celibacy and solitude if they did not form connections which the law does not allow, and who make excellent husbands and wives still.* Yet they are considered as living in adultery, because a rigorous and unyielding law, from motives of policy alone, has ordained it so.[3]

Bishop was equally vigorous in his condemnation of separation from bed and board. This proceeding, neither dissolving the marriage, nor reconciling the parties, nor yet changing their natures was "one of the most corrupting devices ever imposed by serious natures on blindness and credulity." It was tolerated, Bishop explained, only because men believed as part of their religion, that dissolution would be an offense against God, "whence the slope was easy toward any compromise with good sense, and as the fruit of compromise, we have this ill-begotten monster of divorce *a mensa et thoro*, made up of pious doctrine and worldly stupidity." [4]

On other aspects of the divorce question, Bishop took a similar stand. Since religious bodies differed in their interpretation of the Scriptures, it was impossible for legislation to mirror any common dogma. Therefore, "our legislatures must act on this subject with a view solely to political and social interests."

And if they establish laws permitting divorce, they do not thereby injure, even in the innermost conscience, those who deem marriage a religious sacrament, and indissoluble. Such persons are under no compulsion to use the divorce laws, by appearing as plaintiffs in divorce suits; and, if they are made defendants, having violated their matrimonial duties civilly, they cannot complain of being cut off from their matrimonial rights civilly, while still permitted to retain the seal of the sacrament pure and undefiled in their consciences, and not compelled to marry again. [5]

In his impatience with religious dogmatism and his insistence that the divorce laws should be adapted to the general needs of society, Bishop undoubtedly spoke for thousands of American lawyers and legislators. Yet many excellent people clung to the opposite point of view, that marriage was peculiarly the province of the churches and that the statutes should be brought into conformity with this or that interpretation of the Scriptures. The history of American divorce continued to be a struggle between these rival forces of rationalism and dogmatism.

From November, 1852, to February, 1853, the marriage question was vigorously debated in the columns of the *New York Tribune*. The principal participants were men notable both for brilliance and for eccentricity. Horace Greeley, editor of the *Tribune*, combined a weakness for utopian socialism and other reform fads with a basic political conservatism; Henry James, Sr., the father of Henry James the novelist and William James the psychologist and philosopher, was a writer and lecturer deeply influenced by the religious mysticism of Emanuel Swedenborg; and Stephen Pearl Andrews was a one-time minister who had become a tireless crusader for philosophical anarchism and unrestrained free love.

The debate began after James contributed to the *Tribune* his review of a free-love tract entitled *Love vs. Marriage*. James condemned the author, a certain Dr. Lazarus, because "no person can read this book and dream of any higher divinity of man than his passions." To James, marriage had a divine character: "that is to say," he explained: "the marriage institution embodies the most humane, and therefore the highest or divine idea of the sexual relation." However—and this was the comment that aroused conservative apprehensions—"marriage is very badly administered at present." [6] For this and for other dangerous ideas, James was sharply rebuked by the *New York Observer*, an organ of orthodox Presbyterianism.[7]

Defending himself vigorously against this attack, James published an open letter in the *Tribune*, complaining that he had been charged with hostility to the marriage institution. "This charge," he contended, "is so far from being true, that I have invariably aimed to advance the honor of marriage by seeking to free it from certain purely arbitrary and conventional obstructions in reference to divorce." He had high respect for marriage whether regarded as "a beautiful and very perfect symbol of religious or metaphysical truth" or as an independent social institution. But marriage was in a bad way, James contended:

No doubt there is a very enormous clandestine violation of the marriage bed at the present time; careful observation does not hesitate to say an almost unequalled violation of it: but that is an evil which no positive legislation can prevent, because *it is manifestly based upon a popular contempt for the present indolent and vicious administration of the law.*

The only possible chance of correcting this condition was freely to legitimatize divorce "within the limit of a complete guarantee to society against the support of offspring." [8]

Never so happy as when involved in intellectual swordplay, Henry James continued in subsequent letters to slash at his critics. He completely rejected the idea that the divorce laws should conform to religious dogma. "Our very existence," he wrote, "depends upon the exclusion of religion as an element of government; and we should become a righteous mockery to all mankind if, in face of the open page of history, we should yet allow the foul itch of ecclesiastical ambition to corrupt our present political innocence." He interpreted the New Testament teachings as applying only to the old Jewish practice of private divorce. "Jesus Christ," he concluded, "may be an excellent practical authority for your and my private conscience, but in matters of legislation we are not in the habit of asking any other authority than the manifest public welfare." [9]

Radical though Henry James's ideas were, they were not radical enough to satisfy Stephen Pearl Andrews, who challenged James to say why the government should interfere in marriage matters at all: why not leave both the relations of men and women and the care of their children to the trust of their "inward sweetness without legal bondage?" [10]

In publishing James's controversial letters and Andrews's yet more controversial commentary, Editor Greeley was performing the journalist's role—no doubt aware that these mildly spicy tidbits might improve circulation. A discussion of divorce, Greeley contended, was vitally necessary and had been too long neglected. Yet the editor took pains to dissociate himself completely from his contributors' views. "This," Greeley said, "is preeminently an age of Individualism (it would hardly be polite to say Egotism) wherein 'the Sovereignty of the Individual'—that is, the right of every man to do pretty nearly as he pleases—is already generally popular, and visibly gaining ground daily." This claim of a right to divorce by mutual consent was but another example of excessive individualism: "The general answer to these questions imports that the State does not exist for the advantage and profit of this or that individual, but to secure the highest good of all. . . ." Arguing that freedom of divorce was against the interest of the state, Greeley explained:

Marriage indissoluble may be an imperfect test of honorable and pure affection—as all things human are imperfect—but it is the best the State can devise; and its overthrow would result in a general profligacy and corruption such as this country has never known, and few of our people can adequately imagine.[11]

Ignoring the gadfly Andrews, James directed his reply to Greeley. He turned the editor's charge of excessive individualism around: "It is my identical complaint of the present lax administration of the marriage institution that it allows every brutal and dissolute person 'to do pretty much what he pleases' without, at the same time, allowing his suffering wife and children any adequate redress." James would elevate marriage by excluding from its benefits those who dishonored it. Contrasting the New York laws with those of its neighbors, he wrote:

Our legislators wisely hold with Jesus Christ that all institutions, sacramental or sabbatarian, are made for man, and not man for them, and in some of our sister States accordingly they have already greatly modified the old grounds of divorce. I hear as yet of no bad results. I have an idea that the marriage institution enjoys greater practical honor in Connecticut and Vermont than in our own state. And if so it is only because Connecticut and Vermont have wisely guaranteed its honor by providing for its purity, that is by giving its honest subjects a speedy and complete relief against the *brigandage* which still disfigures it here.[12]

In replying to James, Greeley displayed surprising ignorance of the actual divorce situation. He was not aware, he said, of "any material difference" between the Connecticut and Vermont laws and those of New York; nor did he concede any New England superiority in morals. More to the point was Greeley's argument that most married couples were happy and contented because they assumed their union was for life. "But let it be understood," he warned, "that marriage may be dissolved whenever the parties are tired of each other . . . and we believe more false than true marriages would be contracted; because libertines would resort to marriage as a cloak for lecherous designs, which the legal penalties of Bigamy and Adultery now compel to pursue a more circuitous and less shaded path." Underlining his conservative position, Greeley concluded:

Our own conviction and argument decidedly favor "indissoluble marriage," any existing law to the contrary notwithstanding. But for the express words of Christ which seem to admit Adultery as a valid ground of Divorce, we should stand distinctly on the Roman Catholic ground of no Divorce except by Death. . . .[13]

Refusing to be ignored, Andrews again intervened in the debate. "I regard Marriage," he wrote, "as being neither better nor worse than all other of the arbitrary and artificial institutions of Society—contrivances to regulate nature instead of studying her laws. I ask for the complete emancipation of Woman, simply as I ask the same for Man." [14] Greeley blasted this heresy with his heaviest editorial thunderbolts:

It is very clear, then, Mr. Andrews that your path and mine will never meet. Your Socialism seems to me synonymous with Egotism; mine, on the contrary, contemplates and requires the subjection of individual desire and gratification to the highest good of the community—of the personal to the universal—the temporary to the everlasting. I utterly abhor what you term "the right of woman to choose the father of her child"— meaning her right to choose a dozen fathers for so many different children —seeing that it conflicts directly and fatally with the paramount right of each child through minority to protection, guardianship, and intimate daily counsel and training from both parents. Your Sovereignty of the Individual is in palpable collision with the purity of Society and the sovereignty of God.[15]

This particular divorce debate finally ground to a halt when Greeley refused to accept a new communication from Andrews on the ground that it was unfit for publication. Eventually printed in one of Andrews's pamphlets, the scandalous passage proved to be a curious medical note from a Port Chester doctor's wife attributing uterine tumors to "amative excess." "Be it remembered," the letter commented, "these monstrosities were produced in lawful and indissoluble wedlock." [16] Unsuitable marriages were also blamed for producing murderers, drunkards, and lunatics. Summing up the difference between James's position and his own, Andrews wrote:

Mr. James claims freedom because, for his part, he believes that freedom will lead people to act in just that way which he personally thinks to be right. I, on the contrary, claim freedom for all men and women for no such personal reason, but because they have an inalienable God-given right, high as heaven above all human legislation, to judge for themselves what is moral, and proper, and right for them to do. . . .[17]

This newspaper debate provoked another of some minor interest. In a letter to the *Tribune*, a writer calling himself "Young America" condemned Mrs. Oakes Smith, one of the early champions of woman's rights, for a public lecture in which she had vindicated Cleopatra and certain other historical ladies of dubious character.[18] Greeley chimed in to assert his general sympathy with the woman's rights movement but, nevertheless, to challenge Mrs. Smith to declare "distinctly whether she believes in Divorce or not." [19] Mrs. Smith turned on her tormentors with vigor. What she wanted, she said, was real equality between husband and wife but not divorce: "I would say, guard the conditions of contract. Demand equality in the contracting parties, but forbid Divorce *in toto*. I would have it erased from the statute book. People marry at their peril at best; let them abide the consequences." In her experience, she observed, it was not the women but the men "who go about like grown babies, whining, crying over domestic discomfort, and devising laws to set themselves free from other laws of their own making." [20]

But not all crusaders for woman's rights felt this way. Susan B. Anthony's championship of the right of divorce may have been rooted in dour spinsterhood and contempt for the male sex, but Elizabeth Cady Stanton's feelings need more explanation. A happily married woman who had uncomplainingly given birth to seven children, she might have been expected to defend the indissolubility of marriage. Instead she became the most consistent American advocate of liberal divorce laws. She herself attributed her passionate dedication to this cause to a girlhood experience. One of her youthful friends had made a tragically unhappy marriage. One month after the wedding the husband brutally told his bride that he had married her for her money, that he had already spent the dowry that her father had given them, and that she must live in poverty unless she could extract more money from her family. "When she told the story of her wrongs to me," recalled Mrs. Stanton, "the abuse to which she was subject and the dread in which she lived, I impulsively urged her to fly such a monster and villain, as she would before the hot breath of a ferocious beast of the wilderness; and she did fly, and it was well with her." [21] Shocked by this experience, Mrs. Stanton became a student of the whole marriage problem and a fervent admirer of John Milton—despite that great poet's rather deprecating attitude toward Eve and her daughters.

Mrs. Stanton found her first opportunity to speak her mind in January, 1852, when she addressed a letter to a temperance convention at Albany. She condemned the wife who stayed chained to a drunkard:

> Such companionship . . . is nothing more or less than legalized prostitution. Let us encourage, yea, urge those stricken and who are suffering in such degrading bondage, held there by crude notions of God's laws and the tyranny of a false public sentiment, to sunder all such holy ties, to save themselves from such demoralizing influences, and to escape the guilt of stamping on the brow of innocence the low carnal nature of the confirmed drunkard.[22]

Undeterred by criticism, the feminists continued to urge that the New York legislature recognize habitual drunkenness as ground for divorce. The famous Mrs. Amelia Bloomer declared: "Drunkenness is good ground for divorce, and every woman who is tied to a confirmed drunkard should sunder the ties; and if she do it not otherwise the law should compel it—especially if she have children." [23]

Throughout the 1850's, the feminist leaders engaged in a behind-the-scenes discussion of the so-called "marriage question." In March, 1853, Mrs. Stanton wrote to Miss Anthony: "It is vain to look for the elevation of woman so long as she is degraded in marriage. I say it is a sin, an outrage on our liberal feelings, to pretend that anything but deep fervent love and sympathy constitute marriage. The right idea of marriage is at the foundation of all reforms." She admitted that the world did not seem to be ready for a frank discussion of the question, yet sooner or later it must come: "I would not hurry it on, neither would I avoid it." [24] Mrs. Stanton was convinced that debauched fathers transmitted their faults to their children. In a memorial to the New York legislature in February, 1854, dealing with the whole problem of woman's inequality, she said:

> Instead of your present laws, which make the mother and her children the victims of vice and license, you might rather pass laws prohibiting to all drunkards, libertines and fools, the rights of husbands and fathers. Do

not the hundreds of laughing idiots that are crowding into our asylums, appeal to the wisdom of our statesmen for some new laws on marriage— to the mothers of this day for a higher, purer morality?[25]

Even before Lucy Stone made her famous protest against wives' inequality by refusing to adopt the name of her husband, Henry Blackwell, when she married in 1855, she was deeply interested in the marriage question. "I think we agree in all," she wrote Mrs. Stanton in August, 1853, "except it be the time to strike." Lucy was particularly distressed by the arrogant male assumption that a man owned his wife's body. "One noble woman told me how she fled from her husband to the *Shakers*, because he gave her no peace. . . ."[26] Two years later she wrote: "I *very much* wish that a wife's right to her own body should be pushed at our next convention." [27] But other letters show that she feared to have questions of marriage and divorce raised at woman's rights meetings lest this bring down a storm of censure on the already unpopular feminists. "It seems to me," she wrote Mrs. Stanton in 1856, "that all that pertains *intrinsically* to marriage is an entirely *distinct* question from ours, but one to which this leads just as naturally as rivers run to the ocean. Its magnitude is immeasurable and there ought to be a convention especially to consider that subject but it ought not to be mixed with ours. . . ."[28] And in 1859 she made the specific suggestion to Mrs. Stanton: "I wish you would call a convention to discuss divorce, marriage, infanticide, and their kindred subjects." [29]

The feminists' determination to take up the marriage question was strengthened by the eruption of a new divorce debate in the columns of the *New York Tribune*. This time Greeley found a stubborn antagonist in Robert Dale Owen, son of the utopian socialist and himself a well known champion of radical reform. The *Tribune* editor provoked the controversy by an editorial of March 1, 1860. "Our Legislature," Greeley observed, "is again importuned to try its hand at increasing the facilities of Divorce. We trust it will ponder long and carefully before it consents." He pointed to Indiana as a state whose laws enabled men or women "to get unmarried nearly at pleasure." Indiana, he said, was "the paradise of free-lovers," and this scandal was to be attributed, in large part, to the "lax principles of Robert Dale Owen." [30]

Owen wrote a stinging reply. It was not in Indiana that free love prevailed; there he had never even heard the name. The "paradise of free-lovers" was in states like New York "refusing reasonable divorce."

You have elopements, adultery, which your law . . . virtually encourages; you have free-love, and that most terrible of all social evils, prostitution. You may feel disposed to thank God that you are not as other men, or even as these Indianians. I think that we are justified in His sight, rather than you.

Owen denied that the Indiana divorce laws had been shaped under his influence. While he was in the legislature, he had sponsored only one important change and that was to recognize habitual drunkenness as a ground for divorce. Owen defended the justice of such a provision in an eloquent passage:

See the young creature, "virtuous and worthy," awaiting, late in the solitary night, the fate to which, for life, you consign her; and that for no sin more heinous than that her girl's heart, believing in human goodness, had trusted the vows and promises of a scoundrel. Is it her home where she is sitting? Let us not so desecrate the hallowed word. It is the den of her sufferings and of her shame. A bloated wretch, whom daily and nightly debauch has degraded below humanity, has the right to enter it. In what temper he will arrive, God alone knows—all the animal within him, probably, aroused by drink. Will he beat her . . . ? Likely enough! Ah well if that be all! . . . He has the command of torments, legally permitted, far beyond those of the lash. . . . He is authorized to commit what more resembles an infamous crime—usually rated second to murder, and often punished with death—than anything else. . . .

God forgive you, Horace Greeley, the inhuman sentiment! . . . God send that you may never, in the person of a daughter of your own, and in the recital of her tortures, practically learn the terrible lesson how far you have strayed from the right.[31]

Greeley pounced upon Owen's letter with joyous ferocity. Citing the dictionary definition of marriage as the act of uniting a man and woman *for life*, he declared: "There may be something better than Marriage; but nothing *is Marriage* but a solemn engagement to live together in faith and love *till death*. Why should not they, who have devised something better than old-fashioned Marriage, give their bantling a distinctive *name*, and not appropriate ours?" Greeley didn't question the morality of the people of Indiana, but attributed this to the fact that most of them came from states which maintained the indissolubility of marriage. The population of Indiana was still sparse and not exposed to the temptations born of "crowds, luxury, and idleness."

But let Time and Change do their work, and then see! Given the population of Italy in the days of the Caesars, with easy divorce, and I believe the result would be like that experienced by the Roman Republic, which under the sway of easy divorce, rotted away and perished,—blasted by the mildew of unchaste mothers and dissolute homes.[32]

Owen responded with a second letter reviewing the history of marriage to prove that "there is no absolute right or wrong about this matter of divorce, but . . . it may properly vary in its details at different stages of civilization." Jesus' teachings on divorce, according to Owen, were those appropriate "to the low grade of morality then existing in Judea." Moreover, Jesus' idea of conjugal fidelity was not that entertained by American courts of law; to look on a woman lustfully was adultery by Jesus' definition. "The fair inference seems to be," Owen argued, "that the proper cause for divorce is not the mere physical act of infidelity, but that adultery of the heart which quenches conjugal love, thus destroying that which, far more than your cohabitation till death, may be regarded as 'the very essence of marriage.'" As for Greeley's praise of judicial separation, "of all the various kinds of divorce it has been found, in practice, to be the most immoral in its tendency." [33]

Greeley dissented entirely from the notion that the words of Jesus might have been intended to have a local and temporary application. "On the contrary," the editor wrote, "I believe he, unlike Moses, promulgated the eternal and universal law, founded, not in accommodation to special circumstances, but in the essential nature of God and man." There might be temptation involved in judicial separation, "but I judge this evil far less than that which must result from the easy dissolution of Marriage." According to Greeley, Owen's theory overlooked a vital truth:

The Divine end of Marriage is parentage, or the perpetuation and increase
of the Human Race. To this end, it is indispensable—or at least, eminently desirable—that each child should enjoy protection, nurture, sus-
tenance, at the hands of a mother not only but of a father also. In other
words, the parents should be so attached, so devoted to each other, that
they shall be practically separable but by death.[34]

The debate continued for some time with both disputants tend-
ing to repeat the arguments of their earlier letters. Despite the usual
quibbling over the meaning of Biblical texts, the two men raised the
discussion to a higher level than most such controversies. Owen denied Greeley's assumption that parenthood was the chief purpose of
marriage; the higher end, he believed, was to call forth "all that is
best and purest in the inner nature of man, love, in the broadest ac-
ceptation of that much profaned word." Therefore, when love
ceased, the marriage should also cease.

I do not merely say, in cases where the holiest purposes for which God
ordained Marriage are frustrated, its divinest ends defeated, and its in-
most sanctuary defiled by evil passions, that the relation, thus outraged,
may not improperly cease. I say that for the sake of virtue and for the
good of mankind, in all such demoralizing cases, it *ought* to cease.[35]

Greeley's best argument was that strict divorce laws had a deter-
rent effect. Thoroughly characteristic of the man was this passage:

"It is very hard," said a culprit to the judge who sentenced him, "that
I should be so severely punished for merely stealing a horse." "Man,"
replied the judge, "you are *not* so punished for merely stealing a horse,
but *that horses may not be stolen*." The distinction seems to me clear and
vital.

To the "wedded in soul" to live together till death do part had no
terrors.

But to the libertine, the egotist, the selfish, sensual seeker of personal and
present enjoyment at whatever cost to others, the Indissolubility of Marriage is an obstacle, a restraint, a terror; and God forbid that it should
ever cease to be.[36]

The Greeley-Owen debate steeled the will of Mrs. Stanton to raise the divorce question at the next annual woman's rights convention in New York City. On May 11, 1860, she proposed a set of ten resolutions, most of them closely paraphrased from her hero, John Milton. The seventh, for example, declared "that an unfortunate or ill-assorted marriage is ever a calamity, but not ever, perhaps never, a crime—and when society or government, by its laws or customs, compels its continuance, always to the grief of one of the parties, and the actual loss and damage of both, it usurps an authority never delegated to man, nor exercised by God himself." [37] Supporting her resolutions with all her well known wit and eloquence, Mrs. Stanton ridiculed the theory of indissoluble marriage. She referred to recent newspaper accounts of wife murders and suicides, and asked:

> What say you to facts like these? Now, do you believe . . . that all these wretched matches are made in heaven? that all these sad, miserable people are bound together by God? I know Horace Greeley has been most eloquent, for weeks past, on the holy sacrament of ill-assorted marriages; but let us hope that all wisdom does not live, and will not die with Horace Greeley.[38]

The trouble with marriage, Mrs. Stanton insisted, was that the male sex had had the sole regulation of the matter. "He has spoken in Scripture, he has spoken in law. As an individual, he has decided the time and cause for putting away a wife, and as a judge and legislator, he still holds the entire control." If either party in marriage could claim a right to stand supreme, she said, it ought to be the woman, "the mother of the race." [39]

Although Mrs. Stanton's speech was greeted with loud applause, some of the other feminist leaders strongly opposed her position. The Reverend Antoinette Brown Blackwell, an ordained Congregational minister, introduced a set of counterresolutions upholding "the permanence and indissolubility of marriage." She argued that if a woman's husband were wretched and degraded it was her duty to stick with him and endeavor "to win him back to the right." Yet even the Reverend Antoinette's spirit rebelled at the thought that a wife was obligated to bear children in such circumstances. "I say to her, 'No! while the law of God continues, you are bound never to make one whom you do not honor and respect, as well as love, the father of any child of yours." [40]

To the well known Polish Jewess, Ernestine Rose, Mrs. Blackwell seemed to be treating woman "as some ethereal being." This was all very well, but it was necessary to be "a little material also." Practical considerations demanded that divorce be granted for cruelty, willful desertion, and habitual intemperance. "I ask for a law of Divorce," Mrs. Rose said, "so as to secure the real objects and blessings of married life, to prevent the crimes and immoralities now practiced, to prevent 'Free Love,' in its most hideous form, such as is now carried on but too often under the very name of marriage, where hypocrisy is added to the crime of legalized prostitution." [41]

Wendell Phillips never shied away from an issue merely because it was controversial. But the famous radical believed that it was a mistake to mix radicalisms. "This Convention," he argued, "was no Marriage Convention." Wise or unwise, the divorce laws were the same for men as for women. "Certainly, there are cases where men are bound to women caracasses as well as where women are bound to men carcasses." [42] He moved, therefore, that the divorce resolutions be excluded from the journal of the convention. William Lloyd Garrison attempted to play the unaccustomed role of peacemaker: he agreed, he said, with Phillips that the marriage problem was not properly before the convention, yet he opposed Phillips's motion, because he believed that Mrs. Stanton had a right to present her resolutions.[43]

Susan B. Anthony met the issue more directly. Totally dissenting from the contention that the divorce question did not belong in a woman's rights platform, she said:

Marriage has ever been a one-sided matter, resting most unequally upon the sexes. By it, man gains all—woman loses all; tyrant law and lust reign supreme with him—meek submission and ready obedience alone befit her. Woman has never been consulted; her wish has never been taken into consideration as regards the terms of the marriage contract.[44]

When the issue came to a vote, the convention rejected Phillips's motion, thus upholding the position taken by Mrs. Stanton.

Horace Greeley, sympathetic with many of the feminist goals, was of course unhappy at the latest turn of events. In an editorial on May 14, he wrote:

> On the subject of marriage and divorce we have some very positive opinions, and what they are is pretty generally known. But even were they less positive and fixed, we should none the less protest against the sweeping character of the resolutions introduced at the Woman's Rights Convention . . . by Mrs. Elizabeth Cady Stanton. We can not look upon the marriage relation as of no more binding force than that which a man may make with a purchaser for the sale of dry-goods, or an engagement he may contract with a schoolmaster or governess. Such doctrine seems to us simply shocking.[45]

Two weeks later the *Tribune* published a letter from Mrs. Stanton, replying not so much to Greeley as to Phillips. Denying that the laws of marriage and divorce bore equally upon men and women, she said that "an immense difference rests in the fact, that man has made the laws, cunningly and selfishly, for his own purpose." [46]

In February, 1861, when the New York legislature was considering the Ramsey Bill to liberalize the divorce laws, Mrs. Stanton was invited to address the senate judiciary committee. She used this opportunity to make a spirited presentation of her case before an assembly chamber full of curious legislators.[47] Her eloquent speech was warmly applauded, but did not save the Ramsey Bill from defeat a few days later.

The determination shown by Mrs. Stanton and Miss Anthony in pushing the divorce question to a place of high priority in the woman's rights movement was highly significant. Whereas divorce in earlier periods of history had been primarily a prerogative demanded by men to rid themselves of unwanted wives and open the way for new marriages, nineteenth century American divorce was becoming more and more a right demanded by women on humanitarian grounds. The day was passing when wives would meekly submit to all kinds of abuse from brutal husbands. The early compilers of divorce statistics were impressed by the fact that women far outnumbered men as plaintiffs. In part, no doubt, this reflected a kind of male gallantry. When a marriage failed and both parties wanted a dissolution, many times the husband encouraged his wife to seek the divorce, thereby saving her from being publicly branded as the guilty party. This was particularly true in New York State where the charge of adultery had to be made. But women's increasing resort to divorce was too pronounced a tendency to be explained by this factor alone. Despite the stigma involved in many social circles, more and more women accepted divorce as a lesser evil than continued suffering in an unhappy marriage. And in such situations the wife's former economic dependence upon her husband had now been much reduced by the opening up of new opportunities for employment.

CHAPTER 8

The Shoals of Free Love

During the 1850's and 1860's free love had become a familiar phrase. In New York City a little group of defiant intellectuals including Dr. M. Edgeworth Lazarus, Josiah Warren, and Stephen Pearl Andrews wrote tracts denouncing the tryanny of marriage and championing the right to complete freedom in sexual relations. A scandal of 1855 was the publication of Mary Gove Nichols's autobiographical novel *Mary Lyndon,* characterized by the *New York Times* as an attempt to convince the world of "the reforming influence of fine art and fornication." [1] Fourier socialism and free love were favorite subjects for discussion at the biweekly meetings of the society known simply as "The Club." According to the newspapers, this was the headquarters of the whole Free Love movement, where its disciples not only propagated their heresy but met each other socially—an obvious convenience for men and women who were looking for partners in "passional attraction." [2] Egged on by the press, the police raided the premises in October, 1855.[3] But the free lovers were alleged to have found a new front for their iniquities in the "Unitary Household," founded in 1858. According to the *New York Times,* "the serving-maids were debauched, children of tender years fell victims to the art of accomplished seducers, lust raged, and decency was banished." [4] Fortunately for the morals of the city, the Unitary Household became insolvent and had to close shop in 1861. After these lurid episodes, local champions of morality kept vigilant watch against any new cult of Venus.

To advocate liberal divorce laws was obviously not the same thing as to preach free love. What need, after all, had free lovers of either marriage or divorce? Nevertheless, champions of the right of divorce always ran the risk of being denounced as enemies of marriage, and Mrs. Stanton and Miss Anthony found themselves under especially virulent attack on this ground in the years between 1868 and 1875. At times it seemed that the whole woman's rights movement might be wrecked upon the rocks of pious prejudice. For the situation that developed, the feminist leaders were in part to blame, since they had deliberately sailed their ship into dangerous waters. But their moments of greatest peril occurred when they encountered treacherous hidden reefs. How could they have foreseen that they could not safely steer by such trusted lighthouses as Theodore Tilton and Henry Ward Beecher?

In January, 1868, Mrs. Stanton and Miss Anthony were in a rebellious mood. They and their sister leaders had put the woman's rights movement into cold storage during the Civil War, while they spoke and worked tirelessly for Union victory. Having done so much, they looked for their reward after Appomattox in Radical Republican support for woman suffrage. But the radical leaders gave priority to the Negro, refusing to concede that women also should be guaranteed the right to vote. Mrs. Stanton and Miss Anthony had a further rebuff at the New York Constititional Convention of 1867, when the dominant Republicans refused to support woman suffrage. The two women embarrassed Horace Greeley, the presiding officer, by arranging for the presentation of a woman's rights petition signed by none other than Mrs. Horace Greeley. On the next occasion when Editor Greeley met Mrs. Stanton and Miss Anthony he called them "the most manuevering politicians in the State of New York"; he had given instructions, he told them, that the *Tribune* should never again award a word of praise to Mrs. Stanton.[5]

Mrs. Stanton and Miss Anthony became further alienated from the Radical Republicans as a result of their campaign in Kansas, where important referenda on both Negro and woman suffrage were held in November, 1867. Convinced that the Republicans were only lukewarm for their cause, the feminists scandalized their eastern friends by allying themselves with George Francis Train, a flamboyant Irish Democrat, who had made a fortune in clipper ships and railroads. A natural spellbinder, Train combined a genuine sympathy for woman suffrage with an equal enthusiasm for such miscellaneous radicalisms as paper money, the eight-hour day, and Irish freedom. When the Kansas voters rejected both Negro and woman suffrage, old line abolitionists like William Lloyd Garrison and Wendell Phillips blamed the twin defeats upon the folly of Miss Anthony and Mrs. Stanton in joining forces with such a mountebank.[6]

Completely unrepentant, the two women accepted Train's money for their next venture, the publication of a weekly paper with the defiant title *The Revolution*. The new periodical provided a platform for uncompromising advocacy of woman's rights and other controversial causes. Train was a regular contributor and continued to jar the orthodox with his political and financial heresies.[7]

Among the subjects thrown open for discussion in *The Revolution* was that of the marriage laws. On June 18, 1868, Eleanor Kirk contributed an article entitled "A Word to Abused Wives," in which she bitterly condemned the New York divorce laws. "Here a woman may not be legally separated from a man—never mind how much personal abuse she may bring witnesses to testify to—unless she has proof positive of his infidelity. *That* statute . . . needs fixing; and I trust that those compelled to suffer its extremity will give it an overhauling." [8]

In her own editorials Mrs. Stanton repeatedly raised the divorce question. Showing the influence of Milton, she wrote: "The wisest possible reform we could have on this whole question is to have no legislation whatever. The relations of the sexes are too delicate in their nature for statutes, lawyers, judges, jurors, or our public journals to take cognizance of, or regulate." [9] She complained that the divorce laws were unequal: if the husband were the guilty party, he still retained the greater part of the common property; if the wife were guilty, she went out of the partnership penniless.[10] In an editorial entitled "The Man Marriage," Mrs. Stanton denounced the "present system" of marriage as based on creeds and customs to

which women had never given their consent. Male interpretation
of the Bible, male lawmaking, and male-orientated social customs all
combined to make the wife the mere possession of her husband.[11]

Mrs. Stanton's radicalism on this and other matters caused growing concern to more conservative advocates of woman's rights. In
May, 1869, an open storm blew up at a convention of the Equal
Rights Association. Organized to work for both Negro and woman
suffrage, the Association bitterly debated which should come first.
Miss Anthony and Mrs. Stanton condemned the pending Fifteenth
Amendment because it provided that the right to vote should not
be denied on account of race, but did not prohibit discrimination
on the basis of sex. The convention overrode their objections and
endorsed the Amendment. The delegates also rebuked Mrs. Stanton
by passing a resolution upholding the sanctity of marriage. Mrs.
Mary Livermore of Chicago wanted to substitute still stronger
language to save the movement from its disgraceful reputation of
favoring free love. Mrs. Ernestine Rose, on the other hand, wanted
no resolution at all; the character of the feminist leaders was un-
tainted; certainly it was not necessary for them to declare that
"they were not prostitutes." [12]

Deciding that the Equal Rights Association was too conservative,
the more aggressive faction now organized the National Woman
Suffrage Association with Mrs. Stanton as president. All this was
deeply disturbing to a New England group that included Lucy
Stone and her husband Henry Blackwell as well as such other lead-
ers as Julia Ward Howe, Wendell Phillips, and Thomas Wentworth
Higginson. Unwilling to follow the radical leadership of *The
Revolution*, the moderates founded a new periodical, the *Woman's
Journal*, and organized the American Woman Suffrage Association
with the widely-admired Henry Ward Beecher as first president.
The new association was committed to work for woman suffrage
through state rather than Federal action.[13]

Already in serious trouble because the effervescent Train had
withdrawn his support, *The Revolution* was mortally wounded
by the establishment of this rival suffrage organ. But for their few
remaining months of journalism, Mrs. Stanton and Miss Anthony
continued to fly all their banners, including that of liberalized divorce.

The woman's rights crusaders found a focus for their indignation in the tragic McFarland-Richardson affair of December, 1869. As a trusting New England girl, Abby Sage had married Daniel McFarland to whom she had borne two sons. McFarland proved to be a highly undependable husband. He drank too much and was unable to earn a steady income in any of his successive ventures as lawyer, land speculator, and political spoilsman. Forced to find something to do to support the family, Abby began to give dramatic readings, a vocation for which she appeared to have some talent. In her new career she became friendly with several prominent New York women, who helped her to get a job as an actress, doing bit parts in Edwin Booth's company. Meanwhile Abby's relations with her husband became increasingly unhappy, as he drank more heavily than ever and displayed a sullen and abusive temper. Abby's plight won the sympathy of Albert D. Richardson, a well known correspondent for the *New York Tribune*, who roomed in the same lodging house with the McFarlands.[14]

Fearing that the moody McFarland was about to kill either himself or her, Abby left him in February, 1867, and found refuge in the home of Samuel Sinclair, the publisher of the *New York Tribune*. Richardson immediately offered his help to the fugitive wife and the two soon reached an understanding that they would marry if Abby were ever free. Like many another New Yorker of this period, Mrs. McFarland sought the easiest way out of her marital troubles by taking up temporary residence in another state. She lived for sixteen months in Indiana, where she finally obtained a divorce in October, 1869. She then returned to New York with the obvious intention of marrying Richardson, but before she could do so, the vengeful McFarland surprised his rival in the offices of the *New York Tribune* and shot him through the stomach. Richardson was carried to the near-by Astor House, where he lingered for a week, finally dying on December 2, 1869. Two days before the end, Richardson was married to Abby McFarland by Henry Ward Beecher, the most famous preacher of the day, assisted by Octavius Brooks Frothingham, a well known Unitarian minister.[15]

The Richardson case provided all the sensation that greedy newspaper readers could ask. The victim had been a well known Civil War correspondent and a friend of such prominent Republi-

cans as Vice-President Schuyler Colfax. The whole editorial staff
of the *New York Tribune* was deeply involved. Not only had the
shooting occurred in the *Tribune* office, but Horace Greeley and
his associates had ministered devotedly to their stricken colleague,
even making the arrangements for his deathbed marriage—an obvious
irony in view of Greeley's fame as an opponent of divorce. Greeley,
Beecher, and Frothingham were all savagely flogged by editorial
pens. "We doubt," said the *New York Times,* "whether a more disgraceful outrage on public morals has ever been committed in this
community than is involved in the open scorn of the marriage tie
and the total disregard of all principles of justice, which professed
ministers of religion and public writers have managed to display." [16]
Self-righteous moralists smeared the widow with innuendoes concerning her relations with Richardson and her out-of-state divorce.

These sensational events struck off sparks from the radical wing
of the woman's movement. At a meeting of the National Woman
Suffrage Association on December 8, 1869, two resolutions of opposing tendency were adopted. The first praised the leaders of the
New York Tribune for their recent conduct in connection with the
McFarland-Richardson affair; the second condemned the same paper
for its "pernicious influence on the divorce question and the civil
rights of women," which had contributed to the unhealthy state of
mind reflected in McFarland's crime. Still more provocative ground
was taken by Mrs. Stanton in a letter published in *The Revolution:*

> You ask what I think of the Richardson affair. I rejoice over every
> slave that escapes from a discordant marriage. . . . My opinion is, that
> a woman has a right to choose between a base, petty tyrant and a noble,
> magnanimous man. . . .[17]

But female indignation did not rise to the explosion point until
after McFarland's trial and acquittal. Although John Graham, the
defendant's lawyer, based his technical case on a plea of temporary
insanity, his real effort was to convince the jury that the injured husband was justified in killing the man who had broken up his marriage. In his closing argument, Graham declared:

When this man Richardson led this woman from her husband's house in Amity street, the husband had as much right to shoot him down as though Richardson had been guilty of her forcible abduction. That is the law of the Bible; for one of the two parties is superior and the other inferior. There is no absolute equality in the Bible between man and wife. As I understand the law of the Bible, it is that man was made for God and woman for man; that woman is the weaker vessel, and is meant to be under the protection of the stronger vessel, man; and that any attempt from any quarter to interfere with that supremacy, even though it be with the consent of the woman, is as much an infraction of the husband's rights as though it were the infliction of absolute violence upon her or upon him.[18]

Reporting the scene, a journalist noted that Graham's argument was greeted with "a distinct hiss from some of the strong minded ladies present." [19] This unhappiness was intensified when McFarland walked out of the courtroom not only a free man but with custody of the elder son. From the woman's point of view this outcome of the trial defied all logic: either McFarland was sane and should be hanged; or he was insane and should be confined to an asylum.

The McFarland case confirmed Mrs. Stanton in her belief that the New York divorce law was intolerable. Addressing a woman suffrage meeting on the final day of the trail, she said:

No matter what the character of the husband—though a bloated drunkard and diseased libertine, leaving his wife and children to poverty and rags to suffer hunger in a New York garret, victims to his daily outbreaks of brutality and passion, or of his stolid indifference or neglect—let him, in fact, be and do as he chooses, no other man shall have mercy on these helpless ones, and the woman shall continue to be his wife as long as he lives, say the laws of New York, though her flesh crawl, and her soul sicken every time he enters her presence.[20]

Female indignation over McFarland's acquittal reached a climax on May 17 when two thousand women crowded into Apollo Hall in New York City to applaud Mrs. Stanton's fiery oration and to approve a petition to the Governor, requesting that McFarland be confined to an insane asylum. Mrs. Stanton addressed another great protest meeting in Brooklyn a few days later. The *New York Sun* and other papers sharply rebuked these demonstrations, but *The*

Revolution was characteristically defiant. These meetings "to protest against the unjust decision in our courts, the scurrility of the press, the popular idea of marriage are the handwriting on the wall, warning our Belshazzars that they are weighed in the balances and found wanting." [21]

The position that Mrs. Stanton had taken on the McFarland case was strongly supported by Theodore Tilton, the liberal editor of the influential religious journal, *The Independent*. He denied that a Christian woman was bound to live as the wife of a drunkard, who made her life "a constant agony." [22] Growing still more explicit, Tilton demanded the enactment in New York of the general divorce code which prevailed in New England. "To say that the only permissible ground for divorce is adultery," he wrote, "is to show a blind allegiance to a superstition which never had any other foundation than a long-exploded interpretation of a Scriptural text." [23]

But the *Woman's Journal*, speaking for the conservatives, deplored these recent developments. Henry Blackwell denied that the McFarland case had any legitimate relationship to the woman suffrage issue. Noting the growing tendency of the newspapers to charge the woman's movement with hostility to the marriage institution, Blackwell wrote: "As friends of Woman Suffrage, we protest against being compromised in this matter by the ultraism of a few individuals. Ninety-nine out of every one hundred of the active workers in our movement are happy husbands and wives, who believe in marriage as a noble and life-long partnership of equals, and who believe in political equality because men and women should go hand in hand as mutual friends and helpers." [24]

Criticism, whether from prosuffrage or antisuffrage sources, only strengthened Mrs. Stanton's resolution to campaign for more liberal divorce laws. In June, 1870, she delivered a lecture in New York City on "Marriage and Divorce," in which she explored the subject more thoroughly than ever before. The battle for woman suffrage, she optimistically declared, was almost won. Therefore, those who felt a deeper interest in "the social problem" should transfer their energy to this "more vital question." Indissoluble marriage, Mrs. Stanton asserted, is slavery for the woman; indeed there is "no other human slavery that knows such depths of degradation as a wife chained to a man whom she neither loves nor respects, no other slavery so disastrous in its consequences on the race, or to individual respect, growth, and development." Citing the authority of the famous Unitarian scholar, Moncure D. Conway, Mrs. Stanton boldly challenged the idea that Christ had condemned all divorce except on the ground of adultery. "The ascetic law of marriage ascribed to Jesus in Matthew," she declared, "has been the means of killing more wives and husbands, the cause of more intrigues, and the training of more children amid daily examples of hypocrisy and meanness than all other causes put together." [25]

Thousands of men and women in all parts of the country heard Mrs. Stanton repeat this lecture. The journalistic phase of the Anthony-Stanton partnership had ended in May, 1870, when the debt-ridden *Revolution* passed into other hands, and the two women now devoted their energies to professional lecturing. Mrs. Stanton had several lectures in her repertoire, but she particularly liked to speak on the divorce question. "Women respond to this divorce speech as they never did to suffrage," she noted in June, 1870.[26] Six months later when she was lecturing in Michigan, she wrote: "I am speaking every night to fine audiences, sometimes on suffrage, sometimes on marriage and divorce. I shall be a reservoir of sorrows. Verily, slavery is nothing to those unclean marriages. The women gladly hear the new gospel so let the press howl." [27]

Radical though her standard lecture sounded to conservative ears, the famous feminist went still further on at least one occasion. Preserved among her papers is a manuscript headed: "Delivered by Elizabeth Cady Stanton before a club of men and women in New York City about 1869." [28] This date is certainly wrong, because internal evidence would place the speech about 1871. Referring to her earlier lecture in which she claimed her views would not destroy but would "improve and perfect" marriage, she declared:

But stop! I will not be guilty of false pretenses. I will not skulk under the pretentious ambiguity in the meaning of the term: marriage in some sense will be disturbed, will be abrogated in fine by the progress of reform. . . . Marriage I mean as a compulsory bond, enforced by law and rendered perpetual by that means.

By advocating a maximum of liberty in these relationships, Mrs. Stanton admitted that she laid herself open to criticism:

Freedom on this subject! Why that is nothing short of unlimited freedom of divorce, freedom to institute at the option of the parties new amatory relationships. We put above marriage in a word the obnoxious doctrine of Free Love. Well yes, that is what I mean. We are all free lovers at heart though we may not have thought so.

This did not necessarily mean transient unions. "If every man selects one woman and every woman one man and if they live together as the most exclusive mates, that is just as much free love as the most unlimited variety or promiscuity." To her critics, she threw out this provocative challenge:

The men and women who are dabbling with the suffrage movement for women should be at once therefore and emphatically warned that what they mean logically if not consciously in all they say is next social equality and next Freedom or in a word Free Love and, if they wish to get out of the boat, they should for safety get out now, for delays are dangerous.

Would The Revolution, now under the editorship of Laura Curtis Bullard, continue to advocate more liberal divorce laws? At first, this seemed doubtful. Under Miss Anthony's management, the masthead legend had been: "The True Republic—Men, Their Rights and Nothing More; Women, Their Rights and Nothing Less." Under Mrs. Bullard, this was discarded in favor of the reassuring Biblical verse: "What therefore God hath joined together, let not man put asunder." [29] Conservatives took this as an announcement that The Revolution would drop its controversial position on the marriage question. Commending the change, Lillie Devereux Blake wrote: "It has been a source of regret to me ever since I joined the Woman Suffrage party, that so many advocates of that measure are advocates also of a greater liberty of divorce." [30]

But The Revolution's backtracking lasted only a few weeks. By August, 1870, the editor was interpreting the new masthead in a radical sense: only those marriages should continue where the mutual love of the parties demonstrated that God had truly joined them. "Man," Mrs. Bullard explained, "has bound in wedlock many whom

God has not joined together. Indeed, it is difficult for a close observer not to come to the conclusion that marriage, as it now exists, is a curse to society and to the human race; it is a source, far more frequently, of misery than of happiness." [31] Over the next three months *The Revolution* became more militant than ever on the divorce question. In enumerating woman's demands in September, it included "freedom to marry, and to be mistress of herself after marriage; freedom to sunder a yoke which she has freely bound." [32] The *Woman's Journal* was indignant:

If this language means anything, it means that woman shall be as free to sunder the ties of marriage as to form them—shall be as free to divorce herself from marriage as to marry—that there shall be as large a freedom in going out of marriage, as in entering it. If this *be* the meaning of the Revolution . . . we dissent from such a demand, *in toto*. We believe in *marriage for life*, and deprecate all this loose, pestiferous talk in favor of *easy divorce*.[33]

Provoked by newspaper reports of one of Mrs. Stanton's speeches, the *Woman's Journal* warned:

Legitimately carried out, these theories abrogate marriage, and we have then the hideous thing known as "free love." Be not deceived—*free love means free lust*. And let all women ponder well how they accept the specious arguments, and follow the leading of even a woman beloved and honored as Mrs. Stanton is, and has been, if her teaching lead in that direction.[34]

As the *Woman's Journal* and *The Revolution* locked horns in journalistic combat, the whole strategy of the woman's rights movement came under debate. In an article in the *Woman's Journal*, Boston's highly respected Thomas Wentworth Higginson argued that the reformers should concentrate all their energies on suffrage, postponing all other demands until women won the right to vote.[35] *The Revolution* heatedly rejected this advice. "The ballot," it said, "is not even half the loaf; it is only a crust—a crumb." The marriage question was of more vital consequence to woman's welfare than "any such superficial and fragmentary question" as woman's suffrage.[36]

In December, 1870, a proposed merger of the rival suffrage organizations failed—in large part because of the divorce controversy. The deliberations of the conservative American Woman
Suffrage Association at Cleveland were disrupted by Susan B.
Anthony, who was present, not as a member, but as a spectator. She
challenged the other party to "talk plain and say what you mean!"
If they opposed union because Mrs. Stanton advocated woman's
right "to free herself from a marriage relation that is worse than
slavery," they should say so. Miss Anthony left no doubt as to how
she felt on the issue. "If a woman makes a mistake or is forced into
marriage and finds that her husband is a drunkard, a gambler, or a
libertine, it is criminally wicked for her to remain bound to him; it is
a sin for her to bear children to sorrow and misery in such a
union." Is momentary pique she alluded to Lucy Stone's shift of
position since the historic day when she had married Henry Blackwell in a defiantly unconventional ceremony. How could such a
marriage have been legal? she asked—only to apologize a moment
later to her old friend whose marriage had been the "greatest protest against wrong the world has ever seen." [37] Susan's peppery per-
formance contributed nothing to harmony, and the split in the
woman's movement continued for two decades.

The National Association's reputation for radicalism was strengthened by the pronouncements of one of its most prominent members, Mrs. Pauline Wright Davis of Providence, Rhode Island. At the
National's annual meeting at New York on May 11, 1871, Mrs. Davis
moved a somewhat enigmatic resolution, asserting "that the evils,
sufferings, and disabilities, of women as well as of men, are social
still more than they are political, and that a statement of Woman's
Rights which ignores the right of self-ownership, as the first of all
rights is insufficient to meet the demand and is ceasing to enlist the
enthusiasm, and even the common interest, of the intelligent portion of the community." [38] When there was some question after
the convention as to just what this meant, Mrs. Davis became em-
barrassingly explicit. "The law," she said, "which makes obligatory
the rendering of marital rights and compulsory maternity on the
part of Woman in the absence of love, and of congeniality, of
health, and of fitness, is a deadly despotism; and no woman thus
subjugated can be pure in soul and body." Greeley's *New York*

Tribune at once scented in Mrs. Davis's words the trail of its most feared enemy: "We cannot understand the above otherwise than as the broadest assertion of the doctrine which we execrate as 'Free Love'—that is, the right of each man and each woman to repudiate the marriage tie whenever he or she shall find a new 'affinity' more to his or her liking." [39]

The *Tribune*'s rebuke to Mrs. Davis precipitated a journalistic exchange in which each side became more and more outspoken. Eventually Mrs. Davis wrote: "I wish to adopt the term 'Free Love,' and avow my thorough belief in the doctrine as high and holy, and hurl back all the foul charges against it, which are made by the ignorant, the corrupt, and the impure, from the purlieus of our cities." [40] The *Tribune* professed itself to be shocked by such theories:

The ignorant and impressionable women whose principles have been shaken by this insidious propaganda will become the easy prey of the first plausible scoundrel who can persuade them of his sympathy. A school which is capable of preparing so baleful a harvest of foulness and misery cannot claim the immunity of silence. Mrs. Davis's vagaries may be fun to men, but they are death to women.[41]

But Mrs. Davis was not in the least abashed by the *Tribune*'s rebukes. Who should determine whether marriage should exist, the man or the woman? she asked, and then replied: "I hold that woman shall make the laws (if we must have laws to govern the affections) not man. On woman falls all the burdens of marriage . . . I am not afraid to trust human nature in freedom. Love will find its own way to take care of children." The *Tribune* shook its head at such heresy. "These are the only two logical results of the doctrines of Free Love," it concluded. "With pure women like Mrs. Davis, it means no love at all. With the other kind, it means the promiscuous license of the beasts that perish." [42]

Throughout 1871, the cause of liberal divorce continued to be complicated with the still more controversial issue of free love. Both became hopelessly involved in the career of Theodore Tilton. First as editor of the *Independent*, then of the new competing magazine, the *Golden Age*, Tilton argued strongly for a liberalization of the divorce laws. Unfortunately this campaign cannot be intelligently discussed without taking note of Tilton's own marital difficulties. In July, 1870, the famous editor's wife confessed to him the shocking fact that she had been having illicit relations with her own pastor, Tilton's closest friend, the great Henry Ward Beecher. At first Tilton followed the Christian course of forgiving the guilty pair and saying nothing, but he lacked the fortitude to persist in this course. During the next several months he confided his secret to several friends including Elizabeth Cady Stanton, and, as knowledge of the affair spread to a gradually widening circle, a time bomb was set ticking in the citadel of New York's most respectable society. For two years the explosion was delayed, but when it came the damage was of sickening proportions.[43]

Under the circumstances it can scarcely be doubted that Tilton's growing radicalism on the marriage question provided some kind of psychological outlet for his own unhappiness. Yet this explanation can be carried too far. Long before this personal problem arose, he had identified himself as a liberal on the divorce question.

"Marriage without love," Tilton wrote in December, 1870, "is a sin against God:—a sin which, like other sins, is to be repented of, ceased from, and put away." [44] Defending the point of view of the Union differs from every other in its laws concerning divorce, we the radical feminists, he said in April, 1871: "While every state of respectfully submit that the time has come when the women of the country should take hold of this subject, with a view to the enlightenment of the public mind, and to a consideration of the proper remedy for a universal grievance." [45] Two months later he wrote: "There is but one ground for divorce in the State of New York. But we have repeatedly insisted that to limit divorce to this one and only cause is to make a legislative mockery of the sorrows and sufferings of human hearts." [46]

As Henry James and Robert Dale Owen had discovered earlier, one of the best devices for focusing attention on the divorce question was to provoke Horace Greeley into debate. This was probably Tilton's motive in devoting an editorial in August, 1871, to "Mr. Greeley's Course on the Woman Question." "Outside of the Roman Catholic Church," Tilton wrote, "we do not know a man so backward in his views on all that pertains to the status of woman, as Mr. Greeley." He alluded particularly to the "absurdity and folly" of the Tribune's views on marriage and divorce.[47]

Greeley accepted the challenge of his old friend with alacrity. Writing "in a spirit of hearty hatred for Free Love and all its infernal delusions," he assured Tilton that the latter was "eminently right" in asserting that his "conviction of the proper indissolubility of marriage" was "the mainspring" of his hostility both to woman suffrage "and to the social philosophy from which many vainly seek to separate the woman movement." [48] Tilton replied by denying that woman suffrage tended to dissolve marriage. But he chided Greeley for having "helped to make or at least to keep the divorce laws of our own State very illiberal and unjust." Alluding to the more rational laws of New England, he asked:

Will you rebuke those States for this legislation, and call their citizens free lovers for adopting it? Or (what would be better) will you join me in an endeavor to import the Masschusetts legislation on this subject into our New York code.[49]

Greeley and Tilton continued their jousting for several months. Tilton denied the charge that he favored free love, but he defined his position in language that seemed to conservatives a reasonable facsimile of that hated doctrine. "I would no more permit the law of the land to enchain me to a woman whom I did not love, or who did not love me, than I would permit the same law to handcuff me as a slave to a master on a plantation. There are higher laws than civil statutes, and I am a rebel against the State's too impertinent interference between man and wife. Love should be like religion—free from the mandate of the civil law." [50] Defining his position more carefully in a later editorial, he called for the sweeping away of all conflicting state laws on divorce in favor of a uniform national statute based upon liberal New England principles. But this was only a first step. Looking at the issue from the standpoint of a doctrinaire—"which every journalist should be"—he asserted "that the best civil law concerning divorce would be *no law at all*; and this will one day become the opinion and practice of all intelligent and refined communities." [51]

In 1872, the erratic Tilton dropped his divorce crusade for a feverish effort to—of all things—elect Horace Greeley President of the United States.[52] This ill-fated venture was probably undertaken as a last gamble to save Tilton's career from the rocks toward which it was drifting. Among those who now knew the dangerous secret of Elizabeth Tilton's relations with Henry Ward Beecher was the lovely and unscrupulous Victoria Woodhull. Once Victoria began to talk, not only were Beecher and Tilton threatened with ruin but so were the whole circle of their friends, including Elizabeth Cady Stanton and Susan B. Anthony.

Victoria Woodhull and her sister, Tennessee Claflin, had appeared like comets in the New York City skies after an earlier career in itinerant fortunetelling and spiritualism. Through the senile patronage of Commodore Cornelius Vanderbilt, they operated a Wall Street stock brokerage house for a time and then began the publication of the sprightly *Woodhull's and Claflin's Weekly*. When Victoria showed up in Washington in January, 1871, for a meeting of the National Woman Suffrage Association, the feminist leaders were hesitant to accept so notorious a personality into the movement. But Victoria's success in presenting her own independent memorial to the House Judiciary Committee convinced the doubting that she was too valuable an ally to be spurned. Soon she was on terms of close friendship with the leaders of the radical wing of the suffrage movement and in this position of confidence she learned the Beecher-Tilton secret. She also became the close friend of Tilton himself. Indeed that harried editor undertook to defend Victoria against the unkind slurs of the New York newspapers. In August, 1871, he wrote: "Mr. Greeley's allusion to a certain lady whom he describes but does not name is an ungentle and gross reflection on a life which has been marked by great suffering, which has been guided by pure motives, and which has flowered into rare worth. Knowing her well, we respect her not less highly than we do Mr. Greeley himself." [53] Tilton followed up this defense by writing a highly laudatory pamphlet for Victoria. His motives were apparently mixed: like many others he was for a time utterly captivated by Victoria's beauty and charm; at the same time he hoped that by flattering her and championing her cause he could prevent the horror of seeing his own marital affairs served up as tasty tidbits for the readers of *Woodhull's and Claflin's Weekly*.

On the marriage question, Victoria Woodhull stood to the left even of such advanced liberals as Elizabeth Cady Stanton and

Theodore Tilton. Her own family affairs were tangled. Within her household lived not only several of the Claflin clan but also Victoria's second husband, Colonel Blood, and her first husband, Dr. Woodhull, from whom she was divorced. Alluding acidly to this situation, Greeley referred to Victoria as "one who has two husbands after a sort, and lives in the same house with them both, sharing the couch of one, and bearing the name of the other (to indicate her impartiality perhaps)." [54] Equally shocking to New York moralists was the fact that she had opened the columns of her paper to Stephen Pearl Andrews, notorious as a preacher of free love. Under the promptings of Andrews and Colonel Blood Victoria herself became an increasingly outspoken advocate of what she called "Social Freedom." To a largely hostile audience in Steinway Hall, New York, she defiantly asserted:

> Yes, I am a Free Lover. [Loud hisses] I have an *inalienable, constitutional* and *natural* right to love whom I may, to love as *long* or as *short* a period as I can, *to change that love every day*, if I please [renewed hisses], and with that right neither you nor any law you can frame have any right to interfere; and I have the further right to demand a free and unrestricted exercise of that right, and it is your duty to see that I am protected in it. [55]

In view of Victoria's strong views, she was hardly shocked by the knowledge that Henry Ward Beecher had had a love affair with Elizabeth Tilton. What disgusted her was Beecher's hypocrisy in continuing to preach a different moral code from that which he practiced. Victoria's resentment became increasingly dangerous throughout 1872, a year in which she was hounded without mercy by all the self-appointed guardians of morality, among whom Beecher's own sisters, Harriet Beecher Stowe and Catherine Beecher, were conspicuous. The year was one of disaster, in which Victoria's campaign for herself as President of the United States was laughed off the hustings and she was repudiated by such former friends as Commodore Vanderbilt, Susan B. Anthony, and Theodore Tilton.

Harassed and bitter, Victoria gushed out the story of the Beecher-Tilton scandal with lurid embellishments in the November 2, 1872, issue of *Woodhull's and Claflin's Weekly*. All the great preacher's admirers rallied to his defense; Victoria was not only denounced as a libelous liar, but was hauled off to jail and prosecuted—unsuccessfully—for issuing an obscene publication. For over a year the great preacher's critics and defenders argued over who was telling the truth. At length the controversy came to a climax, first in an investigation by a hand-picked committee from Beecher's own Plymouth Church, and then in a sensational civil trial.

The results, as symbolized by the jury's disagreement in the latter case, were inconclusive. So extraordinary was Beecher's hold over his adoring public that he survived his ordeal with only slightly tarnished reputation, but the other principals were ruined. Tilton's career in American journalism was ended and he took up residence in France; Mrs. Tilton withdrew from society and lived as an unhappy recluse. Victoria Woodhull cashed in on her notoriety by a few more months on the American lecture platform, then divorced Blood, and settled down to dull respectability as the wife of a wealthy Englishman.

But what had all this to do with divorce? So far as Elizabeth Cady Stanton was concerned, the lesson was obvious. More liberal divorce laws and a more tolerant public opinion would provide a far healthier remedy for unhappy marriages than the heartbreaking hypocrisy of the Beecher-Tilton triangle. In a public statement published in 1874, she said:

If the testimony given in this case be all true, and it be proven that such men as Henry Ward Beecher and Theodore Tilton find the marriage laws of the State of New York too stringent, both being in discordant marriage relations, might it not be well to review the laws, as well as their violations? To compel unhappy husbands and wives, by law and public sentiment, to live together, and to teach them that it is their religious duty to accept their conditions, whatever they are, produces, ever and anon, just such social earthquakes as the one through which we are now passing.[56]

But the general public drew quite different conclusions from the Beecher-Tilton affair. In their desperate effort to save Beecher, the champions of conventional respectability felt it necessary to blacken the reputation of all his accusers. Not only was this true in the case of Theodore Tilton and Victoria Woodhull, but in that of Susan B. Anthony and Elizabeth Cady Stanton as well. Although these close friends of the Tiltons had said little about the case, their silence was in itself a testimonial to their belief in Beecher's guilt. Not for this reason alone were the two feminists under attack. In the nexus of guilty associations set up by the conservative press, the wicked attack on Beecher was the work of free lovers, free love was a corollary of liberal divorce, and liberal divorce was closely connected with woman suffrage. By advocating woman suffrage and the right of divorce, Mrs. Stanton and Miss Anthony had therefore sinned against public morals. Instead of helping to liberalize public opinion on the marriage question, the Beecher scandal like the earlier Richardson-McFarland affair contributed to a conservative reaction against divorce.

CHAPTER 9

Rise of
the Divorce Colonies

Commenting upon the ceremony in which Henry Ward Beecher married the dying Albert D. Richardson to the recently divorced Abby McFarland, the *New York Times* declared: "An Indiana divorce is not only a farce, but a disgusting farce." [1] In an earlier editorial the paper had criticized Abby for not using the courts of her own state.[2] Mrs. Richardson's explanation of her conduct was simple and direct. She went away, she said, because the Indiana laws permitted divorce for drunkenness, extreme cruelty, and failure to support a wife, and the New York laws did not. McFarland had probably also been guilty of adultery, but, she said, "I considered his treatment of me, his personal abuses, his terrible profanity, his outrages of all kinds, an infinitely greater sin against me and my womanhood than if he had committed again and again, unknown to me, the crime against the marriage relation which is the only cause the New York courts hold just grounds for divorce." [3]

The problem of migratory divorce was by no means a new one. Even before the passage of the law of 1787, New Yorkers who found the marriage law of their own state too rigid had been establishing temporary residences elsewhere. Chancellor Kent thus describes the early situation:

. . . for many years after New-York became an independent state, there was not any lawful mode of dissolving a marriage in the lifetime of the parties, but by a special act of the legislature. This strictness was productive of public inconvenience, and often forced the parties, in cases which rendered a separation fit and necessary, to some other state, to avail themselves of a more easy and certain remedy.[4]

One of the early divorce havens was Pennsylvania. Paying tribute to that state's "moral preeminence," a New York legislative committee in 1840 commented: "Yet how many unfortunate 'yoke fellows' annually seek a refuge from our inexorable law, and take up a residence in moral Pennsylvania, for the sole purpose of dissolving a connection which has been productive of nothing but bitter unhappiness." [5]

This was a more patient generation than ours, and divorce seekers did not expect to win their freedom in a mere six weeks. At least a year's residence was required in all eastern states, and in otherwise liberal Connecticut three years were specified. Despite these obstacles, the practice of seeking out-of-state divorces continued to grow. Courts in all the New England states and in Vermont especially had a trickle of business from parties whose permanent homes were in states with more rigorous divorce laws.

After 1840 the flow of divorce seekers began to move westward. The states of Ohio, Indiana, and Illinois all enjoyed the reputation of being reasonably hospitable to migrants in search of freedom. Ashtabula County in northeastern Ohio was highly accessible to temporary residents from New York, Pennsylvania, and Ontario, and this no doubt helps to explain why the courts of a county of only 32,000 inhabitants should have had 174 divorce cases on their dockets in the decade of the 1850's and 442 cases in the 1860's.[6] Other Ohio counties also displayed a rising rate. In the judgment of the *Cleveland Leader*, the statistics of Ohio divorce pointed to the necessity of reform. "The record of Cuyahoga county alone for the year 1870—one hundred and seventy-two applications for divorce, of which fifty-eight were dismissed, ninety-five granted, and the balance held over until next year—ought to awaken our legislators to the necessity of more adequate protection in law for the permanency of the marriage relation." [7]

After the Civil War Chicago gained renown as a divorce Mecca. According to a facetious writer in 1868, husbands wishing to get rid of their wives, or wives of their husbands, had only to take the next train for Chicago. On stepping out at the depot, they would be surrounded by boys shouting: "Step this way, divorce ye'r in five minutes!" and "Want d'voss, want d'voss, put you through by daylight and marry ye'r over again in forty seconds." [8] A more prosaic account reported that 460 cases had been brought in Chicago courts during 1868; 284 of these had been commenced by wives, and 176 by husbands.[9] To explain the high rate, another writer stressed such local peculiarities as the large number of wives left stranded in Chicago by husbands who had wandered off in search of adventure and easy money. But the Chicago situation reflected another factor of greater significance.[10] At the hands of certain unscrupulous New York lawyers, divorce was becoming highly commercialized. Such advertisments as the following were regularly published in the newspapers: "Absolute divorces obtained in any State without publicity or exposure; good everywhere. No fee charged until divorce is obtained. Consultations free. George Lincoln, Lawyer, 80 Nassau Street." [11]

The possibilities for skulduggery were illustrated by a case reported in 1867. In February of that year, a Chicago court granted a divorce to Lieutenant Joseph H. Sylvester of the United States Army on the representation that his wife Emily had deserted him three years earlier. The defendant failed to appear—a circumstance no doubt related to the fact that she was residing in Castine, Maine, while notice of the action was being given in an advertisement published in *Western Merchants' Prices Current* and by a document nailed to the door of the Chicago courtroom. The only supporting evidence for the plaintiff's case came in the form of two depositions taken in New York City, in which witnesses swore that Emily's desertion had taken place in Peoria, Illinois, and that Joseph had resided in Chicago for the past year. In June, 1869, Emily appeared in Chicago to ask for a reopening of the case. According to the indignant wife, she had not deserted her husband and was quite prepared to live with him in Chicago. But she denied that Chicago was his real residence; he had not lived there to her knowledge since his marriage. She had known nothing of the divorce proceedings until a copy of the decree had been sent to her through the mail. The Sylvester case was evidently not unique. "In connection with this cause," said the *Chicago Tribune*, "it is proper to say that a regular business is being carried on in this city for the procurement of divorce for non-residents. This is also a business in New York, whence these cases come, and where the evidence in all these cases is supplied." [12]

Exposing New York City divorce frauds in 1870, the *New York Times* described the faked evidence of adultery that was already common in the city's courtrooms. Even so, divorce lawyers often preferred to bring their actions in other states. About one-quarter of all the decrees issued in Illinois and Indiana and one-sixth of those of Connecticut were alleged to have been arranged through New York City offices. It was a mail-order business of huge proportions, by no means confined to New York clients. "The divorce lawyer," said the *Times*, "keeps his standing card in papers of large circulation, announcing the facility with which he is prepared to get a decree, good for any State in the Union; and a considerable share of his business is transacted on behalf of parties whom he never sees and never expects to see." [13]

Indiana's reputation as a happy hunting ground for divorce arose during the 1850's when out-of-state lawyers began to realize the possibilities of two unusual features of the state law. The first of these was the so-called "omnibus clause" enacted in 1824. In addition to a variety of specific grounds for divorce, the courts were authorized to grant decrees for "any other cause" which they might deem "proper." The second was the virtual absence of any residence requirement. When the Indiana divorce law was revised in 1852, the only requirement laid on the plaintiff was that he should be a *bona fide* resident of the county at the time of filing his petition, and on this point his own affidavit was accepted as *prima facie* evidence. This loophole probably resulted from accident rather than design, but sharp lawyers were not slow to take advantage of the situation.[14] In 1858, the *Indiana Daily Journal* complained: "We are overrun by a flock of ill-used, and ill-using, petulant, libidinous, extravagant, ill-fitting husbands and wives as a sink is overrun with the foul water of the whole house. . . . Nine out of ten have no better cause of divorce than their own depraved appetites." [15] The scandalized Horace Greeley reported that a prominent Easterner came to Indiana, went through the usual routine, obtained his divorce about dinnertime, "and, in the course of the evening was married to his new inamorata, who had come on for the purpose, and was staying at the same hotel with him. They soon started for home, having no more use for the State of Indiana; and, on arriving, he introduced his new wife to her astonished predecessor, whom he notified that she must pack up and go, as there was no room for her in that house any longer. So she went." [16]

Although Indiana lawyers and boardinghouse keepers were happy to accommodate the migrants, many other citizens were disstressed at the state's notoriety. The *Indiana Daily Journal* complained that lax legislation "gave the whole Union a chance to be divorced here, and flooded our courts with the abominations of half the dishonored homes on the continent." [17] The same paper asserted that in 1858 out of seventy-two divorce actions pending in Marion County "more than fifty were brought by non-residents." [18] These protests resulted in the enactment of a one-year residence requirement and some additional safeguards in 1859.[19]

But even after these changes the Indiana situation remained sufficiently inviting to bring many divorce seekers to the state. Describing matters in 1865, an Indiana state senator alleged that there were "mercantile businesses" along the Atlantic seaboard "whose stock in trade was Indiana divorce." Fraudulent affidavits of plaintiffs and falsified retainers purporting to come from defendants were placed in the hands of conniving Indiana lawyers. These men referred the issues to a third lawyer selected by them to further their fraud and to avoid judicial examination of the case, and the courts accepted these referees' findings without question. This system produced "hundreds of divorces . . . in the courts of this state annually by non-residents, and in no case were the defendants probably . . . aware of the fact until long after the same had been procured." [20]

The Richardson-McFarland affair focused national attention on the Indiana divorce situation. Abby's loyal supporters defended her action in establishing temporary residence in Indiana and argued that the state's liberal laws were evidence of Hoosier enlightenment. But conservatives drew quite different conclusions from the case. Devoting a portion of his annual message of 1871 to a review of the divorce laws, Governor Conrad Baker said: "We might well hope that Indiana divorces would cease to be advertised in any of the Atlantic cities; and that refugees and fugitives from the justice of other States would no longer come to Indiana in quest of divorces to be used on their return to their homes as licenses to violate the laws of our sister states." [21]

Despite the strong demand for reform, the Indiana legislators were too much divided on the issue to permit important new legislation until 1873. In that year, however, the pressure for a change became overwhelming. Sternly lecturing the lawmakers on their duty, the *Indiana Daily Sentinel* said: "They will not forget the universal notoriety of Indiana on the matter of divorce, and that the legislation of the present session will interest the country at large quite as much as any work that shall go upon the record." [22] The new Indiana law, passed March 10, 1873, was strict. Not only did it extend the required period of residence from one year to two, but it demanded adequate proof. New safeguards were added to give defendants more effective notice; and, in cases where notice had to be given by publication, plaintiffs were forbidden to remarry for a period of two years during which the case might be reopened on motion of the defendant. The famous omnibus clause was eliminated.[23]

Indiana's decision to close her courts to the migratory divorce business was apparently effective. Direct statistics on the issue are unavailable, but an indirect index is provided in the number of divorces dissolving marriages celebrated elsewhere than in the divorcing state. From 1867 through 1871, Indiana stood first among the states in this category; from 1872 through 1876, it was fourth; from 1877 through 1881, it was seventh.[24]

Rebuffed in Indiana, seekers for divorce continued to patronize not only Chicago but a number of other localities, where the laws were reputed to be liberal. Rhode Island, Iowa, and the District of Columbia all shared to a minor degree in the migratory divorce business of the 1870's and 1880's.[25]

But the path of divorce—like that of empire—seemed destined to move westward. The mining country had the reputation of taking a decidedly relaxed attitude toward the laws of matrimony. If a woman in Idaho was dissatisfied with her husband, reported the *Cleveland Leader* in 1864, she went to see the president of the mining district. The latter called a miners' meeting which untied the matrimonial knot without further formalities. "Idaho," the paper asserted somewhat enigmatically, "is decidedly the last country." [26] When the period of informal association gave way to the legalized forms of territorial and state government, divorce became the business of the legislatures and the courts. But liberal principles continued to prevail. California's pioneer law of 1851 was overhauled in 1874, when six grounds for divorce were carefully defined— adultery, cruelty, desertion, nonsupport, alcoholism, and felony conviction. This California statute was of wide influence, serving as a model for laws passed in Nevada in 1875, Dakota Territory in 1877, Idaho in 1887, and Montana in 1895.[27]

Much more important to out-of-state divorce seekers than a liberal definition of grounds was the short residence requirement of several Western states. In their origin these provisions had nothing to do with divorce. They arose out of the necessary mobility of frontier towns, where prospectors and other adventurers move in, try their luck, and often roll on again without staying more than a year in any locality. If such communities were to have voters, they had to specify periods of residence in terms of months rather than years. And easy voting qualifications found their logical corollaries in easy requirements for beginning law suits.

Utah provided an early example of this laxity. The divorce statute of 1852 provided only that the plaintiff "is a resident of the Territory, or wishes to become one." Also of interest to out-of-state divorce seekers was an omnibus clause that permitted the courts to issue decrees when they were satisfied "that the parties cannot live in peace and union together, and that their welfare demands a separation." Although the Mormon citizens of the state apparently did not abuse the law's liberality, eastern divorce lawyers soon became aware of Utah's attractions, particularly after the transcontinental railroad made this distant haven accessible to wealthy clients. Certain local judges proved to be cooperative, and the Utah divorce business enjoyed a minor boom from 1875 to 1878, but the territorial legislature eventually slammed the door by enacting a one-year residence requirement and abolishing the omnibus clause.[28]

The Dakota Territory with its three-months residence requirement was attracting eastern interest as early as 1879.[29] When North and South Dakota were admitted to the Union as separate states in 1889, each retained the short residence requirement and each attracted a growing number of out-of-state divorce seekers. By 1892, the *Chicago Herald* thought the South Dakota situation sufficiently newsworthy to deserve a six-column article illustrated with pictures of notable judges, lawyers, and divorcees. The lavish spending of the transients was enriching the hotel men and shopkeepers of Sioux Falls. "The notoriety South Dakota has got is doing us no harm," one promient lawyer said. "It advertises us abroad, brings thousands of dollars here, not only to pay expenses of divorce suits, but, for investment as well." Yankton was reported to be eager to divert the divorce business away from Sioux Falls. A new hotel had been erected there, and a beautifully printed circular had been "sent by the hundreds to society in New York, Boston, and Philadelphia." But Sioux Falls was fighting to hold its preeminence. One of its prime assets was reported to be a certain Judge Aikens, who was only thirty-three years old—"just that ardent and susceptible age when woman's distress appeals to man most strongly. In all the cases that Judge Aikens has heard where the fair sex has appeared in complaint, his course has been marked by the tenderest sympathy and the most delicate solicitude for their interests." [30]

Moralists criticized the divorce seekers as a corrupting influence. In 1893, a newspaper complained that Sioux Falls was "getting metropolitan with a vengeance." She now supported ten gambling houses, thirty-seven "holes-in-the-wall," and a hundred prostitutes.[31]

Yet it was by no means clear that these merchants of vice were drawing their patronage from the visitors rather than from the natives. For one thing, the divorce colony was relatively small. Even the conservative secretary of the National Divorce Reform League refused to become unduly alarmed. His investigations indicated that for the twelve months ending September 30, 1891, there had been only 65 applications for divorce in the five counties that made up the Sioux Falls circuit.[32] According to another tally, there were 90 divorces granted in Sioux Falls in 1892.[33] Moreover, despite contrary impressions, the divorce seekers were for the most part well behaved. Basing his judgment on a six-months observation, one writer reported that with three possible exceptions the visitors had been remarkable for the inherent justice of their cases and the dignity of their behavior.[34] Apparently much of the adverse publicity was the work of Chicago reporters jealous of Sioux Falls's encroachment upon what had long been a Chicago speciality.

Developments in South Dakota were strongly reminiscent of the course of events in Indiana twenty years earlier. The state's growing reputation as a haven for divorce seekers scandalized conservatives and created a demand for reform. A Sioux Falls newspaper attributed the rise of a crusading spirit to "the churches and the ladies of the W.C.T.U." [35] Other observers noted that the rising Farmers Alliance movement was suspicious of divorce as an alien urban influence.[36] In 1892, the legislature was under strong pressure to lengthen the residence requirement to a year, but counter influences were also at work. According to a local newspaper:

> The Sioux Falls lawyers, however, as well as various other citizens asked this question, Why should the legislature, on merely sentimental grounds, drive out of South Dakota and into North Dakota and Nebraska a business which brings to Sioux Falls over $100,000 a year? So the legislature defeated the bill to lengthen the term of residence to a year.[37]

But the conservative forces gained a highly effective leader. In 1892, the saintly Episcopal Bishop William H. Hare, known as "the apostle to the Sioux," returned to South Dakota after a trip to Japan and China. In a letter to his daughter-in-law, he confided that his homecoming had been a gloomy one because of "the scandalous divorce mill which is running at Sioux Falls." The good bishop continued: "I despise people who trifle with marriage relations so intensely that the *moral* nausea produces nausea of the *stomach*. I have a continual bad taste in my mouth." [38] Two personal experiences contributed to Bishop Hare's nausea. One involved a wealthy temporary resident who faithfully attended the Sioux Falls Episcopal cathedral and gave $1,000 for memorial windows, only to shock the righteous by remarrying directly after her divorce decree was granted. The scandalized bishop refused to allow the memorial windows to be installed. "I'd as lief paste up the flaming placards of a low circus," he fumed. The second shock came when Hare was invited to dine at a certain house and discovered upon his arrival that his host was equipped with a brand-new wife and that among the other guests were the host's first wife and her new husband. Bishop Hare's chagrin, comments his biographer, was only increased by discovering that his own great embarrassment was "wholly unshared by the strangely assorted quartette." [39]

On Sunday, January 1, 1893, a large congregation, liberally sprinkled with temporary residents awaiting divorce, crowded the cathedral to hear Bishop Hare's New Year sermon. This did not deter the bishop from choosing as his subject "Marriage and Divorce." He condemned "the consecutive polygamy" involved in speedy re-marriages after divorce and the "perjury" committed by those who swore that they were permanent residents of South Dakota and then left town as soon as their decrees were granted. "What better object," the bishop asked, "can the church of Christ have in view, the beginning of this new year, than to work for a new law?" [40]

Bishop Hare followed up his sensational sermon by addressing a pastoral letter to all the churches of his diocese and by co-operating with the ministers of other denominations in circulating a petition to the legislature. Some 900 signatures were obtained within a few days, and 500 more were added later.[41] On January 14, 1893, Bishop Hare was reported to be at the state capital at Pierre, moving about the lobby "with as much unconcern as if lobbying had been his business for years." [42] But the prelate's activities were not confined to the corridors; he was invited to present his ideas to a joint meeting of the judiciary committees of the two houses and to use the chamber of the lower house for a repeat per-formance of his sermon on marriage and divorce.[43]

The newspapers attributed to the bishop's influence a remark-able change in the legislative atmosphere. Before he arrived at Pierre, a bill to lengthen the residence requirement to a year had already been rejected in committee and the prospects for any kind of divorce reform had appeared slight.[44] After the clerical lobbying began, it became evident that a roll call on the issue could not be avoided.[45] In a sharp debate in the senate the advocates of change charged that the three-months residence requirement brought in a crowd of people from other states "who filled the community with foulness and cast discredit on her good name." But their opponents argued that the present law brought relief to hundreds of worthy petitioners and benefited the state by bringing in land purchasers and investors. Liberal divorce laws were of more value than two immigration commissioners.[46]

In the end, the conservative party won a substantial victory. The residence requirement for all divorce plaintiffs was lengthened to six months, and in cases where personal service on the defendant was not made and notice had to be given by newspaper advertisement one year's residence was required.[47]

But the struggle over South Dakota divorce laws continued. Neither side was really satisfied with the 1893 law. The moralists wanted a straight one-year residence requirement; their opponents hoped to go back to the three-months system. On February 9, 1895, Bishop Hare wrote a public letter charging that lawyers, jewelers, innkeepers, and other businessmen were contributing money to establish a prodivorce lobby and that the reporters were in tacit conspiracy to keep the matter quiet until a bill could be slipped through the legislature. The purpose of this plot was to change the law so that the plaintiff could begin proceedings immediately upon arrival in South Dakota. This, he indignantly charged, would make South Dakota a more attractive field for persons tired of their matrimonial obligations, "for *passion* always seeks *immediate* gratification, and passion, as experience shows, is often, if not generally, back of a suit for divorce." [48]

This time the bishop's strictures found an answer from another clergyman. On the evening of February 24, 1895, the Sioux Falls Opera House was crowded to hear the Reverend J. L. Andrews of the Unitarian Church lecture on marriage and divorce. He asserted that it was "idiotic" to believe that there was but one valid ground for divorce. In reply to Bishop Hare's charge that divorces were actuated by "passion," the Unitarian defended passion as essential to happiness. The reason why people came to South Dakota to get divorces was "not because our laws are bad but because their own states have not become civilized enough to enact proper divorce laws." [49]

The actual bill under consideration was one that would have speeded divorce by allowing a plaintiff to begin his action immediately after arriving in the state, even though he could not receive a final decree until he had been a resident for six months. Slightly amended, this bill passed the state senate on February 11, but failed by a narrow margin in the house on March 1. The vote was 41 in favor to 38 opposed, but this was one vote less than the required constitutional majority based on the total membership. The Populists provided the core of the opposition to liberalizing the 1893 law, but they were helped, so a Sioux Falls newspaper asserted, by a Fargo hotel man who spent two weeks lobbying for strict laws in South Dakota so that North Dakota would benefit.[50]

From 1893 to 1899, South Dakota's facilities for divorce seekers were somewhat less attractive than those of North Dakota, which still required only three-months residence. But Fargo's boom period was short-lived, because in 1899 the reformers pressured the legislature into raising the residence requirement to one year.[51] South Dakota with its six-months requirement enjoyed a temporary revival of its divorce business, but in 1907 the forces of righteousness, led once more by Bishop Hare, gained the upper hand and extended the residence period to one year.[52] The Sioux Falls lawyers and hotel men warded off the evil day for almost two years more by petitioning to have the issue submitted to the voters at the next general election in November, 1908.[53]

Regarding this referendum as the crucial battle in his long crusade, the venerable bishop worked tirelessly to round up support from as many different religious and civic groups as possible. A strongly worded appeal was published in most of the state's nearly three hundred weekly newspapers, while a hundred thousand pamphlets were distributed through the churches.[54] As defined by Bishop Hare and his colleagues, the issues were these:

First, Shall the people, now that the matter is referred to them, nullify, or shall they confirm, measures approved by the Bar Association and passed by the Legislature? Second, Do we want our young people's minds defiled, and our State disgraced, any longer by the nasty importations of the divorce traffic? There are two signs which persons stick up on their town lots. One is, "Dirt Wanted." The other, "Dump No Rubbish Here." The question now is, which of these signs shall South Dakota present to persons who purpose bringing hither from other states their hateful conjugal follies and sins. Is it, "Dirt Wanted! Come!" or is it, "Dump No Rubbish Here! Keep Off!"[55]

Once again the militant bishop carried the day. The 1907 divorce law with its one-year requirement was ratified by a substantial majority.[56] Even in Minnehaha County, where Sioux Falls was located, the conservatives enjoyed a 747-vote margin over their opponents. Those who had shared Bishop Hare's philosophy on the divorce question were generous in their praise of the Episcopal prelate's pertinacity. The Roman Catholic Bishop of South Dakota, Thomas O'Gorman, said: " I joined forces with him in the fight he led against this evil thing. We were allies in doing away with it. He led the fight, step by step he fought, forcing the limit of residence from three months to six, from six to twelve. . . . Morally and financially we are all the better for the Christian courage of Bishop Hare. To him, the Defender of the Home, honor and the gratitude of South Dakota." [57]

As new barriers to migratory divorce were being erected in the Dakotas, the welcome sign was hung out elsewhere in the West. In 1894, lawyers in Oklahoma Territory were sending out circulars proudly proclaiming the local divorce possibilities. "Service upon a non-resident defendant," they pointed out, "may be made personally or by publication. There is no statute requiring corroborative proof as in South Dakota." [58] Oklahoma City and Guthrie were eager rivals in catering to the temporary residents.[59] The situation became so scandalous to eastern reformers that they put pressure upon Congress in 1896 to enact a statute providing that "no divorce shall be granted in any Territory for any cause unless the party applying for Divorce shall have resided continuously in the Territory for one year next preceding the application." [60]

Wyoming also took a short flier into the divorce business, particularly after the extension of the North Dakota residence requirement in 1899. Wyoming's six-months residence was publicized as the most lenient in the country, and New York divorce lawyers established branch offices in Cheyenne. Many rich clients spent the summer of 1899 enjoying the great open spaces. At least fifty important divorce cases were on Wyoming court dockets for the following winter.[61] But the boom was short-lived, for in 1901 the Wyoming legislature extended the residence period to one year.[62]

After 1908, only Texas, Nebraska, Idaho, and Nevada still retained the six-months residence requirement. Of these Nevada became the most inviting Mecca for out-of-state divorce seekers for reasons that will be discussed in a later chapter.

CHAPTER 10

The Conservative Reaction

The tightening of the divorce laws in Indiana, the Dakotas, and the Federal territories reflected a general reaction against divorce that was sweeping the country during the late nineteenth century. The pre-Civil War trend toward more liberal laws was reversed, and the tide began to move in the opposite direction.

This conservative reaction gained its initial impetus in hitherto liberal Connecticut. As we have seen, Congregational tolerance on divorce had already been rebuked by individuals like Benjamin Trumbull and Timothy Dwight, but the liberal trend had nevertheless continued until it culminated in the 1849 law with its omnibus clause permitting divorce for "any such misconduct as permanently destroys the happiness of the petitioner and defeats the purpose of the marriage relation." Conservative clergymen regarded this "general misconduct" clause with horror and called for its repeal. Although the legislature resisted this demand for many years, it did authorize a legislative committee to investigate the divorce situation.

This study resulted in the collection of the first important divorce statistics for any American state. The figures were highly disquieting to the moralists, since they revealed a steady rise in Connecticut divorces from 544 for the four-year period 1849-1852 to 1,253 for the Civil War Years 1861-1864.[1] Leadership in the movement to tighten the state law was assumed by President Theodore Woolsey of Yale, who published in 1867 a series of articles in the *New Englander* tracing the history of divorce from Roman to moddern times. He issued a somber warning:

> Rome is a most interesting study for us Americans, because her vices, greed for gold, prodigality, a coarse material civilization, corruption in the family, as manifested by connubial unfaithfulness and divorce, are increasing among us. We have got rid of one of her curses, slavery, and that is a great ground of hope for the future. But whether we are to be a thoroughly Christian nation, or to decay and lose our present political forms, depends upon our ability to keep family life pure and simple.[2]

Gaining strength over the next decade, the Connecticut movement achieved its immediate objective in the repeal of the general misconduct clause in 1878. This conservative victory stirred the clergy of other New England states to action. A sudden passion for statistics revealed the situation summarized in the following table:

Divorces 1860-1878 *

	1860	1865	1870	1875	1878
Massachusetts					
Number of divorces	243	333	379	577	600
Ratio—divorces to marriages	1:51.0	1:39.2	1:38.8	1:23.6	1:21.4
Vermont					
Number of divorces	95	122	164	171	197
Ratio—divorces to marriages	1:22.9	1:21.0	1:18.4	1:15.8	1:14.0
Connecticut					
Number of divorces	282	404	408	476	401
Ratio—divorces to marriages	1:14.1	1:11.1	1:11.6	1:9.2	1:10.6
Rhode Island					
Number of divorces	Not available		200	158	196
Ratio—divorces to marriages			1:11.8	1:15.7	1:11.8

* Based on Nathan Allen, "Divorces in New England," *North American Review*, CXXX (June, 1880), 549.

It was obvious from these figures that the general trend was toward a rise both in the absolute number of divorces and in the ratio of divorces to marriages. Although more sophisticated scholars might have suspected that a variety of social and economic factors were at work, the clerical reformers laid almost exclusive emphasis on the alleged laxity of the divorce laws. "Among no Christian or civilized people at the present day," mourned the Reverend Nathan Allen, "do we find divorces sought and obtained to such an extent as now in New England." [3]

Following the tradition of earlier American reform movements, these viewers-with-alarm organized to combat the dreaded evil. On January 24, 1881, the New England Divorce Reform League was founded. Dr. Woolsey, now retired from college administration, was elected president, but the most dynamic officer was the secretary, the Reverend Samuel W. Dike, a Congregationalist from Royalton, Vermont. Although a conservative on the divorce issue, Dike avoided fanaticism. Through his insistence that no action could be taken until the facts were known, he asserted a major influence on the collection of American divorce statistics.

The work of the New England group attracted attention elsewhere, and on February 16, 1885, the pioneer league was reorganized as the National Divorce Reform League. Among its sixty charter members were representatives of all the leading Christian bodies, including the Roman Catholic.[4] In 1897, the organization changed its name to the National League for the Protection of the Family.[5]

The activities of the divorce reformers bore fruit in a substantial crop of legislative changes during the 1880's. In 1883, the Maine law was radically revised: an earlier omnibus clause was abolished and specific grounds were carefully defined on the Massachusetts model, while restrictions were imposed on the remarriage of both parties. The result, according to Dike, was to cut the Maine divorce rate by more than half. Vermont also reduced its divorce rate by 14 per cent by stiffening its residence requirements, restricting the defendant's right to remarry, and improving procedures. Massachusetts and New Hampshire made procedural changes and authorized the systematic collection of divorce statistics.[6] In 1887, Dike applauded what he called the "most important gain" since the Maine reform of 1883, the passage of a Michigan statute discouraging divorce by safeguards against collusion, providing for the defense of certain cases by the state, and making other procedural changes.[7]

Whenever some dramatic episode focused attention on the migratory divorce problem, newspaper editorial writers would deplore the fact that there was no uniform national law of marriage and divorce. At the time of the McFarland-Richardson affair the *New York Times* expressed its regret that the framers of the Federal Constitution had not reserved to the Federal government sole jurisdiction in matters affecting marriage.[8] Ten years later when Dakota Territory was the scene of a widely publicized divorce case, the *New York Tribune* said: "Truly the land needs a reform in the law of divorce. If it cannot be attained by a uniform, National law, let it be sought by some concurrence of legislation, and some reasonable comity of courts in administration of their local laws." [9] Having altered the Federal balance through the enactment of the Thirteenth, Fourteenth, and Fifteenth amendments, many Republicans were hospitable to the idea of adding still another constitutional amendment that would permit Congress to legislate in the field of marriage and divorce. Democrats, on the other hand, tended to oppose Federal action but applauded the idea of achieving uniformity through the cooperation of the states. Dike believed that both demands were premature. Much more information about the subject was necessary. Through his initiative Congress was besieged by petitions from local groups, who stressed the evils growing out of the diversity of state divorce laws and argued that "the magnitude of these evils, their bearing upon our general social conditions, and the best methods of guarding against their increase can be fully apprehended only by a careful collection and comparison of the facts and statistics of divorce." [10]

Dike visited Washington in 1884 to lobby for this proposal and received an encouraging response.[11] The Senate gave unanimous support to a bill "providing for the collection of statistics touching marriage and divorce," and the House Judiciary Committee brought in a favorable report. But Congress adjourned without taking further action. Two years later the proposal was revived by Senator George Edmunds of Vermont, only to suffer a similar fate.[12]

In January, 1887, the issue was raised once again, this time through a petition from a special committee of the Protestant Episcopal Church. Congress responded by including in the general appropriation bill, passed March 3, 1887, the sum of $10,000 "to enable the Commissioner of Labor to collect and report to Congress the statistics of and relating to marriage and divorce in the several States and Territories and in the District of Columbia." A further appropriation for the next year increased the total amount to $17,500. The sum was far from adequate for such an ambitious project, but Carroll D. Wright, the Commissioner of Labor, stretched these resources by assigning his regular staff to the divorce study whenever their services could be spared from other duties. Wright was ideally equipped for his task. Not only was he a pioneer American statistician, but he had participated in an earlier Massachusetts study of divorce data. In formulating the questions for investigation he leaned heavily on Dike's advice.[13]

Considering the difficulty of obtaining accurate national statistics on marriage and divorce—a difficulty still encountered today—Wright's study was impressively thorough. He endeavored to accumulate data from about 2,700 American counties for a twenty-year period. Knowing the carelessness of many clerks of court, he depended as little as possible on questionnaires. Instead he sent agents to all the more populous counties to collect data through direct inspection of the records. Even this method had its limitations. Chicago's Cook County Court House had gone up in flames during the great fire of 1871, Cincinnati's Hamilton County Court House burned down in 1884, and 158 other depositories had suffered a loss of all or part of their records. Despite such frustrations, Wright felt that he had obtained a substantially complete record of divorces.[14] Much more formidable were the problems in collecting marriage statistics; only twenty-one of the then thirty-eight states required the registration of marriages and even in these states the law was poorly enforced; Wright acknowledged his data on marriages to be "thoroughly incomplete and unsatisfactory." [15] In the fat volume of statistics that Wright submitted to Congress in February, 1889, there was a wealth of data. For the country as a whole, the number of divorces had risen from 9,937 in 1867 to 25,535 in 1886—an increase of 157 per cent. Divorce was increasing much faster than population: between the census years 1870 and 1880 the population had grown by 30 per cent, but divorces had increased by 79 per cent.[16] Wright did not regard the ratio of divorces to total population to be as important as the ratio of divorces to the number of married couples—hence his disappointment in obtaining such unsatisfactory data on marriages. He overcame this handicap as best he could by estimating the number of married couples in each state in the census years 1870 and 1880 and then comparing this figure with the number of divorces. Measured by this crude standard, the states and territories with the highest divorce rates in 1870 were Wyoming, Utah, and Rhode Island, while those with the lowest were South Carolina, Delaware, and North Carolina. By 1880 the situation had changed somewhat: Colorado, Nevada, and Wyoming now had the three highest divorce rates, with South Carolina, Delaware, and North Carolina still having the lowest.[17] (Actually Delaware's position on this honor roll was a statistical curiosity: the Delaware legislature was still passing a large number of private divorce bills at each biennial session, but the legislature did not meet in 1870 or 1880. Louisiana had a better claim to having one of the lowest divorce rates in the country.)

Two questions of interest to divorce reformers were whether the divorce rate was influenced by legislation and whether most divorces were migratory in character. On the first issue Wright concluded that changes in the divorce laws did indeed influence the number of divorces. The only three states where the divorce rate had declined during the twenty years under study were Connecticut, Maine, and Vermont, where there had been a stiffening of the laws. On the other hand, in Colorado, Dakota Territory, Massachusetts, and Mississippi, where the laws had been liberalized, the rate had risen. Even so, Wright was impressed by the fact that in most states there had been a steady increase in the rate without any substantial change in the laws. Obviously legislation was only one factor in a complex situation.[18] On the question of migratory divorce, the inquiry was inconclusive. Indirect evidence of a sort was provided by the number of couples who were divorced in some state other than the one in which they had been married. Almost 20 per cent of the divorces were of this character, but this was not unnatural in a country where there was so much normal movement of the population. Indeed, 22 per cent of the native-born population in 1880 were living in states other than the one in which they had been born. "In other words," Wright concluded, "the migration shown by the divorce tables . . . is not as great as that of the population at large." [19]

Wright was undoubtedly sympathetic with the divorce reformers, but his findings did not strongly support their presuppositions. Indeed, Walter F. Willcox of Cornell University, analyzing Wright's data in 1891, drew quite different conclusions. Willcox believed that the influence of legislation on the divorce rate had not been proved. Delaware, which permitted divorce on six different grounds, had a lower rate than Maryland and New Jersey, each of which recognized only two grounds. New York with its conservative one-ground law had a higher divorce rate than New Jersey with its two grounds.[20] Summarizing his position, Willcox wrote:

The whole argument of this monograph has gone to show that legal provisions of whatever sort have little direct and permanent influence upon divorce. Restrictions on marriage, restrictions on divorce and restrictions on remarriage after divorce, have been tried in various places and at various times, and have proved of little effect.[21]

To Dr. Dike, already skeptical of the demand for Federal legislation, the Wright report seemed highly significant. On the basis of Wright's figures, Dike thought that probably less than 10 per cent of American divorces were migratory in character. "The center of the problem of divorce legislation," he wrote in 1889, "is now proven to be located elsewhere than in the question of uniformity, though this is by no means eliminated from the problem." [22] The data that Wright had collected seemed to indicate that state legislation was already moving toward the adoption of certain common principles. Could not this tendency toward uniformity be accelerated by cooperative action?

Dike highly approved a suggestion offered by Governor David B. Hill in his annual message to the New York legislature in January, 1889. New York ought to take the lead, the governor said, in proposing a conference of state representatives to consider the question of uniform marriage and divorce laws.[23] When the legislature failed to move, Hill renewed his suggestion in January, 1890.[24]

This time the lawmakers responded with an act authorizing the appointment of three persons to be known as "Commissioners for the Promotion of Uniformity of Legislation in the United States." These were to consider whether it would be wise to invite the other states to send representatives to a convention to draft uniform laws not only on the subject of marriage and divorce, but on such other subjects as insolvency, inheritance, and legal forms.[25]

By 1891, five other states—Massachusetts, New Jersey, Pennsylvania, Delaware, and Michigan—had taken similar action, and two more—Mississippi and Georgia—added their support in 1892. Thereafter, the movement spread rapidly, and by 1898, a total of thirty-two states and one territory were cooperating in the movement.[26]

The state commissioners held their first annual meeting at Saratoga, New York, in August, 1892, where they agreed upon a few tentative principles relating to the divorce problem.[27] But at subsequent meetings the marriage and divorce issue proved too thorny for action, and the commissioners concentrated their attention on other subjects. Their most notable achievement was to draft a uniform negotiable instruments statute, which was adopted by twenty-nine states before 1906.[28]

Progress toward a model divorce law was much slower. In 1897, a committee headed by John C. Richberg of Chicago submitted a proposed statute dealing with matters of procedure but not attempting to define causes.[29] In subsequent years the commissioners gingerly took up a proposal to limit permissible grounds to adultery, extreme cruelty, habitual drunkenness, felony conviction, and desertion.[30] When Episcopal Bishop William C. Doane of Albany, New York, expressed alarm lest the specification of these five causes might liberalize the laws of the more conservative states, Dike explained in a letter to the *New York Tribune* that the commissioners had no such intention. States would be asked not to recognize any ground other than these five, but they might recognize fewer, or, as in the case of South Carolina, no ground at all.[31] In 1901, the commissioners approved a model divorce law along these lines, but only two states—Delaware and Wisconsin—adopted it.[32]

Meanwhile the advocates of divorce reform were agitating strongly within the various Protestant denominations. For the Protestant Episcopal Church the issue was a particularly serious one. The Church had inherited from her Anglican mother a highly conservative attitude toward marriage, yet divorce was increasing among the fashionable sectors of society from which the denomination traditionally drew many of its members. Back in 1808, it had been proposed that the Church should adopt the canon of the Church of England prohibiting the clergy from remarrying divorced persons under any circumstances. But the house of bishops had rejected this proposal and adopted a slightly less rigorous principle: "It is inconsistent with the law of God that the ministers of the Church should unite in matrimony any person who is divorced unless it be on account of the other party having been guilty of adultery." At first this was only an admonition, but in 1868 it was enacted as a law of the church.[33] A strong faction among the clergy disapproved of the canon's provision for the remarriage of the innocent party in cases involving adultery. The conservatives clung to the old doctrine of the indissolubility of a truly valid marriage; also they suspected that the so-called "innocent" party in many a divorce was not innocent at all because of collusion between husband and wife in arranging the case. In 1899, Bishop John Scarborough of New Jersey was quoted as saying: "I am happy in the belief that an ever-increasing number of the clergy and laity of our Church are determined to close the door against the remarriage of divorced persons under any and all circumstances." [34] At the triennial conventions of the Church the conservatives made persistent efforts to obtain such a canon. Although failing in this major objective, they did get minor concessions in the form of resolutions deploring the rising divorce rate and allowing clergymen to refuse to perform the marriage ceremony when doubtful of the moral character of the parties.[35]

The *New York Times* advised the Episcopalians not to push their antidivorce campaign toward unrealistic goals. Commenting on the situation in 1904, the *Times* said:

The Church already stands in this matter on very much higher ground than is taken by the laws of most of the States, or the practice of most of the Churches. To go further and to say that in no case shall a minister of the Episcopal Church give the sanction of that Church to the remarriage of the innocent party to a suit for divorce is to lead whither there is no chance that any other Christian body or any secular Legislature will follow.[36]

Other Protestant bodies also demonstrated a growing conservatism. In 1883 the Presbyterian General Assembly deplored the fact that "divorce laws in many of the states are in direct contravention to the laws of God" and advised the churches and presbyteries "to make use of all proper measures to correct this widespread evil." [37] At subsequent meetings attempts were made to withdraw the Church's historic recognition of willful desertion as a legitimate cause for divorce. This effort failed, but in 1902 the General Assembly admonished ministers to "exercise due diligence before the celebration of a marriage to ascertain that there exists no impediment thereto, as defined in our Confession of Faith." [38] The Methodists moved to a position almost as lofty as that of the Episcopalians. In 1884, their general conference added the following rule to the Discipline:

No divorce shall be recognized as lawful by the Church except for adultery. And no minister shall solemnize a marriage in any case where there is a divorced wife or husband living; but this rule shall not apply to the innocent party in a divorce for the cause of adultery, nor to divorced parties seeking to be reunited in marriage.[39]

In 1904 the American Baptist Home Mission Society went on record as favoring a uniform divorce law for the country based upon Scriptural teachings.[40]

Episcopal Bishop William C. Doane of Albany was the most active worker in a movement to organize a united religious front. In 1901, the Protestant Episcopal general convention directed that a commission be established to confer with the representatives of other religious bodies "with a view to establishing uniformity of practice on the subject of Holy Matrimony and Divorce." Meeting first in January, 1903, the Interchurch Conference on Marriage and Divorce eventually included representatives from some twenty-five Protestant denominations. As one line of attack, the Interchurch group recommended that ministers refuse to marry any person whose marriage was forbidden under the rules of the church to which he belonged.[41] This proposal provoked sharp debate at the Presbyterian general assembly of 1904. The Reverend Henry C. Minton of Trenton, New Jersey, opposed any prohibition on marrying Roman Catholics who had defied their Church's laws. The Roman Catholic Church did not recognize divorce, but Jesus Christ and the Presbyterian Church did, Dr. Minton argued. The proposed rule was rejected by the close vote of 262 to 244, but a compromise was passed, advising ministers not to marry persons whose marriage was prohibited by the laws of their own church "unless the minister believes that in the peculiar circumstances of a given case his refusal would do injustice to an innocent person who has been divorced for scriptural reasons." [42]

The Interchurch Conference infused new life into the languishing campaign to achieve uniform divorce laws. It endorsed specific proposals of the Commissioners for the Promotion of Uniformity and of the American Bar Association. On January 26, 1905, Bishop Doane and a committee from the Interchurch Conference called on President Theodore Roosevelt to enlist his support.[43] Four days later the President sent a special message to Congress asking for authority to collect divorce statistics to bring the Wright report up to date. Roosevelt placed himself squarely behind the movement to obtain uniform legislation:

The hope is entertained that co-operation among the several States can be secured, to the end that there may be enacted upon the subject of marriage and divorce uniform laws, containing all possible safeguards for the security of the family. Intelligent and prudent action in that direction will be greatly promoted by securing reliable and trustworthy statistics upon marriage and divorce.[44]

The President's message brought results of two kinds. Congress passed the necessary legislation to provide for a new compilation of Federal statistics.[45] And Governor Samuel W. Pennypacker of Pennsylvania took the initiative in planning for a National Congress on Uniform Divorce Laws to concentrate on this single problem. The Pennsylvania legislature appropriated $10,000 toward the expenses of such a meeting, and Governor Pennypacker sent out invitations during the summer of 1905.[46] Most of the governors promised to cooperate, often appointing as their delegates men who had already studied the divorce law problem as Commissioners for the Promotion of Uniformity.[47]

With the ground thus prepared, the National Congress on Divorce Laws met in Washington in February, 1906, with over one hundred delegates responding to the initial roll call. Of the forty-five states then in the Union, all but five—South Carolina, Mississippi, Kansas, Montana, and Nevada—were represented.[48] The state of Pennsylvania, which had sponsored the Congress, took a leading role in the proceedings. Governor Pennypacker was elected President, and Attorney Walter George Smith of Philadelphia served as chairman of the seventeen-state committee on resolutions.

On most issues the conservatives were in firm control. Without serious opposition, they obtained approval for a variety of procedural safeguards: a two-year residence requirement, adequate notice, court-appointed attorneys to represent defendants in uncontested suits, open trials before regular courts, and no remarriage for one year after the final decree. They also agreed that these goals should be sought through uniform state legislation, because no Federal divorce law was "feasible" and all efforts to secure the passage of a constitutional amendment would be "futile." [49]

Despite these points of agreement, the delegates displayed significant differences on other issues. There was a sharp debate on a Pennsylvania-proposed resolution reading: "The following causes for divorce seem to be in accordance with modern views . . . ," and then listing five grounds for annulment, five for absolute divorce, and four for legal separation.[50] The New York delegates objected to this statement as implying that the conservative law of their own state was not in accordance with modern views. Asserting New York's claim "to stand on full equality with the other states," Walter S. Logan insisted "that nothing can be said to be in accordance with American legislation which is contrary to the legislation of New York State." [51] He moved to strike out the whole section except the statement that the Congress "does not at present recommend any attempt at uniform legislation as to causes for divorce." [52]

John C. Richberg of Illinois took a diametrically opposed position. "How can you have a uniform bill of divorce," he asked, "when the meat of the entire subject is the cause for divorce, and we leave this out?" [53] He demonstrated that the ultraconservative states like South Carolina and New York were out of line:

> We have representatives in this Convention from the different states, and there are at least six causes for divorce that are uniform in three-fourths of the states of the Union. Now, when three-fourths of the states of the Union, represented here, have legislation in their states upon this question of causes, are we to go out and say that this Congress will do nothing simply because one state objected to any legislation upon this subject, great as she may be?[54]

In the end, the Congress accepted a compromise that stressed the delegates' conservative intention. "While the following causes . . . seem to be in accordance with the legislation of a large number of American states, this Congress, desiring to see the number of causes reduced rather than increased, recommends that no additional causes should be recognized in any state; and in those states where causes are restricted, no change is called for." [55] The six causes recognized under this cautious formula were adultery, bigamy, conviction of felony, intolerable cruelty, willful desertion for two years, and habitual drunkenness.

The sharpest controversy grew out of the following proposal for preventing migratory divorces:

> When the courts are given cognizance of suits where the plaintiff was domiciled in a foreign jurisdiction at the time the cause of complaint arose, it should be insisted that relief will not be given unless the cause of divorce was included among those recognized in such foreign domicile.[56]

This meant, for example, that if a husband deserted his wife while they were residing in New York, she could not obtain a divorce by moving to another state. In her new home she could obtain a divorce only on the one ground recognized in New York. Many delegates believed that the proposed resolution went too far in denying relief to abused wives who went back to the states from which they had originally come. If a woman married in Michigan were so cruelly treated by her husband in New York that she fled to her parental home, should she not be entitled to sue for a cause recognized in Michigan even though it were not recognized in New York? This was the issue on which the moderates and the conservatives parted company.

The moderates rallied around a substitute proposal that would make an exception in "the case of a wife's returning to her original domicile." [57] This wording appealed to all those who believed that divorce was in many circumstances fully justified. "It seems to me," said the Reverend Caroline Bartlett Crane of Michigan, "that the aim of this Congress should be to prevent people from getting divorces who ought not to have divorces, and not to put endless obstacles in the way of those who have a moral right to freedom from the bonds of matrimony." [58] E. D. Leach of West Virginia asserted that it was the physicians, not the lawyers, who knew the truth about unhappy marriages. Oftentimes "sexual anesthesia, sexual perversion, dread of child-bearing, impotency, and venereal disease" were involved. Since this was so, Leach argued:

It does not make any difference how high you make the ground for divorce, people are going to meet it, if they cannot live together by the laws of nature. You cannot suspend those laws by any Act of Legislature; and until we come in this country to understand that the main duty, the chief purpose, and end of an organization of this kind is to increase the sum total of human happiness in the country, I think we are searching after false gods. If we can do so by increasing the standard of divorce, well and good; if we cannot, better lower it.[59]

Many of the moderates believed that the archaic laws of South Carolina and New York were the real nub of the divorce problem. "What is the source of the evil of the migratory divorce?" asked Dean Thomas Sterling of the University of South Dakota Law School. "You will find the greatest source of that evil . . . in the extreme laws adopted by such states as New York, because people say, 'We are driven to a State where we may free ourselves from this intolerable bond.' " [60]

But the conservatives were unwilling to abandon a position that they claimed had the support of the Commissioners on Uniform State Legislation, the American Bar Association, and the Interchurch Conference. Dean Ernest Huffcut of Cornell University Law School argued that cruelly treated wives had an adequate remedy in legal separation without divorce.[61]

When the vote was finally taken, the liberalizing amendment was voted down by the narrowest of margins, 15 states in favor to 16 states opposed. The original resolution was then passed by a vote of 26 to 4.[62]

The conservatives won another victory when the Congress resolved that:

An innocent and injured party, husband or wife, seeking a divorce, should not be compelled to ask for a dissolution of the bonds of matrimony, but should be allowed, at his or her option, at any time, to apply for a divorce from bed and board. Therefore, divorces *a mensa* should be retained where already existing, and provided for in states where no such rights exist.[63]

The resolutions passed at the Washington Congress were committed to the committee on resolutions to be worked into a model statute. When this work had been completed, Governor Pennypacker summoned the delegates back into session at Philadelphia in November, 1906. Many of the issues that had divided the experts at Washington were fought out again, but in the end the proposed divorce statute was approved in pretty much the form in which it had been drafted. The heart of the suggested legislation was contained in Section 21 dealing with the matter of out-of-state decrees, which read:

Full faith and credit shall be given in all the courts of this state to a decree of annulment of marriage or divorce by a court of competent jurisdiction in another State, territory or possession of the United States when the jurisdiction of such court was obtained in the manner and in substantial conformity with the conditions prescribed in . . . this act. . . . Provided, That if any inhabitant of this state shall go into another state, territory or country in order to obtain a decree of divorce for a cause which occurred while the parties resided in this State, or for a cause which is not ground for divorce under the laws of this state, a decree so obtained shall be of no force or effect in this state.[64]

Dr. Dike, Bishop Doane, and other advocates of divorce reform applauded the results of the Congress and called upon the various legislatures to bring their laws into harmony with the model statute.[65] But realists knew that this would be no easy task. The *New York Tribune* doubted whether the proposed bars to migratory divorce were compatible with the "full faith and credit" clause of the Federal Constitution. It commended the divorce congress for crystallizing public sentiment on a "national scandal," but it doubted that any practical result would follow. "States which have strict laws will hardly relax them so as to recognize six causes in place of one cause for divorce. Easy Western states will hardly see any reason for making their laws more severe." [66]

The *Tribune* proved to be an accurate prophet. Despite prompt endorsement of the model statute by the Commissioners for the Promotion of Uniformity, only three states—New Jersey, Delaware, and Wisconsin—adopted it.[67] Even in Pennsylvania the reformers met a crushing disappointment. A bill embodying the model statute passed the state senate in 1907, but failed in the house.[68]

As the effort to get uniform state legislation petered out, the alternative strategy of seeking a Federal law began to attract more support. As early as 1884, two constitutional amendments to empower Congress to regulate marriage and divorce had been introduced—one by Representative George W. Ray of Norwich, New York, and the other by Representative Lewis Beach of Cornwall, New York.[69] For more than sixty years thereafter, similar proposals were made at almost every session of Congress. In the early days the sponsors appeared to be as much concerned with curbing Mormon polygamy as with regulating divorce. This was particularly true of Senator Joseph N. Dolph of Oregon, who introduced a constitutional amendment in 1887.[70] Also conspicuous in the early movement for Federal divorce legislation were Senator James H. Kyle of South Dakota and Representative Frederick H. Gillett of Springfield, Massachusetts.[71]

None of these proposals ever came to a vote in either house, and only once were they considered important enough to require formal committee action. In 1892, the House Judiciary Committee passed adversely on a constitutional amendment proposed by Representative Ray of New York. The majority report, signed by the chairman, William C. Oates of Alabama, reflected the prejudices of the Southern Democrats. Congress, Oates complained, was already exercising too many powers and should not be entrusted with any such dangerous authority as might permit it to legalize interracial marriages. Ray himself and five other committee members—all but one of them Republicans—signed a minority report favoring Federal action.[72]

Despite Congressional coolness to Federal regulation of marriage and divorce, the idea did not lack for distinguished champions. In 1897, the *New York Tribune* called attention to "the ridiculous and disgraceful complications of marriage and divorce in the United States" and invited Congress to test its powers by passing a regulatory bill without waiting for a constitutional amendment.[73] And in December, 1906, President Theodore Roosevelt unexpectedly took up the issue in his annual message to Congress:

> I am well aware of how difficult it is to pass a constitutional amendment. Nevertheless in my judgment the whole question of marriage and divorce should be relegated to the authority of the National Congress. At present the wide differences in the laws of the different States on this subject result in scandals and abuses; and surely there is nothing so vitally essential to the welfare of the nation, nothing around which the nation should so bend itself to throw every safeguard, as the home life of the average citizen.[74]

Five years later, another Roosevelt committed himself to the proposal. Franklin D. Roosevelt, beginning his political career in the New York state senate in 1911, introduced a resolution requesting the state's delegation to Congress "to use their best endeavors for the adoption of . . . an amendment to the Constitution of the United States, delegating to Congress power to establish uniform laws on the subject of married persons throughout the United States." [75] Writing to Eleanor, his wife, the young politician exulted: "By great good luck the divorce resolution passed the Senate *unanimously* last night and the Assembly *unanimously* today!" [76] The *New York Times* reported that Roosevelt did not believe that a Federal divorce law should be as rigid as the New York statute, but he thought, on the other hand, that "the divorce laws of Nevada and some other Western states are too lax." [77]

Although neither Roosevelt won any large number of converts to the idea of Federal regulation of divorce, the general political climate was not unpromising. While the progressives and the prohibitionists were winning the series of victories represented by the Sixteenth, Seventeenth, Eighteenth, and Nineteenth amendments, the divorce reformers tried to put over their own pet project. The movement was particularly strong in California, where the official governing bodies of the Methodist Episcopal and Protestant Episcopal churches had endorsed the idea of Federal regulation of marriage and divorce as early as 1902 and 1904. To lobby for divorce reform both at the state and national level, a California Commission on Marriage and Divorce had been organized. The California movement inspired similar activity in Illinois and New York. Finally representatives from these three states united to form the International Committee on Marriage and Divorce, incorporated under the laws of New York in 1914.[78] This organizaion and other similar ones were able to win at least nominal support for their program from many quarters. The California legislature passed resolutions favoring a Federal divorce law in 1911 and 1915; the New York legislature in 1911 and 1916; the Oregon and Illinois legislatures in 1913. Among the political leaders who endorsed the movement were Governors Hiram W. Johnson of California, Samuel W. McCall of Massachusetts, Charles S. Whitman of New York, and former governors Samuel W. Pennypacker of Pennsylvania and Edward F. Dunne of Illinois. Boards of bishops, both Episcopal and Methodist, passed favoring resolutions, as did also the Roman Catholic bishops of the Western and Middle Western dioceses.[79]

Although Congress failed to give serious attention to the divorce issue, individual legislators continued to push for a constitutional amendment. Between 1913 and 1920 the most active sponsors of the project were Representative George W. Edmonds of Philadelphia, Representative Andrew J. Volstead of Granite Falls, Minnesota (of Prohibition fame), Senator Joseph Ransdell of Louisiana, and Senator Wesley L. Jones of Washington.[80] Each had his own formula for the wording of the desired amendment, but the phraseology most acceptable to the conservatives was that proposed by

Representative Edmonds and later adopted by Senator Jones. This read:

> Congress shall have power to establish and enforce by appropriate legislation uniform laws as to marriage and divorce: Provided, That every State may by law exclude, as to its citizens duly domiciled therein, any or all causes for absolute divorce in such laws mentioned.[81]

This pleased conservatives, because it would permit the Federal government to put a curb on states like Nevada, but allow states like South Carolina and New York to retain their so-called "higher standards."

But more moderate students of the issue perceived that the unrealistic laws of the conservative states were at the heart of migratory divorce problem. Unless the same grounds were recognized in every state, unhappy South Carolinians would continue to seek release in Georgia and New Yorkers in Nevada. After 1920, therefore, attention began to shift to proposed constitutional amendments that would give Congress unlimited power in the field. One such amendment was introduced in 1922 by Representative George P. Codd of Detroit, who had come to Congress with much experience as a Michigan judge.[82]

But the most carefully formulated program was one that originated with Mrs. Edward Franklin White, the chairman of the committee on legislation of the General Federation of Women's Clubs. Mrs. White was an able lawyer, then serving as Deputy Attorney General of Indiana. Through her initiative, the General Federation went on record in 1922 as favoring "a national uniform marriage and divorce law which will prevent hasty and ill-considered marriages, preclude inter-state confusion, and provide a proper justice for all members of the family when divorce becomes necessary." [83] To implement this, Mrs. White drafted both a constitutional amendment and a Federal statute, the latter incorporating many features from the model statute of the American Bar Association's uniform laws committee.[84]

Mrs. White found an enthusiastic sponsor for her program in Senator Arthur Capper of Kansas. In 1923, Senator Capper introduced a constitutional amendment worded thus:

The Congress shall have power to make laws, which shall be uniform throughout the United States, on marriage and divorce, the legitimation of children, and the care and custody of children affected by divorce.[85]

At a hearing before the Senate Judiciary Committee in January, 1924, Senator Capper claimed impressive support for his amendment. Favoring resolutions had been passed by the National Congress of Parent-Teachers, the National Federation of Business and Professional Women, the Woman's Christian Temperance Union, and the Daughters of the American Revolution.[86]

But the Capper program soon ran into stormy weather. It was strongly opposed by the Reverand Walker Gwynne, spokesman for the Association for the Sanctity of Marriage, a Protestant Episcopal group committed to ultraconservative principles. "There are, or were according to the report of 1906," Gwynne asserted, "more than fifty different causes for absolute divorce in the 48 codes, any or all of which, under an unlimited amendment, could be forced by a single Congress upon unwilling states—surely an unprecedented and dangerous power."[87] Another severe critic was Iredell Meares, Washington counsel of the Sentinels of the Republic, a strongly nativist organization of the day. Meares complained that the proposed legislation contained no prohibition against interracial unions, while the five grounds recognized for divorce included adultery, cruelty, desertion for one year, incurable insanity, and conviction for an infamous crime. Meares condemned the desertion and insanity clauses as unduly lax. He also raised constitutional objections against the provision that the Federal divorce law was to be administered through the state courts.[88]

With the advocates of Federal regulation thus divided between conservatives and moderates, it is little wonder that only a few senators and congressmen took a definite stand. Refusing to give up, Senator Capper offered his amendment and bill to eleven different congresses. His final effort came in 1947 when he told his fellow senators:

During World War II it was understood that no action on constitutional amendments would be taken until most of our veterans returned to their homes. The time has come for action, and I firmly believe this matter should be given prompt consideration and—I trust—early approval.[89]

The Capper amendment of 1947 was identical with that first proposed in 1923; the accompanying Capper bill differed from its earlier prototypes largely in recognizing six instead of five grounds for divorce. (The additional ground was habitual intoxication.)[90]

But Congress was no more ready to take the Kansas senator's advice in 1947 than it had been in 1923. Indeed the likelihood of Federal action seemed less in 1947 than in 1884 when Representatives Ray and Beach first proposed to give Congress the power to regulate marriage and divorce. For better or for worse, responsibility for the law of domestic relations seemed destined to remain with the states.

The conservative reaction obviously failed. Despite stiffening of the laws, the number of divorces in the United States rose during the fifty years between 1870 and 1920 from about 11,000 annually to 170,000—more than fifteen times as many. During the same fifty years the total population increased by only two and one-half times. In 1870, there had been .3 divorces per thousand population; in 1920, there were 1.6, more than five times as many.[91]

Even while the conservative reaction was at its height, many public figures continued to defend the right of divorce. In 1889, when conservative moralists like Cardinal Gibbons and Justice Joseph P. Bradley of the United States Supreme Court were deploring the rise of divorce, Colonel Robert G. Ingersoll took the other side, writing with impassioned eloquence:

Is it possible that an infinitely wise and compassionate God insists that a helpless woman shall remain the wife of a cruel wretch? Can this add to the joy of Paradise, or tend to keep one harp in tune? Can anything be more infamous than for a government to compel a woman to remain the wife of a man she hates—of one whom she justly holds in abhorrence?[92]

Mrs. Stanton was as radical on the marriage question at the age of eighty-six as she had been a half century earlier. "The States that have more liberal divorce laws," she wrote in 1902, "are for women today what Canada was for the fugitive in the old days of slavery." [93] And in 1915, William E. Carson argued that "the increase of divorce is, in reality, a healthy sign, proving, as it does, that people have become less tolerant of evils which were once endured and for which divorce is the only remedy." [94]

CHAPTER 11

Divorce and
the Tourist Trade

The earlier divorce colonies had lasted for only brief periods of time. When local peculiarities in the law had induced eastern divorce seekers to establish residences in places like Indiana, North and South Dakota, and Utah, the result in each case had been to attract such unfavorable publicity that the conservatives mobilized their forces and obtained a change in the laws. The first state in which this familiar pattern of developments broke down was Nevada. Here the champions of respectability tried to smash the "quickie" divorce business, but failed, because the state so desperately needed additional income. Reno's success in this specialty was so great that other states and countries were tempted to offer competing inducements to divorce-seeking tourists.

As more and more western states lengthened their residence requirements for divorce to one year, attention inevitably focused on the few places where the older six-months requirement still held. Nevada was such a state—not because its founding fathers had set out to attract divorce seekers, but because a short residence provision for citizenship and voting privileges had suited the needs of the early mining population and six-months residence had likewise seemed logical for divorce.[1] Only slowly did Easterners become aware of Nevada's possibilities. In 1900, Earl Russell, member of a famous English family, established residence in Nevada, divorced his first wife, and married another woman, with whom he returned to England. Denying the validity of these transactions, the first wife sued him for divorce on the grounds of adultery, thereby precipitating a litigation climaxed by his Lordship's indictment for bigamy, trial by the House of Lords, and imprisonment in the Tower of London.[2] This may seem to have been an inauspicious precedent for Nevada divorces, but it at least called attention to the liberality of the Nevada law.

Nevada received publicity of a more favorable kind in 1905 when Mrs. Laura B. Corey, a wealthy Pittsburgh woman, won a Reno divorce from her husband who had neglected her for a chorus girl. Public opinion sided with Mrs. Corey, and Nevada's prompt and easy surgery won wide applause.[3]

As more and more outsiders began to come to Nevada for divorces, enterprising lawyers sought to capitalize on the situation. In January, 1907, William H. Schnitzer moved from New York City to Reno, where he established a law office. Two years later he published a twenty-four-page pamphlet under the title *Divorce Practice and Procedure*, in which he summarized the peculiar attractions of the Nevada law. Not only was the six-months residence requirement now the shortest in the nation, but the seven grounds for divorce included those that were "simplest and least difficult" to prove. Extreme cruelty, for example, could be established if the defendant had been guilty of acts "producing mental anguish and threatening health." In uncontested cases, there might be private hearings without "embarrassing cross-examinations" and without the need of corroborative proof for the plaintiff's charges. There were no bars to the immediate remarriage of the parties. In a section entitled "Your Selection of a Lawyer," Schnitzer coyly set forth his own qualifications, naming as references not only several Nevada lawyers and judges but a United States senator and the acting governor of the state. Schnitzer placed advertisements in eastern newspapers like the *Brooklyn Daily Eagle* and the *Washington Post*, offering to send free copies of his pamphlet, and he also inserted a particularly blatant spread in a San Francisco theater program, reading as follows:

Have You Domestic Trouble?
Are You Seeking DIVORCE?
Do You Want Quick and Reliable Action?
Send for My Booklet
Contains Complete Information

FREE

Shortest Residence
Address Counselor, P.O. Box 263, Reno, Nevada
Correspondence Strictly Confidential[4]

When the Reno Bar Association objected to Schnitzer's advertising as unethical, the Nevada Supreme Court in 1911 suspended his license to practice for eight months, but this slap on the wrist was not enough to check the state's rapidly expanding divorce business. Alarmed by Reno's growing notoriety, local reform groups began to agitate for extending the residence requirement to one year, but this proposal was strongly opposed. A Reno journalist argued the matter thus:

Prosperity reigns in Reno. Isn't it wiser to cling to it than to take a chance on losing it? Regrets don't amount to much when the consequences of a rash act stare one in the face. Better slow up a bit, Disgruntled one, and think twice. Sioux Falls sank into obscurity in a very short time and Sioux Falls had size and industry in its favor. Has Reno anything to swap equal to the Colony? Not yet! [5]

The same argument was more attractively packaged in verse:

Have you ever thought about the Reno Colony
And what we owe this little fad, divorce?
    Fair plaintiffs oft advising,
    Forever criticizing,
Yet their money helps us on a bit, of course.

If you legislate against the Reno Colony,
To other fields the fair ones you will drive
    For ill-advised propriety
    Brings poverty with piety,
And some of us would much prefer to thrive.

Does Reno really know how much the Colony
Contributes to the cafés and the stores?
    Hotels would soon be closing,
    The population dozing,
If broken hearts should favor other shores.

A necessary evil is the Colony.
It must exist when Love has sullen grown,
    So quit the foolish knocking,
    Your own prosperity blocking,
And learn to let what's well enough alone.[6]

But in 1913 the demand for reform became so insistent that the legislators felt it necessary to listen. Reno's leading newspaper, the *Nevada State Journal* argued: "This state and this city cannot advance permanently unless they be fortified not only in self-respect, but in the respect of all who think of us. Any work too damaging for any other state to do is certainly too damaging for Nevada to do." [7] Reno women undertook to marshal the forces of respectability through meetings of church societies and mothers' clubs and door-to-door circulation of petitions. A mass meeting in the high school auditorium unanimously called upon the legislature to amend the divorce statute "to the end that divorce colonies with all their attendant evils and resulting undesirable notoriety may no longer flourish in our midst." Clergymen spurred on the campaign with fiery sermons.[8]

On February 7, 1913, the antidivorce crusade came to a climax when 160 passengers crowded onto the little Virginia and Truckee Railroad train running from Reno to Carson City, the state capitol. Arriving at their destination, the militant visitors marched straight to the capitol building where they crowded into the assembly chamber, overflowing the gallery and standing in every available space on the floor of the house itself. The clergyman who made the opening prayer called God's attention to the fact that the eyes of the commonwealth and the nation were upon Nevada and asked "that strength be given that the state be freed from the curses which beset her." In such an atmosphere the prodivorce majority melted away, and the one-year residence bill was expedited toward final passage.[9]

The reformers' victory was bitterly resented by the lawyers, hotel-keepers, and merchants who had profited from the divorce colony. Republican Governor Tasker Oddie, who had signed the one-year residence bill, was defeated for reelection in 1914, as were also several of the assemblymen who had voted for the measure.[10]

When the legislature met for its next biennial session in January, 1915, the divorce issue was at once reopened. Spokesmen for the Reno Businessmen's Association asked for a return to the six-months requirement, even though a Reno banker argued that real estate values had gone up after the stricter divorce law had been passed. The women's organizations again took the conservative side. With both factions mobilizing their forces, the strain on the Virginia and Truckee was even greater than two years before. On February 3, more than a thousand strangers were reported to be in Carson City.[11] In the assembly, the six-months bill won an easy 40 to 12 victory, but in the senate the supporters of the bill had to resort to trickery to win. One vote short of the constitutional majority that they needed, the prodivorce faction delayed a final showdown by committing the bill to the friendly committee on railroads and internal improvements. The proponents also gained time by going into hiding to avoid quorum calls. Meanwhile Humboldt businessmen, hopeful of getting a share in the divorce business, put pressure on their senator to change his vote. This maneuver was successful, and the bill was pushed through on February 17.[12] Democratic Governor Emmet D. Boyle signed the bill, accompanying his action with a Pilate-like declaration, in which he suggested that the final decision ought to be made by popular referendum. "Moral and social questions on which the people are divided," the governor explained, "should, if possible, be kept out of the legislature where they tend to obscure legislation of even greater moment to the serious detriment of good government." [13]

The divorce law again became a political issue in 1922, when two propositions were put on the ballot in the November election. By a three to one margin the voters rejected a proposal to lengthen the residence requirement to one year; by a two to one margin they indicated their desire to retain the existing law for at least three more years.[14]

By 1927, more Nevadans than ever had reached the conclusion that the state's prosperity depended on the tourist's dollar. It was imperative to keep Nevada's divorce attractions bright in competition with those of France, Mexico, and other potential competitors. Bills were introduced in the legislature to reduce the residence requirement to three months and to enact wide-open gambling laws to keep the temporary residents amused. The gambling bill failed, and the three-months proposal also seemed doomed to defeat. By a brilliant last-minute maneuver, however, the divorce measure was put through. In the early hours of the morning of March 18, 1927, when the assemblymen and senators were dozing in their seats after an all-night session, a conference report embodying the three-months residence requirement was hurriedly read and adopted without a roll call. Judge Patrick A. McCarran, of later United States Senate fame, was one of the lobbyists who helped arrange this transaction. Before 8 A.M. Governor Fred B. Balzer signed the bill, explaining that he wanted to get it off his hands before individuals and organizations had time to protest. The *Nevada State Journal* summarized the transaction in an indignant editorial:

> One of the most amazing legislative performances of record happened early yesterday morning when a three months divorce law was jammed through and given executive approval before the public had any inkling of the proposal. The plans of the proponents were evidently well laid and worked with absolute precision. The only astonishing thing is why the wide open gambling bill was not handled in the same efficient manner. Regardless of the merits of the measure, the indecent haste in passing and signing the three months divorce law should be roundly condemned by every good citizen. Such procedure is repugnant to the principles of free government and forms a most dangerous precedent.[15]

In 1931, Nevada felt itself threatened by the news that Idaho and Arkansas intended to reduce their one-year requirements for divorce to three months. Effective countermeasures were at once proposed. The *Nevada State Journal* carried a banner headline: "REVIVAL OF GOLD RUSH DAYS PREDICTED. BEAT THIS ONE, IF YOU CAN." [16] If Idaho and Arkansas reduced their residence requirements, Nevada would outbid them by passing a six-weeks bill. Things worked out as predicted: the assembly passed the measure by a 34 to 0 vote on March 6 and the senate by a 13 to 1 vote on March 16. The cooperative Governor Balzer signed the measure three days later.[17] To round out Nevada's defenses in this hour of crisis, the legislature specified that divorce cases were to be tried behind closed doors, liberalized procedure in other particulars, and sanctioned wide-open gambling. The *Nevada State Journal* was less critical than on earlier occasions. "No one denies," it said, "that the 'business of divorce' has brought millions of dollars into the state annually, and no one is to be blamed for desiring to continue this income." But it went on to warn that divorce was a precarious resource, largely dependent on visitors from New York State. If that state should ever modernize its statutes, Nevada would be in trouble.[18]

As streamlined in 1931, Nevada procedure permitted her courts to grant a final decree of divorce to a plaintiff on the forty-third day of residence in the state, provided the defendant would cooperate by filing an appearance through a Nevada lawyer. If the defendant refused to appear but could be served with a summons, the divorce could be granted after 73 days; if notice had to be given by publication, the case required 102 days for completion. The strictest requirements of the law had to do with the initial six weeks of residence. Corroborative proof that the plaintiff had actually lived in the state for this period was required, both to protect the interests of Nevada innkeepers and to give the divorce as strong a standing as possible in case it were challenged in the courts of other states. The nine grounds on which a divorce action could be based—adultery, cruelty, desertion, nonsupport, alcoholism, felony, impotency, five years' separation without cohabitation, and five years' insanity—were no more liberal than those of many other states, but proof was made easy in uncontested cases by accepting the unsupported testimony of the plaintiff and by not requiring specific instances to support a general charge of cruelty.[19]

Statistics testified to the success of this fond nurture of the divorce business. By the 1920's the Nevada courts were granting about 1,000 divorces a year; after the residence requirement was reduced to three months, production more than doubled with over 2,500 divorces in 1928. The effect of the 1931 law reducing residence to six weeks was equally dramatic. The rate again doubled, and in 1931 there were 5,260 Nevada divorces. Annual production fell off somewhat during the later years of the Great Depression, but soared wildly under the impact of World War II, reaching 11,000 in 1943 and 20,500 in 1946. Thereafter, it subsided to a more or less stable level of between 9,000 and 10,000 a year during the later 1950's.[20]

Although to most Easterners a Nevada divorce usually meant a trip to Reno, the more glamorous night life of Las Vegas began to attract divorce seekers from Los Angeles and southern California. Las Vegas divorces, less than 100 a year before 1928, rapidly grew in popularity, passing the 1,000 level in 1940, and hovering around 4,000 a year in the late 1950's. Reno still granted more divorces than Las Vegas, but the ratio had been reduced to about 1.2 to 1. Ironically, the newer divorce capital was beginning to wish for a reduction in its divorce business. The luxurious hotels and night clubs of the newer city found more profit in catering to visitors who came for a few days of gambling and easy spending or a "quickie" marriage than in accommodating the divorce seekers who had to spread their spending over six weeks.[21]

Despite Nevada's strong inducements, many divorce-seeking Americans were exploring other fields. To rich Easterners, sophisticated Paris possessed attractions that brash Reno could never hope to rival. Since 1884, French law had permitted absolute divorce for four causes: adultery, physical cruelty, serious insults, and imprisonment for crime. More realistic in their procedure than most American courts, French tribunals did not cling to the fiction that divorce was always an adversary proceeding involving an innocent and a guilty party. French judges regarded indications that both parties wished the marriage to be dissolved, not as evidence of collusion, but as strengthening the case for divorce. The court was required to make an effort to reconcile the parties, but if this failed, the judge would usually grant the divorce, often relying upon the broad possibilities offered by the serious insult provision. Newspaper publicity was minimized, it being illegal to print more than the names of the parties and the fact that the decree had been granted.[22]

The French had enacted these liberal laws for their own citizens, and Americans only slowly came to a realization of their possibilities. In 1914, Clarence H. McKay, the president of the Postal Telegraph Company, and his wife, Katherine, obtained separate

Paris divorces, each charging the other with the "serious insult" of desertion. The McKays were ruled to have a French domicile, since they maintained a Paris apartment. Other wealthy Americans followed this precedent, filing suit for divorce in French courts and presenting leases or rent receipts as evidence of an intention to reside in France indefinitely.[23]

At first only a few Americans sought divorce in France each year. But in 1922, interest in this avenue to freedom was heightened by a sensational case involving the socially prominent Frank J. Gould and his wife Edith. Frank obtained a Paris divorce and married another woman; Edith challenged the legality of these transactions by suing Gould for divorce in New York. But the American court upheld the validity of the Paris decree. Not only had it been based upon a charge of adultery, but Mrs. Gould was alleged to have committed her indiscretion in France.[24] Although these were highly special circumstances, this American recognition of a French divorce was followed by a rush of divorce seekers to Paris. About one hundred cases were heard in 1922, and at least as many the following year. One of the marriages dissolved in 1923 was that of the highly popular dancer, Irene Castle, and Captain Robert E. Tremain of Ithaca, New York. While their case was pending in a Paris court, observers reported the Tremains had been seen dining and walking together at Deauville, a display of camaraderie that might have compromised an American divorce suit but did not shock the French.[25]

Had the French wished to exploit divorce to the fullest, Paris might perhaps have displaced Reno in this specialty. But the French found this an appalling thought. A few discreetly handled divorces each year were readily tolerated, but the new flood of cases congesting Paris court dockets amidst cynical reports in the American press were an offense to French national pride. In 1924, Premier Raymond Poincaré was reported to have ordered an investigation of the situation and a tightening of procedure in the French courts.[26]

Apparently this first attempt at reform was not very effective, because in 1927 French and American newspapers published a list of some three hundred American couples who had been divorced in French courts the preceding year. More than half of these were from New York State.[27] Another investigation was ordered, and this time effective countermeasures were taken. A report made public in 1928 revealed numerous irregularities in the administration of the divorce law and some petty grafting. Three American lawyers practicing in Paris were reprimanded.[28] Meanwhile Minister of Justice Louis Barthou issued strict orders that in handling divorce suits brought by foreigners the French courts were to follow the letter of French law. First evidence that the old easygoing days had passed came on February 29, 1928, when the distinguished Bainbridge Colby, who had been Secretary of State under Woodrow Wilson, was denied a divorce at Versailles on the ground that he had not established a genuine French domicile.[29]

The hurdles placed in the way of American divorce seekers were not based on new French legislation, but upon stricter enforcement of existing law. French courts now required convincing evidence that the plaintiff had resided in France for at least six months and intended to remain indefinitely. Moreover, they were much more scrupulous in scrutinizing the "certificate of custom," that is, the document summarizing the marriage laws of the foreign litigant's home state. The principle was enforced that divorce would not be granted unless the ground on which it was claimed was recognized both in French law and in the law of the state of permanent domicile —for example, no divorce for New Yorkers except for adultery. As a final blow to the divorce trade, French judges made it much more difficult for American lawyers with Paris offices to get their cases considered. Although it was still possible for an American to get a French divorce, the difficulties were now so great that by 1934 the annual number had fallen off to about twenty-five.[30]

Unlike France, Mexico hung out the welcome sign to American divorce seekers and left it there. Before the overthrow of Díaz absolute divorce had not been permitted but, on December 29, 1914, the victorious First Chief, Venustiano Carranza, issued a decree authorizing divorce for valid cause or by mutual consent. He directed the governors to modify the laws of the respective territories. Under Mexico's Federal Constitution, her divorce laws thereafter evolved with a complexity rivaling that of her northern neighbor. There were twenty-nine different jurisdictions, each with their local peculiarities. In 1918, the state of Yucatán enacted a very liberal divorce code, which soon began to attract Americans. Three other states—Campeche, Morelos, and Sonora—presently followed this example.[31]

Once the possibility of attracting gringo dollars had been demonstrated, the Mexicans learned fast. Since the visitors were unhappy in lodgings where beds were dirty and plumbing was nonexistent, there was a speedy revolution in Mexican hotelkeeping. Agencies were maintained in New York City, where the curious could not only get information on Mexican divorce law, but make reservations and purchase tickets. These bureaus offered "tours of divorce," just as other tourist agencies sold package deals to visit European cathedrals. A newspaper account of 1928 describes the experiences of a Boston woman who made such a trip to Hermosillo, the capital of Sonora. When she arrived, she was put up at an attractive Swiss villa. Her Mexican attorney drove her to the judge's chamber, where he presented her petition for divorce and her written statement setting forth the essential facts that she had been married for more than one year and had lived apart from her husband for more than six months. There was no oral examination, and no outsiders were present. For the next three days she enjoyed the sights and fiestas of the city. Then she executed a power of attorney authorizing her Mexican lawyer to represent her to the conclusion of the case and returned to the United States. Two weeks after the complaint was filed, the Mexican judge called in the attorney to inquire whether a reconciliation might be made, and the latter replied that this was impossible. In another two weeks a divorce decree was mailed to the eagerly waiting Bostonian. This de luxe tour of divorce had cost $2,500, but there were other less expensive ones available.[32]

In a magazine article written in 1930, it was noted that such well known public figures as Homer S. Cummings, Democratic National Committeeman from Connecticut and future Attorney General of the United States, opera singer Frances Alda, novelist William McFee, and movie star Dolores del Rio had all obtained Mexican divorces. Unlike Reno, where female divorce seekers had always outnumbered male, more men than women went to Mexico in quest of freedom. This was attributed in part to feminine timidity in venturing alone into a country where acts of violence had once been common. But a more important reason was supposed to be the lack of any rigid residence requirement. For a busy husband to spend six weeks of residence in Nevada might be difficult to arrange, but the few days necessary to institute proceedings in Mexico could be easily spared. Zealots for efficiency could combine business with pleasure by planning to hunt, fish, and attend bullfights in the company of congenial comrades visiting Mexico on similar missions.[33]

For those willing to take the risks, it was even possible to obtain a "mail order" divorce without going to Mexico at all. Some of the Mexican states permitted an absentee plaintiff to execute a power of attorney, under which his Mexican lawyer could carry through the divorce case without the personal appearance of either party. In March, 1935, an unhappy husband or wife perusing the classified advertisements of the *New York Daily Mirror* might have discovered this modest notice:

> MEXICAN LAW OFFICE—free consultation.
> American Attorney advising.
> Address:———[34]

If he or she nibbled at this bait and addressed a letter of inquiry to the given address, he would receive a reply setting forth the advantages of Mexican divorces. He would be invited to fill out an enclosed questionnaire, covering "all the information necessary to commence your proceeding." The fee was $225, with the final installment payable "upon the tendering of the certified copy of the final decree of divorce duly translated into English." [35]

Mexican mail-order divorces were cheap and convenient—a little too much so to be a safe investment. Sometimes the purported divorces were entirely spurious. In 1934, it was discovered that a ring in Morelos had been manufacturing divorce documents by an ingenious method. The conspirators would obtain an extra copy of a genuine divorce decree and detach the last page on which were inscribed the signatures of the judge and the state governor together with the official seal. They would then bind this page to a first page containing the names of parties whose cases had never come before the Mexican courts at all. The resulting documents had been so impressive that they had received the authentication of the American consulate in Mexico City.[36]

Even when mail-order divorce decrees were genuine, they were of questionable validity under Mexican law and patently invalid if challenged in an American court. The United States government tried to curb this thriving business, first by warnings issued by its consuls in Mexico, then by asking Congress to pass new legislation prohibiting the use of the mails for the solicitation of foreign divorces. The House of Representatives passed bills of this character in 1936 and 1937, but the Senate failed to act.[37] After a new appeal by Postmaster General James A. Farley, a statute was finally enacted on August 10, 1939, closing the mails to "every written or printed card, circular, letter, book, pamphlet, advertisement, or notice of any kind, giving or offering to give information concerning where or how or through whom a divorce may be secured in a foreign country, and designed to solicit business in connection with the procurement thereof." Violators were liable to fines up to $5,000, or up to five years' imprisonment, or both.[38]

The more responsible Mexican leaders had all along recognized the unwisdom of featuring mail-order divorces. They realized that Mexican decrees would, in the long run, be a salable product only if they had some chance of withstanding attack in American courts. Entering the market somewhat later than other Mexican states, Chihuahua tried to profit by their experience. In its laws of 1932 and 1933 and in the procedure developed in its courts, it tried to provide divorce machinery that was speedy and liberal, yet punctilious in certain particulars on which Anglo-Saxon jurists might be sensitive. In handling American cases, Chihuahua lawyers followed what they called the "Nevada formula." Accordingly, even though the local law permitted divorce by mutual consent and without the personal appearance of the parties, this was not advised for American clients. Their best strategy was to come to Juarez or some other Chihuahua city and establish proof of their residence by obtaining the proper documents from the Municipal Registrar of Residents. Although the Chihuahua law recognized twenty grounds for divorce, the most convenient and respectable for visitors was "incompatibility of characters." The plaintiff would present a written document making this charge; the defendant—if his or her cooperation could be obtained—would file an appearance through a Mexican attorney admitting the truth of the allegation; and the divorce would then be granted.[39]

The number of American parties who sought Mexican divorces fluctuated widely in response to a variety of factors—favorable and unfavorable court decisions, changes in Mexican policy, and the whims of fashion. From an estimated 1,700 in 1935, such divorces fell off to less than 900 in 1940; in 1945, they rose to almost 3,000; in 1950, they declined to 1,500; in 1955, they soared to 4,300.[40] Oftentimes the parties obtained both Mexican and American decrees, the first was prized for its speed, the second for its greater safety. For example, California couples resorted to Mexican courts to get quick divorces, married new mates on Mexican soil to forestall possible prosecutions for bigamy, then went through the slower California divorce procedure that required a year's interval before the final decree was granted.[41]

But Nevada had domestic as well as foreign competitors. During the 1930's, Idaho, Arkansas, Wyoming, and Florida all made open bids for the transient divorce business. In February, 1931, the Idaho legislature took up a bill to reduce the residence requirement from six months to three. There was the usual division of opinion. Ministerial groups opposed the change; many businessmen favored it. On February 20, the state senate voted against the bill, but this decision was reversed the next day by a 27 to 17 vote.[42] On February 25, when the house took up the measure, one faction of women packed the gallery in support of the three-months requirement, while a rival group congregated on the capitol steps to demonstrate their opposition.[43] On the floor of the house the opponents stressed the argument that easy divorce attracted unwholesome visitors, while the other side contended that "there are many desirable people from most social standpoints, all over the United States, who want divorces and many deserve them. They should have an opportunity to come to a nice, law-abiding state and get them." [44]

Even after passing the house, the divorce bill encountered a setback. On February 28, Governor C. Ben Ross vetoed the measure, contending that the three-months visitors were not likely to become permanent residents and that catering to the divorce trade would give the state a bad name.[45] But three days later the governor's veto was overridden in a session that was marked, according to the *Idaho Statesman*, by "swift and silent action." [46]

Idaho's bid for a share in the divorce business was countered by

Nevada's six-weeks law passed the same month. Idaho did not attempt to match this until February 1, 1937, when the legislature cut the residence period to six weeks.[47] Although the 1931 and 1937 laws put the state into the migratory divorce business, it operated strictly at the retail level. In 1955, Idaho courts granted about 2,200 divorces —less than one-quarter the number granted in Nevada.[48]

In 1931, the Arkansas legislature reduced the residence requirement for divorce to three months in an effort to attract visitors to Hot Springs, the state's greatest tourist attraction. Commenting cynically on the plan, the *Arkansas Democrat* of Little Rock offered suggestions for slogans to be printed on the stationery of chambers of commerce and other booster organizations: "Save railroad fare by coming to Arkansas to get a quick divorce, instead of riding all the way to Reno"; and, "Spend your vacation among the lovely hills of Arkansas, where the gals are prettier, yet easier to get, or get rid of." [49]

In the Arkansas house the bill was fiercely debated on February 11, 1931. An opponent shouted: "I want to tell you there is more sin committed by couples awaiting divorces than ever you will find among any other class of people." But one of the bill's supporters was a Methodist minister, who defended the proposal as a means of bringing relief from "a hell on earth" to couples unhappily married. Another legislator asserted baldly that the state needed the extra income which it would get through the residence of "rich Eastern people who will come to our state." He himself had found Reno "a nice little city" in a state populated by "the most hospitable people." He thought that Arkansas would be helped rather than hurt by the influx of divorce seekers. The bill passed the lower house by a vote of 56 to 36.[50]

In the state senate the three-months proposal ran into stormier weather. Calling it "the most vile and vicious of measures," one senator went on to say: "This bill would dump into Arkansas the loose and irresponsible men and women of the nation. A bunch of hotel men are here lobbying this measure through, and if you listen to them and vote this bill through, you will do so over my protest and the protest of the decent citizenship of the state." Another opponent mourned: "It looks as if we have reached the same point reached by Judas Iscariot when he sold the Christ." Supporters of the bill insisted that there was no moral issue involved: the measure simply gave relief to those who wanted divorce without changing the existing grounds. On February 19, the senate passed the bill by a 20 to 12 vote, and a week later Governor Harvey Parnell approved it without comment.[51]

In the short run, Arkansas's attempt to divert a share of the divorce business from Reno, seems to have been successful. In 1946, Arkansas courts granted almost 13,700 divorces, and the state's divorce rate rose to 7.3 per thousand as compared with the national rate of 4.3 and Nevada's fantastic 148.9. But by 1955, Arkansas's annual crop was not much more than 5,000 and her divorce rate of 2.9 per thousand was not much above the national level of 2.3.[52]

Undoubtedly it was the great depression that drove desperate legislators to the expedient of tinkering with the divorce laws in order to attract tourist dollars to hard-pressed local innkeepers and businessmen. This influence was at work in Wyoming, where in February, 1935, the lawmakers reduced the residence requirement from one year to sixty days.[53] Whatever new tourist business was attracted to the state must have been modest in amount. In 1955 Wyoming courts granted about 1,100 divorces, and the state's divorce rate of 3.6 per thousand was only moderately in excess of the national average of 2.3.[54]

Only Florida had the auxiliary tourist attractions to offer real competition to the Nevada pleasure domes. A bill to reduce the Florida residence requirement for divorce from one year to three months was introduced into the state legislature in April, 1935. Representative M. M. Frost of Jacksonville, the sponsor of the measure, frankly described it as a bid for a share in the lucrative divorce trade being enjoyed by Nevada and Arkansas. "If they are going to get divorces," he argued, "we can't stop them and we might as well invite them to Florida to spend the money." The *Florida Times-Union* of Jacksonville linked the new proposal with recent legislation legalizing horse and dog racing and pari-mutuel betting, all being parts of a program to make the state more attractive to tourists.[55] When asked on the floor of the house whether the three-months measure was also related to an effort to attract the movie industry, Frost replied: "If this bill would bring the movie industry to Florida, then I say, for God's sake, let's pass it." [56]

Frost's bill was strongly opposed and appeared to lose by one vote when a roll call was taken on April 30. But several members changed their minds, and on a recount the bill passed the house by a vote of 45 to 42.[57] The senate concurred by an 18 to 14 vote.[58] Governor Dave Sholtz, a former Daytona Beach lawyer, signed the bill gladly. "Florida," he explained, "is a tourist State, extending to the people of the United States an invitation to come here as visitors and remain as residents. If this bill brings additional residents or visitors to Florida, it will be in line with that invitation." [59]

In addition to its short residence period and famous climate, Florida had other attractions for the divorce seeker. Although the nine grounds recognized by the law had not changed much in a hundred years, judicial attitudes had. "Our Courts in Florida," an authority wrote, "have in recent years, through their decisions in matrimonial matters, gotten away from the question of personal or intentional guilt. Florida more and more is treating the question of marriage relations and divorce from not only the external facts, but the internal psychology of the individuals involved." [60] Particularly liberal was the interpretation now placed on cruelty. "What constitutes extreme cruelty depends on the temperament, the culture, and other attributes of the individual," wrote Justice Glenn Terell of the Florida Supreme Court.[61]

Florida's invitation to divorce seekers was eagerly accepted. In 1946, at the peak of the postwar rise in divorce, Florida granted over 26,000 divorces. The rate per thousand population was 12.1, second only to that in Nevada.[62] In 1955, a more normal year, Florida still granted about 20,000 divorces, and the divorce rate was 5.5.[63]

Not all citizens of the state were proud to have Miami in competition with Reno and Las Vegas. In 1957, Governor LeRoy Collins recommended a program of reform that would extend the residence period to one year and require an interlocutory decree, to become final only after sixty days.[64] Submitted to the legislature in separate bills, the governor's proposals were drastically amended but eventually passed. The residence requirement was raised to six months instead of one year, and the provision for interlocutory decrees was dropped in favor of a thirty-day "cooling-off" period between the time of filing the divorce petition and the trial.[65] Although he had received substantially less than he had asked, Governor Collins praised the legislature for taking action that would "enhance the prestige of our state everywhere." [66]

Meanwhile migratory divorce had invaded the Virgin Islands and Alabama. Poverty-stricken and desperately in need of tourist business, the Virgin Islands legislature had in 1939 reduced the residence requirement for divorce from six months to six weeks. This had little effect until after World War II when the islands became much more accessible to the mainland through improved airline service. Even then, however, the business was petty in volume by Nevada or Florida standards, with about 190 divorces being granted to couples from mainland United States in 1950 and about 250 in 1952. One of the islands' selling points had been that their law did not require a plaintiff to state an intention of continuing his residence in the islands indefinitely. But Federal court decisions in 1952 and 1953 ruled that unless such domiciliary intent was established no valid divorces could be granted. The territorial legislature tried to evade this principle in a new statute passed in 1953, but this was held unconstitutional by the Supreme Court in 1955. These judicial roadblocks still made Virgin Islands divorces no more difficult to get than those of Nevada or Florida, but the migratory divorce business nevertheless dwindled to almost nothing by 1955.[67]

Alabama's emergence as a state offering opportunities for migratory divorce was a rather unexpected development of the 1950's. A quirk in the state's divorce law had been that it did not specify any length of residence except for one year in cases where the defendant was a nonresident or where the ground of complaint was voluntary abandonment. In 1945, the legislature waived even this requirement in cases "when the Court has jurisdiction of both parties to the action." This meant that if either party was a *bona fide* resident of the state, the Alabama courts would assume jurisdiction to grant divorce either for or against him, provided the other party submitted to the jurisdiction of the court by making a general appearance. Since no specific period of residence was required, the trial judge had wide latitude in deciding whether any particular party was a *bona fide* resident. In situations where both parties wanted the divorce, this made Alabama a more attractive haven than Nevada or Florida. The prospective party could go to Alabama, file an immediate suit, declare his intention of remaining permanently in the state, and have his case heard at once, provided some Alabama attorney filed an appearance for the absent party. Within a few days the divorce seeker might obtain his decree and be on his way.[68] Grace Metalious, author of *Peyton Place*, Hank Greenberg, former baseball star, and John Daly, well known TV and radio news commentator, were among those reported to have obtained Alabama divorces. But recipients of "quickie" decrees did well not to reopen their cases, as Mrs. John Hartingan of New York State discovered in July, 1960. When Circuit Court Judge George Lewis Bailes of Birmingham learned during a hearing on a motion to modify Mrs. Hartingan's decree that the plaintiff's "*bona fide* residence" in Alabama had lasted no more than four hours, he voided the divorce despite the fact that the husband had already remarried. As further evidence of a local reaction against the state's growing reputation for migratory divorce a Birmingham grand jury petitioned the state legislature in July, 1960, for stricter laws.[69]

American divorce statistics, inadequate on many scores, are particularly unsatisfactory on the matter of migratory divorces. To demonstrate that the problem has been somewhat exaggerated in the popular mind, Justice Felix Frankfurter made this analysis in a Supreme Court decision of 1948:

> Actually, there are but five States, Arkansas, Florida, Idaho, Nevada, and Wyoming, in which divorces may be easily obtained on less than a year's residence. . . . These five States accounted for only 24,370 divorces in 1940, but 9% of the national total. . . . The number of divorces granted in Arkansas, Idaho, and Wyoming is small enough to indicate the normal incidence of divorce among their permanent population, with only a few transients taking advantage of their divorce laws. Nevada and Florida thus attract virtually all the non-resident divorce business. Yet, between them, only 16,375 divorces were granted in 1940, 6% of the total. . . .[70]

The justice might have carried his argument a step further to demonstrate, at least in the case of Florida, that a substantial proportion of even these divorces must have been granted to permanent residents of the state. Paul H. Jacobson, an expert on divorce statistics, says that migratory divorces "probably account for no more than 3 to 5 per cent of the total divorces annually." [71]

To say that no more than 5 per cent of American divorces are migratory does not tell the whole story. Quickie divorces have always found their most eager takers among the unhappily married in the northeastern states. In 1935, it was estimated that transients from New York and New Jersey were the parties in about three-fifths of Nevada's divorce cases. [72] To guess that about one-third of the migratory divorces of any particular year were granted to litigants whose permanent residence was in New York State would probably be on the conservative side. Applying this formula to the divorce statistics of any particular year provides an interesting corrective. For example, suppose we assume that in addition to the 11,700 divorces and annulments reported to have been granted by New York courts in 1950 some 6,400 should be added for divorces granted to New York residents in the courts of other states and countries. Of the new total of 18,100 New York marriages dissolved in 1950, more than 35 per cent would be by the migratory divorce route. Moreover, instead of having the lowest divorce rate in the country, 0.8 per thousand population, New York's rate would be 1.2 per thousand, still substantially below the national level of 2.6 in 1950, but higher than that of several other states—higher than North Dakota's 1.0, or the 1.1 rate of Rhode Island, New Jersey, and South Carolina. [73]

Careful students of divorce statistics agree that New York's boasted low divorce rate is deceptive, because of the unusually large number of migratory divorces obtained by residents of the state. In 1959, Paul H. Jacobson concluded that the total number of New York marriages dissolved each year was probably from one third to one half greater than the number recorded in New York State statistics; "currently," he added, "it may even be double, in view of the marked increase of Mexican divorces to Americans following the 1952 decision of the New York Supreme Court upholding the validity of certain Mexican decrees." [74]

The possibility of gaining out-of-state divorces had a significant influence on the legislation of the conservative states. As Justice Frankfurter pointed out, "The easier it is made for those who through affluence are able to exercise disproportionately large influence on legislation to obtain migratory divorces, the less likely it is that the divorce laws of their home States will be liberalized insofar as that is deemed desirable." And the learned justice went on to give a hint of his own feelings by saying: "For comparable instances, in the past, of discrimination against the poor in the actual application of divorce laws, cf. Dickens, *Hard Times*, c. 11. . . ." [75]

The most unfortunate aspect of migratory divorce was not that it permitted quicker or easier divorce, but that it encouraged the unhappily married to seek their legal remedies thousands of miles from their home communities. When this was done, how could intelligent and humane procedures be followed that would give adequate protection to the interests of both husband and wife and of their children as well? For the situation that had developed, the legislators of the conservative and the lax states were both to blame. The former had repeated the mistake of the prohibitionists: they had kept on the statute books unrealistic laws that offended the moral sense of a majority of their constituents. The latter had taken advantage of this to make the handling of marital disputes a business rather than a humane responsibility.

CHAPTER 12

"Full Faith and Credit"

If John Jones divorces his wife Sally and marries another woman, Jane in State A, it is highly disconcerting to him to discover that in State B the courts may rule that his divorce and second marriage are invalid and that he is still married to Sally. If he is sentenced to prison for living with Jane in State B, his unhappiness will be all the more acute. Under the American federal system this sort of thing is not supposed to happen. To prevent it the framers of the Constitution had made this provision:

> Full Faith and Credit shall be given in each State to the Public Acts, Records, and judicial Proceedings of every other State. And the Congress may by general Laws prescribe the Manner in which such Acts, Records and Proceedings shall be proved, and the Effect thereof.
>
> (Article IV, Section 1)

And in 1790, Congress passed an act prescribing "the mode in which the public Acts, Records, and judicial Proceedings in each state shall be authenticated so as to take effect in every other State." [1]

But there is a catch in the full faith and credit clause. As judicially interpreted, it obligates the courts of one state to recognize the judicial decisions of another, only if the latter properly had jurisdiction in the particular case.[2]

In actual practice, the state courts often failed to recognize out-of-state divorce decrees. As early as 1813, for example, a Connecticut man named Stephen Fitch went into Vermont and obtained a divorce in proceedings of which his wife was alleged to have received no notice. He afterwards married Rebecca Borden of Orange County, New York. The second wife's mother, unhappy with Fitch's conduct, sued him for damages in debauching her daughter and won a verdict of $5,000. This was upheld by the New York Supreme Court on the ground that Fitch's divorce was invalid because the Vermont court did not have jurisdiction over the defendant wife.[3]

In 1851, the marital difficulties of Nicholas and Margaret Vischer were before the New York courts. The couple was married in New York State and lived there until Margaret obtained a divorce from bed and board. Nicholas then went to Michigan where he eventually obtained an absolute divorce on the ground of willful desertion. His wife did not appear, and the notice was given only through publication in a Michigan newspaper. Nicholas returned to New York State and married another woman. Charging that this new union was adulterous, Margaret sued for absolute divorce. She was successful in this, because the New York courts found Nicholas's Michigan decree to be a nullity. Regardless of whether he had established his own domicile in Michigan, his wife was entitled to her own separate domicile because of the earlier limited divorce and she had never submitted to the jurisdiction of the Michigan court.[4]

In 1869, two Jane Kerrs each claimed to be the widow and rightful heir of one Richard Kerr of New York State. The second Jane Kerr's claim was based on the plea that Richard had married her after ridding himself of Jane I by an Indiana divorce. Even though the Indiana record recited that Richard had been a *bona fide* resident of the state for one year and that his wife had filed an appearance through an Indiana attorney, the New York courts ruled that the divorce was invalid, because the Indiana court had no jurisdiction over the defendant.[5]

Summarizing the New York situation as it seemed to be in 1869, the *New York Times* said:

The rule deducible from this series of decisions would seem to be that our Courts will treat as void a divorce obtained in another State, unless the divorced party appeared in those proceedings or was a resident of such other State.[6]

But elsewhere the precedents were different. In 1832, the highest court in Maine upheld the divorce which a wife had obtained in Rhode Island even though the husband's alleged adultery had occurred in North Carolina and he had made no appearance before the Rhode Island court.[7] In 1856, the Rhode Island courts asserted their jurisdiction over divorce cases in which the plaintiff was a Rhode Island citizen, whether or not the defendant was present or absent, provided he had been given notice, either personally or by written summons and publication.[8] In a sweeping decision in 1874, the Massachusetts Supreme Judicial Court ruled that when a husband, whose wife was living apart from him without justifiable cause, removed from Massachusetts to Indiana and acquired a domicile there and afterward obtained a decree of divorce according to Indiana laws, giving notice to the wife by leaving a summons at her Massachusetts home and by publication in an Indiana newspaper, the Indiana courts had had jurisdiction and the divorce was valid in Massachusetts, even though the wife had never been in Indiana, had never appeared in the suit there, had no knowledge that her husband contemplated going to Indiana until after he commenced the divorce action, had never been provided by her husband with a home in Indiana, and had never been requested or furnished with the means by her husband to go to that state.[9]

On this critical issue of recognizing out-of-state divorces in which only the plaintiff had acquired a domicile in the divorcing state, the states were sharply divided in their practice. The conservative rule of not recognizing the divorce unless both parties were domiciled in the divorcing state or had at least appeared in the proceedings was followed by New York, Pennsylvania, North Carolina, and South Carolina. All the other states recognized the validity of divorces where only constructive service on the defendant had been obtained, provided the plaintiff had established a *bona fide* domicile in the divorcing state.[10]

In view of this difference in policy it was inevitable that the

United States Supreme Court would be called upon to lay down
guide rules as to the circumstances under which the divorce decrees
of one state must receive full faith and credit in all the other states.
The issue was prominently before the court in a series of cases between 1901 and 1906—a period when the conservative reaction
against divorce was at its peak.

On April 15, 1901, the Court decided three cases, upholding the
disputed divorce in one and disallowing it in the other two. In the
first, the issue was the validity of a divorce granted by a Kentucky
court to Peter Lee Atherton from his wife Mary. The couple had
been married in Clinton, New York, in 1888, and had then gone to
live in Louisville, Kentucky. Three years later, complaining of her
husband's cruelty, Mary had left him and returned with her child to
live with her parents in Clinton. Peter stayed in Kentucky, where he
sued for divorce in 1893 on the ground of his wife's abandonment.
Mary was notified of the proceedings by a letter addressed to her at
Clinton, to which she made no acknowledgment. Refusing to recognize the validity of the Kentucky divorce, Mary sued successfully
in the New York courts for a limited divorce and support for her
child. The New York courts ruled that she was legally domiciled in
New York and that the Kentucky divorce was invalid for want of
jurisdiction. On this issue, the United States Supreme Court overruled the New York contention. Since Kentucky had always been
the domicile of the husband and had been the domicile of both husband and wife when they last lived together, it was not necessary
to prove that she had been given actual notice of the proceedings
so long as reasonable efforts had been made in accordance with
statutory requirements. She was as much bound by the Kentucky
decree as she would have been by being personally present in the
Kentucky courtroom.[11]

In the second of the 1901 decisions, the Supreme Court refused
to uphold the Pennsylvania divorce awarded to Frederick A. Bell
from his wife Mary. In subsequently suing for divorce and alimony
in New York, Mary denied the validity of the Pennsylvania decree
on the ground that neither she nor her husband had ever been residents of that state and that no process had been served on her. The
New York courts found for the wife, and this decision was upheld by
the Federal tribunal. "No valid divorce from the bonds of matri-

mony can be decreed on constructive service by the courts of a State in which neither party is domiciled . . . the court in Pennsylvania had no jurisdiction of the husband's suit for divorce, because neither party had a domicile in Pennsylvania, and the decree of divorce was entitled to no faith and credit in New York, or in any other State." [12]

The third of the 1901 decisions provided the strongest warning to the divorce mills of the day. Elizabeth Streitwolf had sued her husband August for divorce in New Jersey. While this case was still pending, August had gone quietly to Mandan, North Dakota, and rented a room in a boardinghouse. Staying only a few weeks, he had wandered off to see the wonders of Yellowstone Park and returned to the East to handle some business affairs. Going back to North Dakota, he filed a suit for divorce and took steps to have notice served on Elizabeth in New Jersey. The New Jersey court where the wife's suit was pending issued a temporary injunction prohibiting the husband from proceeding with the North Dakota suit. Despite this, August pressed his case and obtained a North Dakota divorce based upon his wife's alleged cruelty and habitual intoxication. The New Jersey court ruled this decree to be void, since the husband had had no *bona fide* domicile in North Dakota and the judgment there had been obtained by fraud and imposition upon the court. The United States Supreme Court upheld the New Jersey decision.[13]

Taken as a group, the 1901 decisions were believed to offer valuable guidance. In an editorial entitled "A Step Toward Divorce Reform," the *New York Tribune* said: "Whether or not the whole business of divorce should be relegated to Federal legislation and the Federal courts is an open question. But there can be no possible question of the urgent need of making the marriage and divorce proceedings of every State such that it will deserve and command full faith and credit in every other State." [14]

The Supreme Court had more difficulty with the case of *Andrews* v. *Andrews* in 1903. Here the contestants were Kate and Annie Andrews both claiming to be the lawful widow of Charles Andrews. Charles had obtained a divorce from Kate in 1892 in South Dakota on the ground of desertion. After the husband's suit had been initiated, the wife had filed an answer and a countersuit in the

South Dakota court, alleging cruelty on the part of the husband. But Charles and Kate had then made a property settlement to which the wife had signed an agreement and withdrawn her appearance in the South Dakota case. After the husband's return to Massachusetts he had married Annie, and the two had lived together as husband and wife until Charles's death in 1897. The Massachusetts courts, nevertheless, held the first wife to be the lawful heir. Their decision was based in part upon a Massachusetts statute —much admired by the divorce reformers of the period—which said:

A divorce decreed in another state or country according to the laws thereof, by a court having jurisdiction of the cause and of both the parties, shall be valid and effectual in this commonwealth; but if an inhabitant of this commonwealth goes into another state or country to obtain a divorce for a cause which occurred here, or for a cause which would not authorize a divorce by the laws of this commonwealth, a divorce so obtained shall be of no force or effect in this commonwealth.

The United States Supreme Court upheld the Massachusetts decision. Justice Edward D. White, speaking for the majority, said that domicile in a state was "essential to give jurisdiction to the courts of such State to render a decree of divorce which would have extraterritorial effect, and as the appearance of one or both of the parties to a divorce proceeding could not suffice to confer jurisdiction over the subject matter where it was wanting because of the absence of domicile within the State, we conclude that no violation of the due faith and credit clause of the Constitution of the United States arose from the action of the Supreme Judicial Court of Massachusetts in obeying the command of the state statute and refusing to give effect to the decree of divorce in question." Yet the case was a hard one because of the first wife's apparent submission to the jurisdiction of the South Dakota court, and three of the justices— Brewer, Shiras, and Peckham—dissented from the decision.[15]

Even more difficult was the case of *Haddock* v. *Haddock*, decided in 1906. The New York marriage of John and Harriet Haddock in 1868 had been a curious business from the start. Complaining that he had been tricked into the union, John left his bride immediately after the ceremony. After drifting about the country for several years he finally settled in Connecticut in 1877. Four years later he sued for divorce in a Connecticut court, charging his wife with willful desertion. Notice of the proceedings was given in accordance with Connecticut law by addressing a letter to the wife at her last known address and publishing a copy in a Litchfield, Connecticut, newspaper. The divorce was granted, and the next year Haddock married another woman, with whom he continued to live in Connecticut for the next seven years. Not until 1891, when John inherited considerable property, did the first Mrs. Haddock attempt to go after him in the New York courts. In 1894, she obtained a legal separation and alimony order, but was unable to collect anything because of John's absence from the state. But in 1899—thirty-one years after the marriage—she began a new suit based upon personal service upon the defendant within New York State. John offered in defense his Connecticut decree, but the New York court refused to recognize it, granting Harriet a legal separation and $780 a year in alimony.

The Haddock case resulted in a five to four split in the United States Supreme Court. Speaking for the majority, Justice White upheld the first wife's contention.[16] Although the husband's *bona fide* residence in Connecticut seemed to make this case resemble the Atherton one where the Kentucky decree had been upheld, White found one significant point of difference. Kentucky had been the matrimonial domicile of the Athertons, but New York, not Connecticut, had been the matrimonial domicile of the Haddocks. Since the wife had continued to live in the state of matrimonial domicile and the Connecticut divorce had not been based upon personal service, the New York courts were not required to give full faith and credit to the out-of-state decree. Haddock's divorce and remarriage were of undisputed validity in Connecticut, but their status in New York was a matter for the New York courts to decide.

Justices Oliver Wendell Holmes, Jr., and Henry Brown wrote vigorous dissenting opinions. Justice Holmes said: "I think that the decision not only reverses a previous well considered decision of this court but is likely to cause considerable disaster to innocent persons and to bastardize children hitherto supposed to be the offspring of lawful marriage." Refusing to concede that the Haddock case was materially different from the Atherton one, Holmes wrote: "After that decision any general objection to the effect of the Connecticut decree on the ground of the wife's absence from the State comes too late." [17] Justice Brown wrote: "I regret that the court in this case has taken what seems to me a step backward in American jurisprudence, and has virtually returned to the old doctrine of comity, which it was the very object of the full faith and credit clause of the Constitution to supersede." [18]

The uncertainty concerning out-of-state divorces that resulted from the Haddock case was slightly relieved by the Davis case of 1938. The couple involved in this marital hassle had been residing in the District of Columbia in 1928 when the husband charged the wife with cruelty and obtained a separation from bed and board—the only remedy then available in the District on this ground. The District judge ordered Davis to pay $300 a month for the support of his wife and daughter. The husband thereafter established a residence in Arlington County, Virginia, where he sued his wife for absolute divorce in 1929. She was personally served in the District and filed an answer in the Virginia court stating that she appeared there "specially and for no other purpose than to file this plea to the jurisdiction of the court." On this basis she attempted to challenge the husband's contention that he was domiciled in Virginia, but the Virgina court ruled against her. Davis was granted a divorce and his financial obligation was cut to $150 a month. But in subsequent litigation the District court refused to recognize the validity of this Virginia divorce and ruled that the husband was still bound by the earlier District decision. On this issue the Supreme Court reversed the lower courts and ruled that Davis's Virginia divorce was entitled to full faith and credit. The case was differentiated from the Haddock precedent, because Mrs. Davis had submitted to the jurisdiction of the Virginia court and was bound by its decision.[19]

In 1942, the Haddock case was explicitly overruled in the first round of the famous Williams case—one of the most perplexing divorce tangles ever to confront the United States Supreme Court. In 1916, Otis B. Williams had married Carrie Wyke in the state of North Carolina; in 1920, Lillie Shaver had married Thomas Hendrix in the same state. Whether happily or unhappily—who can say?—the Williamses and the Hendrixes had continued married life together until June, 1940, when Williams and Lillie Hendrix left their respective spouses and trekked out to Las Vegas. After residing six weeks in the Alamo Motor Court, each filed a suit for divorce on the ground of extreme cruelty. Notice was given to the defendants in accordance with Nevada law. In the case of Carrie Williams, a North Carolina sheriff delivered a copy of the summons and complaint; in that of Thomas Hendrix, a copy of the summons was published in a Las Vegas newspaper and another copy was mailed to him at his post office address. Neither defendant took any action, and in due course the Nevada courts granted decrees of divorce. On October 4, 1940, the day on which Lillie Hendrix finally gained her freedom, she married Williams and the couple returned to North Carolina. But their dream of happy domesticity was shattered by the unexpected thunderbolt of an indictment and prosecution under a North Carolina statute prohibiting "bigamous cohabitation." Ruling the Nevada divorces to be fraudulent and void, the North Carolina courts sentenced Otis and Lillie to prison for three-year terms.[20]

Under these circumstances North Carolina's refusal to give full faith and credit to a Nevada divorce decree was obviously of much more than academic interest. On December 21, 1942, the United States Supreme Court decided that the North Carolina courts had erred. "Nevada Divorces Valid Over Nation" was the usually accurate *New York Times*'s headline summary of the decision.[21] Actually, however, the point decided in this first Williams case was much narrower. Speaking for the majority, Justice William O. Douglas carefully identified two issues. He stressed the fact that the North Carolina judge had instructed the jury that it might consider the Nevada divorce to be invalid on either of two grounds: (1) that the defendants had not been served in Nevada and had not entered any appearance there; or, (2) that the petitioners went to Nevada not to establish a *bona fide* residence but solely for the purpose of taking advantage of the laws of that state to obtain a divorce through fraud upon the Nevada court. Justice Douglas concentrated on the first issue, the one on which the North Carolina attorneys primarily based their case. Were the Nevada divorces invalid in North Carolina, because the defendants had never submitted to the jurisdiction of the Nevada courts? The Court answered no, thus explicitly overruling the Haddock case. Each state, wrote Justice Douglas, "by virtue of its command over its domiciliaries and its large interest in the institution of marriage can alter within its own borders the marriage status, even though the other spouse is absent. There is no constitutional barrier if the form and nature of the substituted service meet the requirements of due process." And these decrees must be given full faith and credit in other states. "Such is part of the price of our federal system." [22]

But Justices Robert Jackson and Frank Murphy sharply dissented. "It is not an exaggeration," the former wrote, "to say that this decision repeals the divorce laws of all the states and substitutes the law of Nevada as to all marriages one of the parties to which can afford a short trip there." [23] Both dissenting justices believed that the North Carolina decision should have been upheld on the ground that Otis and Lillie had not acquired *bona fide* domiciles in Nevada. Justice Murphy conceded the "tragic incongruity" in the fact that an individual might be validly divorced in one state but not in another. Yet in the absence of a uniform divorce law this could not be avoided. The Supreme Court must not force Nevada's policy upon North Carolina, any more than it must compel Nevada to accept North Carolina's requirements. "The fair result," Murphy said, "is to leave each free to regulate within its own area the rights of its own subjects." [24]

But Otis and Lillie were not through with their legal tribulations. The state of North Carolina brought them to trial again, this time basing the contention that the Nevada decrees were invalid upon the allegation that the defendants had not established *bona fide* domiciles prior to suing for their divorces. Once again the couple were convicted of bigamous cohabitation and sentenced to prison—this time to one year in the case of Otis and eight months in that of Lillie.[25] The second Williams case eventually reached the United States Supreme Court, where it was decided on May 21, 1945. This time a majority of the judges upheld the North Carolina decision. "The decree of divorce," Justice Frankfurter wrote, "is a conclusive adjudication of everything except the jurisdictional facts upon which it is founded, and domicil is a jurisdictional fact. To permit the necessary finding of domicil by one State to foreclose all States in the protection of their social institutions would be intolerable." Since the record supported the contention "that the petitioners left

North Carolina for the purpose of getting divorces from their respective spouses and as soon as each had done so and married one another they left Nevada and returned to North Carolina to live there together as man and wife," the North Carolina courts were not obliged to give full faith and credit to the Nevada decrees.[26]

Three justices—Rutledge, Black, and Douglas—dissented in this second Williams case. Justice Rutledge attacked the majority view as contributing still more confusion to the already confused divorce situation. Justice Black characteristically focused his concern on the injustice involved for these particular litigants. "It is my firm conviction," he wrote, "that these convictions cannot be harmonized with vital constitutional safeguards designed to safeguard individual liberty and unite all the states of this whole country into one nation." Making his point more specific, he said that the majority decision sent people to prison "for lacking the clairvoyant gift of prophesying when one judge or jury will upset the findings of fact made by another." [27]

The second Williams case repeated earlier warnings that out-of-state decrees might not be given full faith and credit, if it were decided that the party who had obtained the divorce had never been actually domiciled in the divorcing state. Just how far this principle would be carried was the problem in two cases decided by the United States Supreme Court on June 7, 1948. The essential facts in the two cases were similar. *Sherrer* v. *Sherrer* involved the validity of a divorce obtained by a Massachusetts woman during a temporary residence in Florida; *Coe* v. *Coe*, that of a divorce granted to a Massachusetts man during a temporary residence in Nevada. In both cases the defendants had appeared personally in the proceedings; and in both the Florida and the Nevada courts had specifically ruled that they had jurisdiction. But in both the validity of the divorces had been attacked by the defendants in new litigations in Massachusetts, and the Massachusetts courts had refused to recognize the out-of-state divorces on the ground that the plaintiffs had not actually established Florida and Nevada domiciles.

Speaking for the highest court in the land, Chief Justice Fred Vinson overruled these Massachusetts decisions.[28] The requirements of full faith and credit, he said, "bar a defendant from collaterally attacking a divorce decree on jurisdictional grounds in the courts of a sister State where there has been participation by the defendant in the divorce proceedings, where the defendant has been accorded full opportunity to contest the jurisdictional issues, and where the decree is not susceptible to such collateral attack in the courts of the State which rendered the decree." Because vital interests were involved in divorce litigation, said the Chief Justice, it was of great importance that there should be a place to end such litigation. "And where a decree of divorce is rendered by a competent court under the circumstances of this case, the obligation of full faith and credit requires that such litigation should end in the courts of the State in which the judgment was rendered." [29]

But as usual in these cases the justices were divided. In a dissenting opinion with which Justice Murphy concurred, Justice Frankfurter wrote:

But the crux of today's decision is that regardless of how overwhelming the evidence may have been that the asserted domicile in the State offering bargain-counter divorces was a sham, the home State of the parties is not permitted to question the matter if the form of a controversy has been gone through. To such a proposition I cannot assent. . . . I cannot bring myself to believe that the Full Faith and Credit Clause gave to the few States which offer bargain-counter divorces constitutional power to control the social policy governing domestic relations in the many States which do not.[30]

But what was the effect of a husband's out-of-state divorce on his wife's right to support for herself and her children, on her right to a share in her former husband's estate after his death, or on her right to the custody of her children? Could a divorced woman be stripped of all these things through distant court proceedings in which she had not been represented? In an effort to deal with this problem, Justice Douglas developed a concept that he called "divisible divorce." First suggested in a concurring opinion of 1945,[31] this line of reasoning was more fully developed in the Estin case of 1948.[32] This involved the obligation of a husband, whom a New York court had ordered to pay $180 a month for the support of his wife and children after separation proceedings. The husband subsequently obtained a Reno divorce under constructive service and used this as a justification for stopping his alimony payments. The wife sued for the arrears, and the New York court gave a verdict in her favor, ruling that the Nevada divorce was valid but that the husband was nevertheless still bound by the earlier support order. The United States Supreme Court upheld this decision. "The result in this situation," explained Justice Douglas, "is to make the divorce divisible—to give effect to the Nevada decree insofar as it effects marital status and to make it ineffective on the issue of alimony. It accommodates the interests of both Nevada and New York in this broken marriage by restricting each state to the matters of her dominant concern." [33]

In dissenting opinions Justices Frankfurter and Jackson rejected this concept. If the Nevada divorce was valid, they reasoned, it terminated the support order under the New York law that should have controlled the decision. Jackson ridiculed the majority's position in these words:

The Court reaches the Solomon-like conclusion that the Nevada decree is half good and half bad under the full faith and credit clause. It is good to free the husband from the marriage; it is not good to free him from its incidental obligations. Assuming the judgment to be one which the Constitution required to be recognized at all, I do not see how we can square this decision with the command that it be given *full* faith and credit.[34]

Logical or not, the Court persisted in the policy that it had adopted, ruling that out-of-state divorces in which the defendant had not appeared in the proceedings might be valid as regards the marital status of the parties but did not preclude the courts of another state from upholding some incidental right arising out of the marriage. Thus in 1949, the Court upheld a Connecticut decision under which a divorced wife had been recognized as the widow entitled to inherit certain Connecticut real estate.[35] In 1953, it recognized the right of a divorced mother to the custody of her children as a personal right which could not be cut off by an *ex parte* divorce decree in another state.[36] And in 1957, it upheld a New York decision in which a wife obtained a support order even after a Nevada divorce had already been granted to her husband.[37]

In numerous dissents, the minority justices protested against the whole idea of divisible divorce. In the Rice case of 1949, Justice Jackson said: "This Court is not responsible for all the contradictions and conflicts resulting from our federal system or from our crazy quilt of divorce laws, but we are certainly compounding those difficulties by repudiating the usual requirements of procedural due process in divorce cases and compensating for it by repudiating the Full Faith and Credit Clause." [38] And in 1957, Justice Frankfurter acidly remarked: "We have thus reached another stage—one cannot say it is the last—in the Court's tortuous course of constitutional adjudication relating to dissolution of the marriage status." [39]

Meanwhile a few reformers kept alive the hope that the divorce situation might be clarified either through the passage of uniform state laws or some Federal statute. In 1947, commissioners from the various states approved a Uniform Divorce Recognition Act, but this was adopted by only nine states.[40]

Senator Patrick McCarran of Nevada proposed a different course of action. As early as 1892, a Congressional committee had pointed out that without any new grant of power Congress could pass legislation defining the conditions under which state courts would be required to grant full faith and credit to the divorce decrees of other states.[41] Recent Supreme Court decisions had pointed to the same possibility. In 1948, Senator McCarran proposed the following bill:

That, where a State has exercised through its courts jurisdiction to dissolve the marriage of spouses, the decree of divorce thus rendered must be given full faith and credit in every other State as a dissolution of such marriage, provided (1) the decree is final as to the issue of divorce; (2) the decree is valid in the State where rendered; (3) the decree contains recitals setting forth that the jurisdictional prerequisities of such State to the granting of the divorce have been met; and (4) the State wherein the decree was rendered was the last State wherein the spouses were domiciled together as husband and wife, or the defendant in the proceeding for divorce was personally subject to the jurisdiction of the State wherein the decree was rendered or appeared generally in the proceedings therefor. In all such cases except cases involving fraudulent conduct of the successful party which was practiced during the course of an actual adversary trial of the issues joined and the effect of which was directly and affirmatively to mislead the defeated party to his injury after he announced that he was ready to proceed with the trial, the recitals of the decree of divorce shall constitute a conclusive determination of the jurisdictional facts necessary to the decree.[42]

No doubt dismissed in the minds of many legislators as no more than a device for protecting Nevada's special interests, the McCarran bill attracted little interest until 1952. But in that year the proposal gained substantial support as a feasible step. Recommending passage, the Senate Judiciary Committee summarized the bill's merits:

The committee believes the enactment of this bill would insure, with respect to divorce decrees, the certainty and finality which the Constitution intended should be inherent in the judgments of the courts of any State; and would accomplish this without legalizing, or condoning, or encouraging fraud in the procurement of divorces. The Congress has been partly to blame for the present divorce muddle through its failure, for more than a century and a half, to exercise fully its responsibility under the full faith and credit clause of the Constitution, and should be anxious to enact such legislation as here proposed.[43]

Explaining the bill on a later occasion, Senator McCarran emphasized that it did not derogate from the right of another state to question a decree based on fraud where the fraud would vitiate such a decree under the laws of the rendering state. Moreover, a default judgment entered without an appearance by the defendant or without his being personally served would be open to attack in the courts of another state to the same degree as at present.[44]

The McCarran bill twice passed the Senate without a roll call vote, on June 21, 1952, and on May 6, 1953.[45] But in neither case did the House of Representatives take any action.

Thus neither the state legislatures nor the Federal Congress did anything to clarify the problems arising from out-of-state divorces and the degree to which they were entitled to full faith and credit in other than the divorcing states. The unsatisfactory condition of the law was eloquently summarized by Justice Jackson in his 1948 dissent to the Estin decision:

If there is one thing that the people are entitled to expect from their lawmakers, it is rules of law that will enable individuals to tell whether they are married and, if so, to whom. Today many people who have simply lived in more than one state do not know, and the most learned lawyer cannot advise them with any confidence. The uncertainties that result are not merely technical, nor are they trivial; they affect fundamental rights and relations such as the lawfulness of their cohabitation, their children's legitimacy, their title to property and even whether they are law-abiding persons or criminals. . . .[46]

CHAPTER 13

New York's Twisting Path

Although conservatives on the divorce question loved to praise New York for its "high standard," more independent observers were not so sure that rigid divorce statutes had a healthy influence on domestic morals. As early as 1870, a writer commented:

It would be truly instructive to know what the influence of such laws is on the frequent seductions, elopements, adulteries, and other crimes in the metropolis. It would be equally instructive to know what proportion of the applications for divorce in Connecticut, Indiana, and other States are made by those who, not willing to avail themselves of the fraudulent divorces so common in New-York, where they reside, temporarily remove to some other State to obtain a legal release from bondage which they cannot obtain at home.[1]

Thirty-six years later a magazine article on the migratory divorce problem made the same point. Contending that abuses in Illinois and South Dakota had been largely corrected, the author went on to say: "A more serious drawback than the legislative antics of any raw community is the incorrigible Bourbonism of a mature State, like New York, in permitting dissolution of a marriage . . . only for adultery or if one of the spouses has been sentenced to life imprisonment. That policy inevitably drives its own citizens into other

189

forums to obtain the relief which justice and the average moral sense
sanction their seeking." [2]

New York's one-ground divorce law had the effect, not of preventing divorces, but of corrupting the whole machinery of justice.
In cheerful disregard of legal ethics, lawyers specializing in divorce
baited their hooks with such advertisements as this:

> DIVORCES quietly; desertion, drunkenness; any cause; advice free.
> REED's American Law Agency, 317 Broadway.[3]

Often these firms passed their clients on to allies operating in whatever states were currently catering to the migratory business. But
they also utilized the New York courts, trapping the defendants in
adultery if this were possible or else faking evidence against them.
As early as 1869, the *New York Times* complained:

> Among the more recent creations of knavery is a trade which ought to
> become as infamous as some other callings which the law visits with its
> severest penalties. . . . The object of it is to procure divorces by means
> of fraud and perjury. The husband or wife who wishes to get rid of a dis-
> agreeable partner has only to go to some sharper calling himself an attor-
> ney, who advertises his readiness to get divorces without publicity, and
> who at once undertakes to do all the dirty work incidental to the case.
> If there is no evidence he forges or invents as much as he wants. If the
> man or woman against whom he is employed is innocent, he finds someone
> to lay all sorts of crime to their charge.[4]

In 1870, the *Times* explained in detail how these divorce rings
were operating. Their headquarters were in palatial law offices located along Wall, Nassau, and Pine streets and lower Broadway. Clients were charged from $25 to $100—or as much as could be extracted from them. For each case, it was shrewdly calculated whether
to bring suit in New York or in some other state like Indiana. The
allegation to be charged was tailored to fit the jurisdiction. It might
be anything from incompatibility to adultery, but many specialists
preferred to charge the latter. "It is just as easy to prove," they explained, "and holds good in any state." If the case were to be tried
in New York, there was often the delicate problem of how to serve
the summons and yet keep the defendant in ignorance of what was

going on. One way was to have the process server met at the defendant's residence or place of business by an accomplice who would pretend to be the wanted party. The process server would then sign an affidavit that he had served the defendant in person and disappear, "to be forever unfindable." Or if the plaintiff claimed to be in ignorance of the defendant's whereabouts, the summons would be printed once a week for a month "in the obscurest sheet that can be selected." After waiting a reasonable time for the defendant to reply, the plaintiff's lawyer would ask the court "with all privacy" to appoint a referee. This having been done, the referee would take the testimony of two or three witnesses, "who thereafter will never appear under the same names again." They would swear that they had seen the defendant "in improper places with improper persons." The referee would render a verdict for the plaintiff, and the court would confirm the decree. The *Times* charged that the judges were involved in the business, because they found in the appointment of referees petty patronage to hand out to their relatives and friends.[5]

For the next ninety years, shady dealings in the procurement of divorces appear to have abounded in New York. Now and again some shyster would make a misstep and get caught. The newspapers would play up the scandal; the public would demand reform; one or two culprits would be disbarred or sent to prison; courts and prosecutors would warn against further violations—and then the excitement would subside, not to be renewed until the next episode. Newspaper accounts of these perennial scandals provide a melancholy record of knavery, brightened only by the occasional novelty in the methods employed. In 1870, John M. Holt, a professional perjurer in divorce cases was sentenced to nine years' imprisonment in Sing Sing. "Bearing False Witness in Divorce Causes—A Punishment Richly Deserved," the newspaper headlines pronounced.[6] In 1884 John W. Law, a deputy clerk in a Brooklyn court, got caught in an ambitious swindle. Forging the name of one of the judges, Law would appoint himself a referee, hear the manufactured evidence, recommend a divorce, and then forge the name of the judge to the decree. He was alleged to have ground out some fifty fraudulent divorces.[7]

Such faking of decrees was frequent. In 1890, when William Coppersmith sued his wife Mary for divorce, naming one August J.

Fechter as corespondent, Mary based her defense on the contention that she was already divorced from Coppersmith and legally married to Fechter. Investigation revealed that Mary had paid $150 to a Broadway legal firm, had been assured from time to time that her case was in progress, and had eventually received an imposing-looking divorce decree on a large sheet of paper. Over the word Judge an undecipherable signature had been scribbled, and a large red seal with the words Cook County had been affixed. But poor Mary was told that her precious charter of freedom was worthless and that she had been living in unwitting adultery with her second husband.[8]

Only a month later the legal partnership of Hughes and Butner was discovered to have been selling bogus divorces in large numbers. By advertising in the newspapers and distributing pamphlets through the mails, this firm had obtained the names of hundreds of potential clients. Selecting the most promising victims, the partners collected their fees and avoided time-wasting court proceedings by simply manufacturing their own divorce decrees with the help of a good supply of the printed forms used in Cook County, Illinois, and a spurious seal.[9]

More common, however, than the counterfeit document was the divorce decree properly signed, sealed, and recorded—but based on perjured evidence. In 1900, Henry Zeimer and W. Waldo Maison were arrested for operating a divorce mill. Testifying against them was Mrs. Byrde Herrick, who related how she had gone to Zeimer to get a divorce, had been unable to pay his $150 fee, and had consented to work for him as a professional corespondent. She would testify against defendants whom she had never seen before. On the days when she was to appear on the witness stand, she would meet her lawyer employers for a rehearsal of the fabricated story. Mary Thompson, who was similarly employed, gave additional details:

When I was corespondent I used to say that I had known the defendant. Then I had to blush and cry, and refuse to answer other questions. Of course I never really had to degrade myself, but I had to carry on in such a manner that the whole case would seem clear to the referee. When the suit was brought by a man I was the private detective. I used to say I was a dressmaker who worked in the same house and saw things that were not intended for me to see.

The two women testified that they received five dollars a day for their services. When Maison and Zeimer wanted new faces for the witness stand, they advertised for secretaries and office helpers. Then they tested the applicants by asking them highly personal questions. The women who were not embarrassed by this interrogation were trained as professional witnesses. Zeimer would quiet any scruples that they might have by arguing that no harm was done to anybody. "If people want divorces," he would say, "why shouldn't they get them?" [10]

In 1934, the *New York Mirror's* Sunday magazine featured a sensational series entitled "I Was the 'Unknown Blonde' in 100 New York Divorces!" A woman calling herself Dorothy Jarvis claimed that she had been a respectable stenographer in a lawyer's office until she lost her job during the depression. Her former employers sent her to a firm of private detectives who employed many girls as professional witnesses in divorce cases. At first Dorothy received from $25 to $100 for each job, but the field became overcrowded and she could get only $10 to $50. With a cooperative husband, the procedure was routine. She would accompany the man to some hotel room and remove a few outer garments. Then a raiding party would break in and surprise the guilty couple. Usually the interlopers were three in number—a private detective, some person who knew the husband (about half the time the wife herself), and a professional process server who would later hand the defendant the summons and complaint in the divorce suit. The eventual hearing before the referee would be routine, even to following a mimeographed list of questions.

Cases in which the husband would not cooperate were more difficult, but Dorothy described three standard ways of framing the potential defendant. "Push and raid" involved finding some excuse for pushing a woman into the victim's room. She would quickly pull off her fur coat, underneath which she was wearing little or nothing. The detective would break in and collect the "evidence." "Shadow and shanghai" consisted of shadowing the victim until the conspirators could seize him and spirit him off to some place where a raid could be staged. "Dance and dope" required the ingenious female to dope the victim's drink and arrange to have him pass out in her apartment, near which the vigilant raiding party would be waiting for a signal.

Dorothy's chatty confessions were written upon the occasion of her retirement from the ranks of the professional corespondents. She settled down to quiet married life as the wife of her last client! [11]

In an earlier chapter we have shown that when true divorce was unavailable, the ecclesiastical courts of medieval Europe found themselves under increasing pressure to grant annulments. Much the same thing occurred in New York, where the unhappily married, faced with the unpleasant options of intrastate divorce based upon faked evidence, and out-of-state divorce based upon fictitious residence, were eager to find some more respectable road to freedom. Whereas medieval lawyers conjured up juridical marvels with the concepts of consanguinity, affinity, and precontract, their New York successors demonstrated equal ingenuity with the word "fraud."

Since 1829, the New York statutes had provided that the courts might declare void a marriage "if either party thereto consents to such marriage by reason of force, duress, or fraud." Just what constituted fraud was left a matter for the judges to decide. During the early 1890's the courts showed a tendency to interpret the word broadly. In 1893, for example, Eliza Keyes was able to get her marriage annulled because her husband had represented himself to be an honest, industrious man, when in fact he was a professional thief. The next year Martha M. King had similar success, based upon her plea that she would not have married her husband had she not believed him to be of excellent character, but she had since discovered that he was operating a poolroom. [12]

The increasing number of annulment cases alarmed the more conservative judges, and in 1896 an attempt was made to choke off this stream by construing the word "fraud" much more narrowly. According to the old ecclesiastical law, the kind of misrepresentations that vitiated a marriage must go to the very "essence" of the marriage contract—factors that would make marital cohabitation either impossible or improper. [13] This so-called *essentialia* doctrine had been adopted by most states, and certain judges were determined to bring the New York law into line. For this reason, the Appellate Division of the Supreme Court in June, 1896, ruled against the attempt of Stephen R. Fisk to get his marriage annulled on the ground that he had discovered his wife, Mary, to be a divorced woman, whereas he had supposed that she had never been married. The decision emphasized that the kind of fraud which would induce a court to set aside a contract of marriage was different from that which would lead it to set aside an ordinary contract. "It is well settled," the court ruled, "that no fraud will avoid a marriage which does not go to the very essence of the contract." [14] In a lower court decision of that same year, the same point was made: "The notion is not to be entertained that the marriage relation, the stability of which is sedulously cherished and supported by the law as a cardinal principle of public policy, is to be dissolved by those false pretenses that suffice for the rescission of the ordinary contracts of commerce." [15]

But in April, 1903, the state's highest tribunal, the Court of Appeals, rejected the *essentialia* doctrine in an important case. This involved the plea of Gregorio di Lorenzo for an annulment of his marriage on the ground that his wife, Johanna, had tricked him most shamefully. According to Gregorio's story, when he had returned to New York City after a period of absence, Johanna had shown him a baby boy and told him that she and Gregorio were the parents. In order to do right by mother and son, Gregorio had married Johanna, only to discover that she had never given birth at all and had borrowed the baby that she had shown to him. Brushing aside the more conservative recent precedents, Justice John C. Gray, speaking for the court, said:

I think it is sufficient that we rely upon the plain provision of our statute and upon the application to the case of a contract of marriage of those salutary and fundamental rules which are applicable to contracts generally when determining their validity. If the plaintiff proves to the satisfaction of the court that, through misrepresentation of some fact, which was an essential element in the giving of his consent to the contract of marriage and which was of such a nature as to deceive an ordinarily prudent person, he has been victimized, the court is empowered to annul the marriage.[16]

The *essentialia* doctrine was not entirely dead, and from time to time some lower court would refuse annulment on the ground that the alleged misrepresentation did not go to the essence of the marriage contract. But the Court of Appeals held to the rule that it had laid down in the di Lorenzo case. The issue was brought into focus again by the Shonfeld case of 1933. Harry Shonfeld had petitioned for an annulment on the ground that his wife had misrepresented her financial assets. Prior to the marriage he had told her that he was in no position to wed because of irregular employment. She had thereupon promised to provide the capital for him to open a jewelry store in New York's Hotel McAlpin. Soon after the marriage he had made the sorrowful discovery that she did not have the promised money. The lower court had refused to annul the marriage on the theory that the wife's misrepresentation had not gone to the essence of the marriage contract, but the Court of Appeals reversed this decision, holding that if these false promises had not been made the husband would not have consented to the marriage.[17]

The alleged misrepresentations under which New York marriages were annulled took an extraordinary variety of shapes. In 1910, Rudolph Domschke rid himself of a wife, whom he had married in the belief that she was a respectable widow, whereas she had, in truth, been another man's mistress and had borne an illegitimate child.[18] In 1947, Loretta Waff won an annulment on her story that her husband had broken his antenuptial promise to treat kindly her three children by a previous marriage. The court ruled that the defendant had made his promise as one of the inducements for her to marry him and had not intended to keep it.[19]

The allegations of fraud sometimes touched the most intimate aspects of married life. According to Harry Miller's story in 1928, he and his intended bride had agreed that they would refrain from marital intercourse for some time in order to avoid having children, but that eventually they would assume normal relations. In violation of this promise, the wife had continued to refuse to consummate the union. The marriage was annulled on the court's finding that the defendant had entered into marriage with the intention of not submitting to marital intercourse and not having children, whereas the plaintiff had believed that she would do these things.[20] Mario Coppo's case in 1937 was somewhat different in that his wife permitted intercourse but not without the use of some means to prevent conception, thereby demonstrating the falseness of her antenuptial agreement to bear children.[21] Even in the absence of explicit promises, the courts ruled that the very fact that the parties entered into marriage implied an agreement to have normal sexual relations and to become parents. In recommending the annulment of a marriage where the wife had refused to consummate the union, an official referee said in 1947:

> There is implied in the promise of marriage, and the making of the contract of marriage, an obligation to perform the duties incident to the marriage status. A refusal to do so implies a fraud that goes to the essence of the contract and entitles the injured party to relief.[22]

The same principle applied to a refusal to cohabit without the use of contraceptives. In the Schulman case of 1943, the court laid down the rule that, if nothing was said on the subject of children before marriage but the wife subsequently insisted on a right to decide when she would have a child, she was injecting into the marriage contract a provision that the law did not place there when the parties entered into the contract silently.[23]

Summarizing the situation in 1946, Joseph R. Clevenger asserted that marriages might be annulled in New York for misrepresentations as to age, business or profession, civil or ceremonial marriage, character, chastity or purity, citizenship, disease or disability, drug addiction, epilepsy, education, love and loyalty, marital relations, mental incapacity, and property. Each category was subject to almost indefinite subdivision so that "the general ground of fraud or misrepresentation has afforded more than one hundred and fifty particular grounds for annulment."[24] In addition to fraud, moreover, some fifty other particular grounds for annulment were available. Indeed, Clevenger's enthusiasm for his subject led him to make the following extraordinary claim:

> Of all 440 Law Titles, the most advantageous to New York lawyers is Annulment of Marriage, in that a New York action to annul a marriage excels every other marital remedy in every other State of all United States, not only in the greatest number and variety of grounds for terminating the

marriage, but also in the surpassing ease and superior mode of proving such grounds.[25]

Although annulment procedure did not invite the grosser forms of perjury notorious in New York divorce cases, it did encourage plaintiffs to stretch their memories in recalling the smooth talk of their suitors and to obtain suspiciously pat collaborations. "It is surprising," wrote Attorney Milton L. Grossman of Rochester, New York, "how many people were present before the marriage when the prospective bride and groom discussed such things as procreation, the desire for a family, or who was to perform the ceremony." [26] The trial was often perfunctory. As Judge Charles S. Desmond of the Court of Appeals described the situation:

A typical case is something like this: a wife brings an annulment action on the ground of fraud; her husband, who is as tired of marriage as she is, does not defend; the wife appears in court and testifies that before marriage her husband told her that he owned considerable property, or had considerable money in the bank, or that he came from a prominent socialite family somewhere in the country, or that he had a good education or a fine war record or something of the kind, or that he was an American citizen, or that he had a good reputation and was a sober hard-working man. She testifies further that these statements of her intending spouse led her to agree to marry him and that she did not find out their falsity until after marriage. She may or may not produce some willing witnesses to corroborate these things, and the annulment is granted.[27]

Although accurate statistics for the state as a whole were lacking, the figures for New York City gave striking evidence of annulment's increasing popularity. In 1932, the city courts granted 576 annulments—about 18 per cent of the total number of marriage dissolutions; in 1942, there were 1,579 annulments—almost 27 per cent of the total marriage dissolutions. And finally in 1946, when divorce records all over the country were being broken, there were 4,169 annulments in New York City—this being over 35 per cent of the 11,802 marriage dissolutions of that year.[28]

The paradox was obvious. When called "divorce," the dissolution of marriage was still restricted to the narrowest of grounds. When called by any other name, marriage dissolution was regarded with easygoing tolerance. This led to a blurring of the proper distinction between annulment and divorce. Annulment logically rested upon conditions existing at the time of the marriage, which made the contract void or voidable. For all conditions that arose subsequent to marriage, divorce was the only logical remedy. Yet this logical distinction was obscured early in New York's legal history, when by statute and judicial interpretation it was ruled that the imposition of a life sentence automatically dissolved the prisoner's marriage and left the former husband or wife free to marry. Even a subsequent pardon did not restore the prisoner's marital rights.[29]

The word "divorce" was also carefully avoided in the so-called Enoch Arden law, enacted in April, 1922. By this statute the New York legislature belatedly dealt with the problem of the long absent and presumably dead husband—a situation for which Connecticut lawmakers had made sensible provision as early as 1667 and their Massachusetts counterparts in 1698. Before the reform of 1922, the New York legal situation had been confused. If a husband or wife had disappeared and his whereabouts had been unknown for five years, the remaining partner might marry again without risking prosecution for bigamy. But he married at his own risk; if the wanderer returned and claimed his spouse, the second marriage might be annulled in the courts.[30] The new statute laid down a procedure whereby a party might file a petition showing that his spouse had been absent for five successive years, that he believed the spouse to be dead, and that diligent search had revealed no evidence that the missing partner was alive. After ordering notice to be given by publication and satisfying itself of the truth of the petitioner's allegations, the court was empowered to make an order "dissolving the marriage." [31]

The *New York Times* thought the Enoch Arden law did not go far enough.

New York has divorce laws of unusual stringency, considerably mitigated by perjury and collusion. It would be a safe guess that in at least a third of the divorces granted in this State the infidelity is fictitious. . . . These things are the natural consequences of a divorce law which is out of harmony with the present opinion of a large part of the public. . . . Until a New York Legislature shall have the courage to revise our divorce laws without beating about the bush we may expect the State will continue to encourage their violation or evasion.

If the new law had made abandonment for five years a ground for divorce, the *Times* said, "it could be commended more heartily." [32]

An even more striking example of the New York politicians' distaste for the word "divorce" was provided in March, 1928, when the legislature amended the domestic relations law to permit the courts to *annul* marriages when the husband or wife had been incurably insane for a period of five years or more.[33]

As for divorce under its proper name, the legislators tinkered from time to time with the procedural machinery but rarely faced up to the more fundamental issues. During the period when the conservative reaction was at its height, the legislature passed several statutes intended to make divorce more difficult. In 1877, the courts were empowered to deny divorce even when adultery was proved, if the plaintiff had condoned the offense, had connived at the procurement of evidence, or was guilty of similar misconduct.[34] In 1899, stricter proof of the plaintiff's charges was required.[35] In 1902, the legislature made it a misdemeanor to advertise for the procurement of divorces and also imposed a three-months waiting period between the granting of a divorce and the issuance of the final decree.[36]

The only significant relaxation of the New York divorce law during these years was to permit the remarriage of defendants convicted of adultery. As early as 1787, the council of revision had pointed out that it was unwise to attempt to prevent such remarriages, but strict moralists insisted upon continuing the ban. The result might have been predicted. More and more individuals prohibited from marrying a second time in New York State simply slipped across the state line to have the ceremony performed. The legality of such unions was somewhat dubious until 1881, when the Court of Appeals ruled that even though a divorced husband went into another state for the purpose of evading the New York law by contracting a second marriage during the lifetime of his former wife, the second marriage was valid.[37]

If the guilty parties to divorce suits could so easily remarry out of the state, it appeared sensible to lift the ban within the state. But a bill for this purpose which passed the New York senate in 1878 was rejected in the assembly by a 58 to 47 vote.[38] The explanation for this defeat appears to lie in the charge that the bill was being pushed "at the solicitation of an eminent politician who desired to marry again." [39] This probably explains the partisan division, with most of the Democrats favoring the measure and most of the Republicans opposing it. But the ways of politics are strange, and at the next session of the legislature the remarriage bill was quietly passed not just once but twice. This was necessary because the bill's author apparently made a serious error. A statute signed April 16, 1879, applied only to future divorces and was obviously worthless to serve the particular case of the "eminent politician" who had been lobbying for the change.[40] So late in the session the same legislator who had introduced the earlier bill—Senator John C. Jacobs, a Brooklyn Democrat—introduced a second measure that slid smoothly through the legislature and received the signature of Governor Lucius Robinson on May 19.[41] Identical with the earlier statute except that it applied to past as well as future divorces, this law provided that the court which had granted the divorce might modify the judgment to permit the defendant to marry again, "which modification shall only be made upon satisfactory proof that the complainant has remarried, that five years have elapsed since the decree of divorce was rendered, and that the conduct of the defendant since the dissolution of said marriage has been uniformly good." [42] This permission to remarry was liberalized in 1897 by eliminating the proviso that the innocent party must have remarried and in 1919 by reducing the probationary period from five years to three.[43]

But the legislature never mustered its courage for a frontal attack on the divorce problem. Between 1900 and 1933 at least fifteen different assemblymen and senators sponsored bills that would have brought New York into line with the rest of the nation by recognizing such grounds for divorce as desertion and cruelty, but almost without exception these bills were buried in committee. The few that reached the roll call stage were snowed under. In 1919, a divorce bill, sponsored by Assemblyman Hermann Weiss, a New York City Republican, was defeated 16 to 76.[44] In 1931, Assemblyman Maurice Z. Bungard, a Brooklyn Democrat, introduced a bill recognizing two new grounds for divorce: cruelty and desertion. The codes committee amended this to include only the single new ground of desertion and then voted seven to five to recommend passage. But the assembly voted down the proposed change 106 to 30.[45] The issue cut across party lines: 23 Republicans and 7 Democrats voted to liberalize the law; 49 Republicans and 57 Democrats were in opposition.

Convinced that their colleagues were too timid to take direct action, some legislators hoped to focus attention on the problem by other means. In 1932 and 1933, Manhattan Assemblyman Meyer Alterman introduced bills for creating a temporary state commission to study the divorce problem.[46] But this proposal never emerged from committee.

For a New Yorker determined to escape from an unhappy marriage, the alternatives continued to be distasteful. He could employ a private detective to shadow his mate, hopeful of catching her in an act of infidelity; he could allow her to sue him for divorce and arrange the phony evidence to deceive a cynical court; he could concoct some plausible claim of fraud upon which an annulment could be granted; or he could entrain for Nevada or Mexico. Actually many individuals followed none of these courses. The husband or wife simply skipped out on his or her responsibilities, leaving the deserted mate to handle the family problems with whatever help could be extracted from public and private welfare agencies. In 1950, it was estimated that desertions cost New York City more than 27 million dollars annually—one half its payments of aid to dependent children.[47] To refuse divorce was obviously no answer to the problems created by broken homes.

CHAPTER 14

Politics and
the New York Divorce Law

Between 1900 and 1933, Democratic senators and assemblymen from the New York City area had been particularly active in intro-ducing divorce bills. Many of these legislators had been Jewish lawyers, men with names like Harold Spielberg, Mark Goldberg, Abraham Greenberg, Harry Samberg, and Maurice Bungard. Yet a rewriting of the New York divorce laws was not likely to be achieved under Democratic leadership for two very obvious reasons. In the first place, the Democrats were seldom in control of the legislature, thanks to an apportionment of representation that discriminated against New York City. Moreover, because of their party's depend-ence upon the urban Catholic vote, most Democrats considered the divorce issue too hot to touch. After 1933, therefore, Republicans were more likely than Democrats to run the political risks involved in proposing fundamental changes in the divorce laws. And even the Republicans preferred to duck the issue.

The first Republican to put up a determined fight was I. Arnold Ross, a thirty-six-year-old lawyer representing the Ninth Assembly District of New York City. When he arrived in Albany in January, 1934, Ross was a political accident, elected because of a feud among the Democrats, who usually carried this district by a two to one margin. Energetic and ambitious, the new assemblyman made proposals enough to occupy any ordinary legislator for several years, as some of his more cynical colleagues complained.[1]

Two of Ross's bills were for the modification of the divorce law. In his home district—located between Riverside Drive and Central Park West—he had been touched by the plight of deserted wives unable to get divorces in New York unless they resorted to fraud and too poor to establish residences in other states. Conservatively drawn, the Ross bills recognized only one new ground, desertion, and they were hedged with every safeguard: the desertion must be "willful" and "without reasonable cause" and must have extended over "the three years immediately preceding the commencement of the action." [2]

At first things went surprisingly well. The bills were committed to the committee on codes, of which Ross himself was a member, and on February 28, 1934, this committee reported favorably by an 8 to 1 vote.[3]

Ross received his first warning of brewing trouble from a confidential source, who showed him a letter from a Catholic bishop to one of the Democratic leaders strongly condemning the desertion bills. The suddenly stiffened opposition came into the open on March 6 when Irwin Steingut of Brooklyn, the Democratic floor leader, demanded that the bills be recommitted to committee for a public hearing. Using a familiar legislative trick, Steingut proposed a date so late that it would probably fall after the end of the session. But Ross acquiesced in the belief that the backlog on the legislative calendar would prolong the session beyond the expectation of the Democratic leader. He hoped to capitalize on the proposed hearing to mobilize public sentiment behind his measure.[4]

The next few weeks were full of hectic activity. Friendly newspapers—particularly the New York Daily News—gave publicity to Ross's campaign, and the assemblyman himself made many speeches and conducted an extensive correspondence in behalf of his program. On March 18, Ross participated in a radio debate with Assemblyman Luke O'Reilly of Brooklyn, a seventy-one-year-old bachelor, whose pious eloquence on behalf of the sanctity of the home charmed some of his listeners and irritated others.[5]

Enthusiastic volunteers circulated petitions in support of the

Ross bills, obtaining some eight hundred signatures. In addition, the assemblyman received some four thousand letters, most of them from husbands and wives who saw in his proposals hope for deliverance from their own unhappy marriages. Many were from Catholics. Written on cheap paper and replete with errors of spelling and grammar, these letters provided a pathetic sampling of the marital problems of the lower-income groups. One "discusted" wife, separated three years from her shiftless husband, wrote: "You can tell Mr. Luke O'Reilly that this letter is from an Irish Catholic whose life is spoiled by meeting a bad husband. I work 18 hours 7 days a week to make a living." Another wife gave a melancholy inventory of the injuries she had suffered: "If I asked money from him I received a broken ear drum, my head put through a closet door, a broken finger, my arm almost slashed off and five black eyes, one of them, I almost lost a eye. From something he did to me I was in bed 3 months and it cost my sister $2000 to save me as I was near death. . . . His habits were that of a degenerate and when I refused I would receive a beating."

From such horrors as these, judicial separation offered a partial escape, yet separation without divorce was full of moral perils, as the letters to Ross made vividly clear. "I'm not willingly a bad woman," wrote one anonymous correspondent, "but I am living with a fine gentleman . . . thats what many Godly folks are up against if the laws are not changed." A husband whose wife had deserted him ten years before admitted that he had subsequently met another woman, with whom he had been living for eight years. The union had resulted in the birth of a child. "I want to do right by the present 'Mrs.,'" he wrote, "and give our little girl a name, but what can we do?"

The poor took it for granted that the New York laws could be circumvented by collusion and perjury—if one only had the money. After Ross's bills had been defeated, "John Doe" wrote: "I waited for the result of the vote as I am anticipating a divorce and I thought I could get it in a decent manner. Next week I am going to be 'framed' at a New York hotel. So you can tell old Reilly I will get my divorce anyhow in spite of his opposition." [6]

The bar associations of Tompkins, Lewis, and Oneida counties passed resolutions favoring the Ross bills, and so did such local groups as the Brooklyn Women's Bar Association, the Lockport Lawyers Club, the Yonkers Lawyers Association, and the New York County Lawyers Association. Supreme Court Justice Salvatore A. Cotillo was a strong supporter, as were several of the official referees with wide experience in divorce matters.[7] Ross's efforts were also endorsed by distinguished religious leaders, including Dr. Sidney S. Goldstein, Chairman of the Committee on Social Justice of the Central Committee of American Rabbis, Dr. L. Ward Foster, Secretary of the Committee on Marriage and the Home of the Federal Council of Churches, and Dr. Harry Emerson Fosdick, nationally famous pastor of the Riverside Church. But Ross did not get what he most needed, a massive endorsement from Protestant and Jewish quarters to counter the formidable Catholic opposition now being mobilized against him.[8]

Hoping to make an impressive showing at the public hearing, Ross telegraphed invitations to a long list of prominent citizens. A respectable number of these responded and were on hand in Albany on March 28. Rabbi Goldstein made the opening plea for the bills and was followed by Supreme Court Referee O. L. Van Horne, Miss Amy Wren of the Brooklyn Women's Bar Association, and George H. Hallett, Jr., of the Citizens Union. Also conspicuously present were many of Ross's humbler supporters with personal stories to tell, dramatizing the need for a change in the law.

Only one person undertook to oppose the Ross bills, but this was the powerful Charles J. Tobin, Secretary of the New York State Catholic Welfare Committee, who declared that passage of the measures would lead to a breakdown of home life and a 100 per cent increase in parentless children. "In time of depression should we legalize the separations that are being threatened by it? What we need is not less personal responsibility but more responsibility in parental relationship." [9] As a member of the codes committee, Ross had an opportunity to question his most formidable opponent. One significant exchange concerned Tobin's contention that there was really no demand for divorce law changes, and that the most the codes committee should do was to recommend the creation of a legislative committee to study the question. As Ross recorded the episode:

I asked him whether he seriously believed that such legislative committee should be appointed and he said he did. I further asked him whether he felt that such committee would make a thorough study of the subject, and he again answered in the affirmative. I then asked him whether he would approve the recommendation of the majority of such committee, regardless as to the nature of the recommendation. He hesitated for a long time, and then stated:

"If you mean that such a committee would report and approve legislation making available divorce in this State on other grounds than adultery, my answer is no."

I then asked Mr. Tobin if his organization would not approve a modification of the divorce laws in this State under any circumstances, and whether his desire for an investigation was a means of ducking the . . . issue, but he failed to answer.[10]

Immediately after the hearing, the codes committee again approved the Ross bills by an eight to five margin. Confronted by this situation, the Catholic opposition took energetic steps. The Brooklyn Catholic Action Council wrote to each assemblyman,[11] while Tobin sent each a nine-page memorandum in the name of the New York State Catholic Welfare Committee. Denying that there was any widespread demand for a change in the law, Tobin asserted that much of the force behind the proposal consisted of "the support of potential plaintiffs and a few lawyers interested in this line of business." He denounced the idea that marriage was a purely private contract:

To weaken the law concerning the marital status is to strike at the foundation of society. The stability of the State itself is involved. Marriage is the basis of the family—and the family is the cornerstone of society. Civilized society either progresses or deteriorates from the moral point of view according as the importance of the family is emphasized in the minds of any civilized people.

The memorandum did not emphasize Catholic doctrine as such, but the assertion that these bills were "directly contrary to the religious faith of more than a third of our people" contained a warning politicians could not fail to note.[12]

In a spirited floor debate on April 10, several Democratic assemblymen quoted directly from the Tobin memorandum. Luke O'Reilly added some characteristic embellishments of his own. "No one wants these bills except a lot of flitterers of the butterfly variety," he said. "We might better make an effort to punish perjury, because our courts are filled with it in connection with divorce cases." Ross countered Catholic objections with the argument that if there was any group in the state who didn't believe in divorce, they didn't have to use it, "but women and children praying for decent homes and prevented by the inadequacy of our divorce laws should not be denied relief." Several Republicans spoke in favor of the measure, as well as a few Democrats like Frank T. Quinn of Oneida County. James E. Stephens, a Harlem Democrat, amused the assembly by declaring: "If I had my way, I would amend the law and charge $250 for a marriage license and 15 cents for a divorce." [13]

The first of the Ross bills went down to defeat on April 10, 1934, by a vote of 52 to 82; the second was beaten on April 18 by a 53 to 80 margin.[14] With their party's strength concentrated in the cities, the Democrats demonstrated great unwillingness to risk offending the Roman Catholic Church. Only eight Democrats ventured to vote for Ross's proposals on April 10 and only six on April 18. The Republicans were sharply divided. On the April 10 roll call, 44 Republicans voted for the desertion bill and 33 against it; on April 18, 47 voted for it and 29 against. Equally significant was the substantial number of legislators, both Democrats and Republicans, who walked off the floor rather than be recorded on so controversial an issue. Fourteen members—many of them personal friends of Ross—absented themselves on April 10, and 15 on April 18.[15]

Ross promised to continue his fight for changes in the divorce law, if he were reelected. But 1934 was an unhappy year for Republicans. The New Dealers swept the November elections, with the Democrats gaining control of the New York legislature for the first time in twenty years. Despite endorsements from such champions of good government as the *New York Times* and the Citizens Union, Ross himself was defeated. He believed that Catholic influence had been used against him, but the extent to which his divorce stand really injured him is difficult to measure. Although he lost by 6,000 votes, he did much better than Robert Moses, the Republican candidate for governor, who ran 14,000 votes behind Governor Herbert Lehman. Given the normally Democratic character of the district, the peak of popularity achieved by the New Deal, and the high personal respect enjoyed by Governor Lehman, it would have required a political miracle for Ross to have won. The divorce issue may have helped more than it hurt him.[16]

Two years after the defeat of the Ross bills another attempt to reform the New York divorce law was launched under the leadership of Assemblywoman Jane Todd of Westchester County. First elected to the legislature in 1934, Miss Todd brought to her position a moral earnestness having it roots in her family background, so thoroughly old-stock American that she could claim eligibility to the Daughters of the American Revolution through each of her four grandparents. She had long been active in welfare work and in Republican party affairs in her native Tarrytown.[17]

In the 1936 session Miss Todd introduced two bills, both in her opinion needed to correct serious abuses. The first, her so-called "hasty marriage" bill, would bring New York into line with most other states by requiring a 72-hour waiting period between the issuance of a marriage license and the performance of the ceremony, thus preventing so-called "gin marriages"—spur-of-the-moment weddings performed by small-town ministers and judges to accommodate tipsy couples, a particular problem in suburban Westchester County. The second Todd bill would recognize three years' desertion as ground for divorce. Miss Todd criticized the existing New York law as class legislation, making honest divorce difficult for the poor while allowing the rich to seek freedom in Reno or Mexico. She deplored the prevalence of staged adultery raids. "For the sake of the children," she declared, "husband and wife should not be forced by law to sully each other's names and besmirch their characters, when actually a record of infidelity has been entered against an innocent person." [18]

The assembly codes committee, to which both Todd bills were committed, held a public hearing on March 4. The occasion was enlivened by a sharp exchange between Miss Todd and Tobin, again representing the State Catholic Welfare Committee. After hearing the latter admonish the committee to consider the effect that liberalized divorce would have on the children of the state, Miss Todd commented that she had received many letters from Roman Catholics on that point. "They were poor Catholics who did not have money enough to go to Reno for needed divorces. They have no one to take care of them and their children. These are women who have been deserted and can't remarry to get help for their children. Mr. Tobin," she asked, "what does your church mean to do with those children?"

"If you will give me the names of those individuals," answered the Catholic spokesman, "I will see that they are provided for."

"Will you provide a father for them?" asked a committee member.

"We do not propose to do that," replied Tobin.

Insisting that the present law was adequate, Tobin argued that to recognize desertion as ground for divorce would throw New York "into a class with Nevada and Wyoming, where the divorce rate is the highest in the country." The desertion bill, he warned, was contrary to the religious beliefs of more than one-third of the state's population. Tobin also opposed the hasty-marriage bill, claiming that there was no public demand for such a change and that it would be more effective to reduce the number of officials authorized to perform the marriage ceremony.[19] Despite this opposition, the codes committee reported favorably on both Todd bills.[20]

Warned that the linking of the two bills might make it impossible for either to pass, Miss Todd arranged to have them considered on separate days. On March 18, the assembly passed the hasty-marriage ban by a vote of 118 to 22.[21] But in the senate—for reasons apparently linked to the divorce bill controversy—the Democrats closed ranks and defeated the bill by a vote of 21 to 25.[22]

Preceding the assembly roll call on the divorce bill on March 31, there was a short but lively debate. "This State," declared Miss Todd, "is dealing unwisely with conditions which it chooses to ignore. Injustice, suspicion, collusion, framed evidence, all tend to debase the courts and destroy respect for our law." She was strongly supported by one of her Republican colleagues, Laurens M. Hamilton of Rockland County. But two other Republicans, Horace Stone and Richard Smith, both of Onondaga County, led the opposition.[23] Miss Todd felt that the action of Stone, one of the most influential leaders in the legislature, was occasioned quite as much by a general distaste for women in politics as by dislike for the bill under consideration.[24]

The Todd divorce bill was defeated 35 to 93—more decisively than the Ross bills two years earlier.[25] Only 3 Democrats and 32 Republicans supported the measure, while 43 Republicans and 54 Democrats opposed it. Miss Todd attributed the outcome largely to the fact that on the day of the vote each assemblyman found in his mail a warning that 400,000 Catholics in the state were opposed to the bill's passage.[26]

The assemblywoman's first inclination was to fight back vigorously through the organization of a citizens' committee for divorce law reform. She was encouraged to do so through the hundreds of supporting letters she had received from individuals and groups. Sober second thought cooled Miss Todd's crusading zeal. The recent roll call provided discouraging evidence of the unwillingness of her fellow legislators to face reality on this issue. Moreover, the failure of her hasty-marriage bill gave warning that persistence in pushing divorce legislation might handicap her in obtaining other measures in which she was interested. In the 1937 session Miss Todd did not reintroduce her desertion bill, and she had her prompt reward in the passage of her hasty-marriage bill—practically without opposition. Behind the scenes, however, Miss Todd used her influence to encourage a more forthright attitude on the divorce issue, particularly in the women's organizations in which she was prominent.[27]

The next serious discussion of New York's divorce problem occurred after World War II. Postwar periods are always hard on family life, and this one was especially so. Hasty wartime marriages went on the rocks; soldiers came home to unfaithful wives; loyal women found their returning mates strangely changed. Throughout the country the divorce rate soared to unprecedented heights.

This postwar situation resulted in intolerable pressures against the flimsy dikes of the New York family laws. It was characteristic of the prevailing chaos that no one knew exactly how many marriages were being dissolved, but Supreme Court Justice Henry Clay Greenberg estimated in 1947 that a thousand divorces a month were being ground out by New York courts. Since adulterers usually try to keep their trysts secret, few of these divorces were based on genuine evidence. Justice Greenberg pointed out that 99 out of 100 New York divorce suits were undefended, and of these he estimated that "75 per cent, at the very least, are based on phony raids and thus involve collusion." [28] For the more fastidious lawyers and clients disliking to dirty their hands in proving adultery, the state's annulment laws offered a welcome alternative. Judge Charles S. Desmond of the Court of Appeals estimated that from July 1, 1945, to July 1, 1946, New York courts granted about 5,000 annulments, many of them on the flimsiest of evidence.[29]

Conscientious judges and lawyers believed that reform was essential lest growing public cynicism toward the divorce and annulment laws undermine respect for the whole judicial process. In 1945, a Committee on Law Reform of the Association of the Bar of the City of New York urged "a liberalization of the divorce laws under proper legal sanctions" in the hope "that we may thus eliminate what has come to be recognized as a scandal, growing out of widespread fraud, perjury, collusion, and connivance in the dissolution of marriages in this State." [30] Specifically, the Committee recommended that six additional grounds for divorce be recognized: extreme cruel and inhuman treatment; such willful conduct as to render it unsafe and improper for the plaintiff to cohabit with the defendant; abandonment; neglect, or refusal of a husband to provide for his wife; conviction of a felony involving two years' actual imprisonment; and habitual intemperance.

This forthright proposal had to wait three years to find a legislator courageous enough to sponsor it in the legislature. But in the 1948 session, Assemblyman William T. Andrews, a Harlem Democrat, introduced a bill embodying the Association recommendations. To support the Andrews bill, the Association created a Special Committee on the Improvement of the Divorce Laws and a broader-based Citizens Committee for the Improvement of the Divorce Laws.[31] This early campaign was abortive: the Andrews bill died in committee and Andrews himself lost his assembly seat as the result of a Democratic primary fight in August, 1948.[32]

Meanwhile, a somewhat different course of action had been proposed in December, 1947, by the Legislative Committee of the Affiliated Young Democrats of New York State. "The restrictions of the divorce laws as they now exist," declared the Young Democrats, "have defeated their own purpose, and, in fact, for those who are willing to bear the stigma of adultery, divorces in New York are easier, less expensive, and more binding than those in Nevada." The proposed road to reform was for the legislature to create "a commission on which will be represented the three principal faiths of the state, the bench, the bar, the women of the state, social scientists and the press to consider and recommend revision and modernization of the state's divorce laws which will restore dignity, decency and self-respect to that branch of our courts." [33] Assemblyman Bernard Austin, a Brooklyn Democrat, introduced a bill along these lines in February, 1948,[34] but this proposal expired in committee.

In December, 1948, the need for reform was dramatized when another of New York's periodic divorce scandals captured the headlines. Twenty-year-old Sara Ellis, the wife of a building superintendent and the mother of three children, had been supplementing the family income by serving as the "unknown woman" in scores of local divorce cases. Piqued by the fact that she received only $10 for each of her acting roles, Sara spilled her story to the *New York Journal-American*. Representatives of that paper took the disgruntled young woman to District Attorney Frank S. Hogan with the result that ten members of this particular ring were arrested.[35] More important was the incentive given to the District Attorney to initiate a grand jury investigation of the whole New York City situation. The records of over 600 recent divorce cases were carefully reviewed and some 1,500 witnesses were examined. This crackdown probably contributed to the 43 per cent reduction in matrimonial actions brought in New York County in 1949.[36]

Yet occasional arrests and disbarments provided no permanent solution of the problem. On December 3, 1948, Robert P. Paterson, former Secretary of War and now President of the Association of the Bar of the City of New York, stated the need for more liberal laws. The pressure for perjury, he declared, was created by the fact that adultery was the only ground recognized for divorce. "Since people believe that the laws are unduly strict . . . you have a condition of law-breaking something like that existing under the prohibition law in the nineteen-twenties and nineteen-thirties." [37] Similar statements came from various Jewish and Protestant sources. Rabbi Jonah B. Wise of New York's Central Synagogue asserted that the state's di-

vorce laws met neither the legal nor the moral requirements of a
modern age,[38] and the State Council of Churches passed the following resolution:

> We would not encourage easy divorce or advocate any legal procedure
> that treats it lightly. We do regard the present New York divorce statutes
> as neither just nor humane and as an occasion for evasion and hypocrisy.
> We therefore commend to the Legislature and to the Governor con-
> sideration of such measures as will provide our state with more just and
> wholesome divorce laws.[39]

But the Roman Catholic Church sternly opposed all such suggestions. Indeed Monsignor Robert E. McCormick, presiding judge of
the Archdiocesan Tribunal of New York, called upon the legislature
to ban divorce entirely. He denounced the movement to liberalize
the law as "a menace to society." [40]

Although the Association of the Bar of the City of New York
had hoped to get a new sponsor for its six-grounds divorce bill, it
proved impossible to find anyone willing to take the risk. Assembly
Speaker Oswald D. Heck advised the Association leaders that a more
hopeful course would be to press for something along the lines of
the earlier Austin bill—a temporary state commission to study the
whole family law situation.[41] The *New York Times* called this "the
soundest approach, and probably the only practicable way from a
political viewpoint." [42] Yet Catholic displeasure was so greatly feared
that even the commission plan did not at first find a sponsor.

This deadlock was broken on February 7, 1949, when Assemblywoman Janet Hill Gordon, a Chenango County Republican, introduced a bill calling for the appointment of a temporary state commission to make a comprehensive study and analysis of the causes
and effects of divorce, separation, and annulment actions, to study
the existing laws of New York and other states, and to report its
findings to the legislature.[43]

Petite and feminine, Mrs. Gordon might not have seemed to the
casual observer strong enough for the rugged task of leading the
fight for a rational approach to the state's family law problems. But
events soon proved that she was well suited for this assignment.
Only thirty-four years old, Mrs. Gordon had the drive and idealism
of youth; her reddish hair and her incisive manner of speaking re-

flected the courage and tenacity that would be required to cope with frequent setbacks. She had other strong assets in background and training. She was the daughter of a widely respected Norwich lawyer and judge, James P. Hill, and was herself a graduate of the Brooklyn Law School. In 1940, she had been admitted to the bar and had begun practice in her home town of Norwich.

Long before she became a lawyer herself, Janet Hill had become familiar with the tangled jungle of the New York domestic relations law through conversations with her father and his friends among the other judges and lawyers. She soon had her own initiation into these matters when she was appointed county attorney. In dealing with cases involving neglected or delinquent children, she was troubled to find that most of these situations arose out of broken homes. Sometimes the problem involved divorces or annulments that had been granted without adequate provision for the children; sometimes the trouble was the difficulty of obtaining a divorce under the New York law, so that the wife or husband long separated from his spouse was unable to provide a new home for the children through a second marriage. Always there was the maddening frustration of a multiplicity of courts, each with partial jurisdiction to handle some segment of the situation but none with a general power to deal with the case as a whole. First elected to the assembly in 1947, Mrs. Gordon frequently discussed these problems with her fellow legislators. Learning that she would be willing to sponsor legislation in this field, the groups dissatisfied with the existing situation naturally sought her out. Hence the commission bill of 1949.[44]

Spokesmen for the Roman Catholic Church regarded the Govdon bill as nothing more than a veiled attempt to put over an "easy" divorce law. In view of the recent effort of the Bar of the City of New York to obtain a liberalized statute, this suspicion was probably inevitable. Yet it involved considerable injustice to Mrs. Gordon, who proceeded on the sincere conviction of the need for a wholly objective study of the situation. She hoped to restore respect for the judicial process, to give more adequate protection to the interests of children, and to set up the machinery for a more rational and humane approach to all types of matrimonial difficulties. Open-minded on the question of whether recognizing additional grounds for divorce would contribute to these ends, she wanted a commission with broad powers to make whatever recommendations seemed wise.

So stubborn was the opposition that Mrs. Gordon had to fight for seven years before she obtained any legislation at all and even then it was far less than she wanted. The long struggle began rather quietly. In 1949, the Gordon bill was painlessly put to sleep in committee.[45] In 1950 Mrs. Gordon herself postponed action out of deference to the Republican strategists who wanted to avoid controversy during an election year.[46]

In 1951, Mrs. Gordon and her allies made their first really serious effort to obtain legislation. The Special Committee on Improvement of the Divorce Laws of the Association of the Bar of the City of New York sprang into activity under the aggressive leadership of Attorney Richard H. Wels. Closely affiliated with this group was the Citizens Committee on Improvement of the Divorce Laws, now headed by Rev. John O. Mellin, pastor of the First Presbyterian Church of New York City. In a speech on February 15, 1951, Wels, a Democrat, sharply criticized Governor Thomas E. Dewey for avoiding the issue.[47]

The need for divorce reform was underlined by two developments early in 1951. On March 6, the grand jury that had been investigating the New York County situation brought in a presentment affirming that "widespread fraud, perjury, collusion, and connivance pervade matrimonial actions of every type." It urged "the enactment of a bill providing for the creation of a state commission to study and analyze the problems relating to marriage, divorce, separation, and annulment of marriage." [48] The second incident pointed up the absurdities of the existing divorce law in an unusually lurid way. Scorning to resort to the usual avenues to divorce, Andrea Gehr had attempted to obtain genuine evidence of her husband's adultery. Accompanied by a private detective, she had tried to surprise her mate in a rustic cabin near Brewster, New York, where he was love-nesting with another woman. This reconnoiter came to a tragic ending, when Herbert Gehr fired a bullet through the screen door, killing his wife. The husband was tried for murder, but the jury acquitted him, accepting his story that he had only intended to scare off unknown prowlers. The jurors addressed a letter to Governor Dewey urging changes in the state's divorce laws, which they asserted were "deplorably antiquated and at times unmoral." When the Governor's office brushed off their plea, they tried to obtain a face-to-face meeting, but this request was ignored.[49]

Despite these developments, the assembly ways and means committee once again killed the Gordon bill without a hearing—much to the disgust of many leading newspapers. In an editorial entitled "Albany's Poor Sense of Smell," the *New York Herald Tribune* called the situation "an outrage to decency" and condemned the legislators for their "ususal exhibition of ostrichism." [50] The *Binghamton Press* placed the blame on "politicians who do a trembling aspen in their pusillanimous brogans every time the stench of the state's divorce statutes comes to their nostrils." [51]

The persistent Mrs. Gordon introduced her bill a third time in 1952. She hoped, she said, that there would be less opposition this time because of a recent pronouncement by the National Catholic Welfare Conference " that Catholics in public life may cooperate in securing amendments to a divorce statute when such amendments would have a substantial probability for reducing the volume of divorces or cutting down on its incidental evils." [52] The State Council of Churches, the Citizens Union, and other civic groups supported her,[53] but once again the bill died in committee.

The proponents of the commission bill made a more energetic fight in 1953. For the first time Mrs. Gordon found a Republican state senator willing to act as cosponsor. Her new ally was Dutton S. Peterson, a Methodist minister who combined farming and preaching in Odessa, New York.[54] Still more encouraging was the changed attitude of the Republican leaders. On February 18, a delegation from the Citizens Committee for the Improvement of Family Laws visited Albany. They found Speaker Heck to be strongly in favor of the commission bill and willing to arrange public hearings. Governor Dewey gave his visitors a somewhat cooler reception. He thought the bill a good one, but he was disinclined to use his influence with the legislature, because he wanted to concentrate his efforts on issues that he considered more important.[55]

Despite the governor's attitude, the Republican leaders obviously decided that the commission proposal could no longer be ignored. At a public hearing on March 5, 1953, Attorney Orrin Judd of New

York City, representing the State Council of Churches, and Richard Wels and William Philo Clark of the Association of the Bar of the City of New York, headed an impressive battery of speakers supporting the commission plan. Methodist, Presbyterian, and Congregational leaders made a strong showing. The Episcopal bishops were more cautious,[56] but Bishop Dudley Scott of Rochester placed his approval on record. Another sector of the religious world was represented by spokesmen for the New York Board of Rabbis and the National Council of Jewish Women. Prominent lawyers expressed the interest of such groups as the Association of the Bar of the City of New York, the New York County Lawyers Association, the Women's Bar Association of New York, and the New York State Bar Association. Three or four judges expressed approval, as did representatives of various social agencies and such civic groups as the American Association of University Women.[57]

Some twenty-eight speakers supported the bill; only two opposed it. One of these hardly counted since his principal interest was in publicizing his own scheme for marriage law reform, but the second, Attorney George W. Wanamaker of Buffalo, representing the powerful New York State Catholic Welfare Committee, commanded the sober attention of every political ear. Alluding to the Association of the Bar of the City of New York, Wanamaker declared that a group "vocal in its sponsorship of this bill" had approved a resolution to establish seven grounds for divorce and "it is the apparent objective of a committee of that group to promote that legislation by first promoting a commission to investigate." The Catholic spokesman contended that "to increase the grounds for divorce is but to multiply opportunities for perjury and subornation." [58] Denying Wanamaker's charge, Wels declared: "I should like to emphasize that we do not seek easy divorce. It could not be easier to get a divorce than it is now in the State of New York. We believe that any changes that are made in existing law will reduce the divorce rate." [59]

Although Mrs. Gordon felt well pleased with the hearing, she was politician enough to know that her bill would not be allowed to come to a vote without help from her party leaders. Speaker Heck remained a firm supporter; Governor Dewey's attitude continued to be described as "wishy-washy." [60] The bill's fate remained in suspense to the end of the session; on March 20 the assembly rules committee finally reported it out,[61] and on the next day—the last of the session—it was voted upon without any opportunity for debate. On this last-minute roll call the Gordon-Peterson bill was defeated 64 to 78.[62] Mrs. Gordon received the support of 57 Republicans and 7 Democrats; she was opposed by 35 Republicans and 43 Democrats. As nearly as can be determined, some 51 of the opposition votes were from Catholics. The influence of the Catholics within the Democratic party was a familiar story; equally impressive was their growing strength among the Republicans. Of the 35 Republicans who voted against the commission bill, all but 8 were Catholic.

Continuing her odd-even year strategy, Mrs. Gordon did not press her bill in 1954. The most important development of the year was the unveiling of a Catholic-sponsored counterprogram. On January 21, 1954, two prominent Catholic legislators, Assemblyman Malcolm Wilson, Westchester Republican, and Senator Francis J. Mahoney, Manhattan Democrat, introduced five bills intended to reduce the state's divorce and annulment rates. The proposed legislation would: (1) set up mandatory conciliation procedures for all seekers of divorce or annulment; (2) provide a special attorney general to act as proctor for the state and to protect the welfare of children in divorce and annulment cases; (3) limit annulment for fraud to matters "essential to the marriage relationship"; (4) fix a three-year limit from the discovery of the fraud for the filing of an annulment suit; and (5) require "clear and convincing" evidence in annulment suits.[63]

On January 20, 1955, the Gordon-Peterson bill was once more introduced. Attorney Orrin Judd of the State Council of Churches master-minded a strategy which it was hoped would finally put the bill across.[64] The latest mobilization of forces was clearly evident at a public hearing on February 24. The State Council of Churches supported the bill even more vigorously than in 1953; there were also more spokesmen for regional Protestant groups in Albany, Buffalo, Rochester, and other cities. Episcopal support was much stronger. Dean James A. Pike of the New York Cathedral of St. John the Divine, once a lawyer, contributed a strong statement:

The present situation is unrealistic and has induced well-known abuses: for example, out-of-state-divorces with fictional establishment of residence, staged adultery, and a perjured basis of annulment on the ground of fraud. All three devices are rapidly gaining the prestige of ac-cepted "legal fictions" to the undermining of respect for law and to the creation of inequities as between particular cases where it would appear that the dissolution of the marriage, though never good, is the lesser of two evils.[65]

Particularly impressive was the point of view presented by the Rev-erend Dennis Lee, an Episcopal rector from Marcellus, New York, and a close friend of Mrs. Gordon. Stressing his own church's be-lief in the indissolubility of marriage, he went on to say: "But, the church has adequate machinery of its own to enforce its canon law upon its own constituents. The state is not the secular arm of the church, and . . . no church has a right under a democratic govern-ment to make its canon law the civil law, or to utilize the legal ma-chinery and authority of the state to impose upon the people of the commonwealth its moral conscience or canon law." [66]

Attorney George W. Wanamaker once again represented the State Catholic Welfare Committee, and this time he was reinforced by spokesmen for the Knights of Columbus, the Catholic War Veterans, the Federation of Catholic Alumnae, and various other lay organizations. The Catholic case was still based on the premise that the commission plan was aimed at liberalization of the law. If the real purpose was to help eliminate perjury and other abuses, said Wanamaker, it was unnecessary, since such purposes already came within the jurisdiction of "two active and highly competent public bodies, the Judicial Council and the Temporary Commission on the Courts." [67] Furthermore, all that was really needed was provided in the Wilson-Mahoney bills.

This contention was vigorously disputed by Roy D. Richardson and Richard Wels of the Association of the Bar of the City of New York, who condemned a "piecemeal" approach to the family law problem. Wels argued against any attempt to limit the commission's mandate:

So far as I am concerned, we want to have a fair open-minded com-mission representing every point of view. . . . We don't want to tie their hands behind their backs and say, "You can go into these problems of a family, but you can only go half way." We don't think they should have blinders, restrictions. They should be permitted to take a complete look and tell you what they recommend, and you, in your wisdom and pleasure, will evaluate their determinations and determine whether they are in the public interest.[68]

The hearings revealed an even sharper religious division than in 1953: the State Council of Churches and other Protestant bodies were more strongly mobilized in favor of the Gordon-Peterson bill; the various Catholic groups were more militantly opposed. In terms of practical politics this made the Jewish position a matter of particular significance. Jewish spokesmen at the hearing firmly supported the commission plan. Speaking for the New York Board of Rabbis, Harold Gordon said:

Judaism throughout the ages has conspicuously upheld the sanctity of law and the integrity of the home and family. It affirms that marriage is a moral and divinely-sanctified union of husband and wife. Therefore, when these elements are no longer present in marriage, Judaism recognizes that divorce may be wise and necessary.[69]

Ironically, Jewish liberalism on the divorce issue was difficult to translate into votes in the legislature, despite the fact that the New York City area contained the largest concentration of Jews in the world. As a Jewish newspaper explained, Jewish legislators represented districts where masses of Jews lived side by side with Catholics, with whom their interests coincided in many respects. "Therefore, the vote of Jewish lawmakers doesn't stray far from the interests of their Catholic colleagues, with whom they are closely bound in local politics too. Therefore, the answer of the Jews in the State Legislature is not much more positive than the Catholics on the divorce issue." [70]

This reluctance of Jewish politicians to risk offending their Catholic allies had been an important factor in the divorce struggle for years. Since these legislators would often express private sentiments very different from their votes on the floor, backers of the Gordon-Peterson bill made a special effort to win them over in 1955. By the middle of March, Mrs. Gordon believed that enough

Jewish votes had been promised to assure a victory, at least in the assembly. Great was her indignation, therefore, when she heard rumors of a last-minute deal whereby certain Jewish legislators had agreed to stick with their Catholic colleagues on the divorce issue in return for a Catholic promise to support a bill that would permit businesses owned by persons observing Saturday as the Sabbath to remain open on Sundays.[71]

When the Gordon-Peterson bill again came to a vote in the assembly on March 29, 1955, the misgivings of its sponsors proved to be well grounded. Getting only 61 votes to the opposition's 85, the proposal was more decisively defeated than in 1953.[72] Only 3 Democrats voted for the bill, while 58 voted against it. In the post-mortems, the rumored deal assumed even more importance. According to information reaching Mrs. Gordon, Catholic representatives had met with Jewish ones in the Madison Avenue office of the attorney for a certain candy company eager for a change in the Sunday closing laws.[73] There the bargain was alleged to have been sealed, but—as Mrs. Gordon noted with grim satisfaction—the promised Catholic support for the Jewish measure failed to materialize in the eventual showdown.

Meanwhile, the least controversial of the Wilson-Mahoney bills, the one setting a three-year limit from the discovery of the fraud for the initiation of annulment suits, had passed the legislature and received the Governor's signature on April 13, 1955.[74]

Despite this minor victory, at least two of the Catholic Republicans felt that their coreligionists had gone too far in their die-hard opposition to any study of the family laws. Each came to Mrs. Gordon on the last day of the session without the knowledge of the other, and each had substantially the same thing in mind—the desirability of some kind of compromise whereby Mrs. Gordon would consent to modify her plan in return for a cessation of Catholic opposition.[75] Speaker Heck advised Mrs. Gordon to enter negotiations with the opposition camp.[76]

Eager to nail things down, Mrs. Gordon sought further conferences during the spring and summer. But these proved hard to arrange. In November, 1955, Mrs. Gordon still had not come to terms with the opposition and was exploring the possibility of utilizing the Episcopal Church to mediate between the conflicting positions represented by the Catholic Church on one side and the State Council of Churches on the other.[77]

But in December—just a month before the 1956 legislature opened—the deadlock was broken when Mrs. Gordon, spending a night in New York City, received a telephone call from one of the Catholic group informing her that she would find an interesting document in her hotel mailbox. Hurrying to inspect this mysterious communication, she found enclosed in a plain envelope the substance of a bill that would overcome objections to her proposal. The suggested formula was for a joint legislative committee instead of the broad commission Mrs. Gordon had wanted; the committee's mandate, moreover, was to be limited to studying matters of procedure and jurisdiction and was to include no authority to make recommendations relating to the grounds for divorce. The terms were hard, but, after consulting with Speaker Heck and other leaders, Mrs. Gordon decided to accept them as the best she was likely to get.[78]

To emphasize the bipartisan character of the new effort, Democratic Senator William Rosenblatt of Brooklyn was substituted for Peterson as cosponsor of the proposal. The Gordon-Rosenblatt bill, introduced January 24, 1956, provided for a joint legislative committee to be composed of three senators and three assemblymen, who were "to make a study and evaluation of, and make recommendations to the legislature with respect to (a) the adequacy of existing laws of procedure in matrimonial actions and actions relating to the family, (b) the jurisdiction, rules, operations, and practices of the various courts in such actions, (c) revision in the laws of procedure, jurisdiction, rules, operations, and practices designed to improve the administration of justice and to preserve the marital relationship and the family unit." [79] With all the legislative traffic lights now turned green, the bill passed the assembly on March 22, 1956, by a vote of 142 to 6, and the senate that same day by a vote of 57 to 0.[80]

Appointed by the temporary president of the senate and the speaker of the assembly, the new joint legislative committee represented a careful balancing of the various political and religious factions. Of the committee's four Republicans and two Democrats, two were Protestant, two Catholic, and two Jewish.

Under the chairmanship of Mrs. Gordon, the joint committee proceeded on a number of fronts. Believing its first function should be that of listening, it offered ample opportunity through public hearings and private conferences for every interested party to state his case. More systematic research was carried on by the committee's own limited staff and through special projects entrusted to the Brooklyn Law School and the St. John's University School of Law —once again discreetly balancing non-Catholic and Catholic agencies.

In its interim reports of 1957, 1958, and 1959, the joint committee covered a wide range of topics—adoptions, fraud in matrimonial actions, alimony, separation agreements, marriage counseling, and conciliation. Among the specific measures recommended were family courts to replace existing children's courts and courts of domestic relations, procedures for the central collection of statistics, court appointment of special guardians to protect the interests of minor children in matrimonial actions, court approval for separation agreements affecting children, requirement of a higher degree of proof in annulment cases, and amendment of the penal law to make fraud upon the court or collusion in matrimonial actions a misdemeanor.[81]

The legislature handled the committee-sponsored bills gingerly. It gave the courts discretionary authority to provide voluntary conciliation services and specified improved procedures in marriage dissolutions based upon incurable insanity.[82] But the lawmakers were slow to implement more important committee recommendations. In 1958, the assembly rejected a bill to make fraud or collusion in matrimonial actions a misdemeanor[83]—a rejection that cast some doubt on the good faith of those who contended that the New York divorce laws needed only rigorous enforcement to make them perfect. The bill to permit the courts to appoint special guardians to protect the children's interest in divorce or annulment cases was also blocked—supposedly out of fear of placing too much patronage in the hands of the judges.[84]

Even if the legislature can be prodded into enacting all the committee-sponsored bills, the reforms are not likely to be effective. The basic difficulty in the New York situation is the unrealistic definition of the grounds for divorce. Under twentieth century

American conditions, husbands or wives deserted by their mates, or cruelly treated, or linked to alcoholics or drug addicts, or continually quarreling, claim a right of legal exit from their unhappy alliances. Once the law recognizes this, then the courts may be required to proceed judiciously, to require honest evidence, waiting periods, conciliation procedures, and adequate safeguards for the interests of the children. Until this basic difficulty is faced, however, all efforts to plug the dikes in New York divorce and annulment laws are likely to be self-defeating.

CHAPTER 15

The Path of Reason

More or less accurate American divorce statistics are now available for one hundred years. During this period the nation's annual crop of divorces has risen from about 7,400 in 1860 to 396,000 in 1959. The divorce rate has gone up from .3 per thousand in 1860 to 2.2 per thousand in 1959.[1] The frequency of divorce varies substantially among the different sections of the country, being generally high in the Far West and certain sections of the South and low on the eastern seaboard and in the agricultural Middle West. The five states with the highest rates in 1958 were Nevada (34.6), Oklahoma (5.5), Arizona (5.0), Florida (3.9), and Alabama (3.9). The five states with the lowest rates were New York (.5), New Jersey (.7), North Dakota (.8), South Dakota (.9), and Connecticut (1.0).[2]

Why has there been this increasing resort to divorce? Not, primarily, because of changes in the statute laws. In most states the grounds for divorce were as liberally defined in 1860 as they are today; in several the laws were more liberal at the earlier date.

The most striking feature to be observed in the accompanying graph is the increasing sensitivity of the divorce rate to economic and psychological factors of a general character. Up to 1913, the rate rose in slow and steady steps. Since then the frequency of divorce has followed the economic cycle, rising in periods of prosperity and falling in years of depression. War's impact has been still more dramatic. The hasty marriages, forced separations, and increased tensions of wartime drove the divorce rate to a high of 1.6 in 1920 and an alarming 4.3 in 1946. But more normal conditions during the 1950's permitted the rate to sink to 2.1 in 1958, the lowest since 1940.

Divorce has provided sociologists with an inviting subject for investigation for many years. Such pioneer works as Walter F. Willcox's *The Divorce Problem* (1891), George E. Howard's *History of Matrimonial Institutions* (1904), James P. Lichtenberger's *Divorce, A Study in Social Causation* (1909), and Arthur W. Calhoun's *A Social History of the American Family* (1917) avoided moral dogmatism and dealt with marriage and divorce as thoroughly human institutions. They explained that in earlier societies divorce had been a luxury available only to the privileged classes; the poor took out their frustrations in noisy quarrels and separated without resorting to the courts. Now divorce had become democratized and was within the means of a larger and larger segment of the population. The rising divorce rate reflected not only the higher standard of living but the changing status of women. The modern wife was less in awe of her husband, expected better treatment, and was quicker to seek relief in the divorce court than her grandmother had been. She was also less dependent economically on her husband and readier to take her chances on self-support.

By the 1930's, the sociological explanations had become more sophisticated. Impatiently brushing aside the historic grounds for divorce—adultery, desertion, cruelty, and the like—James P. Lichtenberger wrote in 1931: "There is but one cause for divorce, namely the culmination of the process of marriage disintegration of which specific incidents, serious or trivial, are but the indices of its regressive trend." [3] In 1941, Kimball Young depicted divorce as rooted in conflicts in the love life and the ego.[4] But why should there have been more ego conflicts in 1930 than in 1860? Here the sociologists had a wide field for gathering data and formulating theories. They demonstrated that divorce was more frequent among Protestants than among Catholics, but that it was still more common among those of mixed religious affiliations or no affiliation at all. They

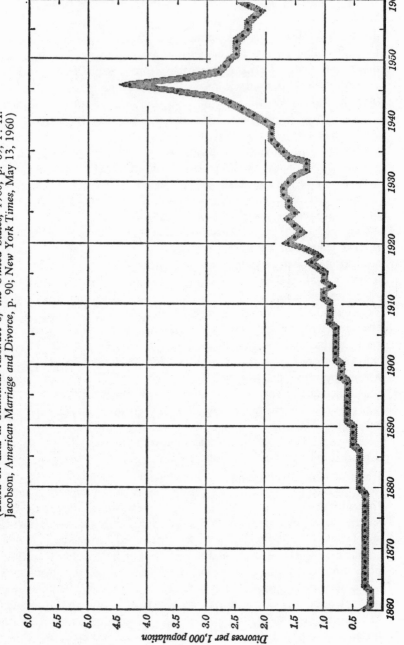

A CENTURY OF AMERICAN DIVORCE: 1860–1959

(Based on data in *Statistical Abstract of the United States,* 1960, p. 69; P. H. Jacobson, *American Marriage and Divorce,* p. 90; *New York Times,* May 13, 1960)

Divorces per 1,000 population

showed that the rate was higher among childless couples than among parents, that it was higher in urban than in rural districts, that it was higher in the earlier than in the later years of marriage, and that it was higher among semiskilled workers than among professional people.[5] Most of this seemed to confirm the common sense of the matter, that the increasing frequency of marriage failure was rooted in the tensions of modern living, in the desperate search for individual happiness, and in the highly differentiated American culture.

Even granting the many sources of friction in modern society, no one could be certain that there were more unhappy marriages in the twentieth century than there had been in earlier periods. But it was undeniable that more people resorted to divorce as a way out of their troubles. Each generation regarded divorce a little more tolerantly than did the preceding one. The social ostracism once imposed upon the divorced person had almost completely disappeared; the moral censure had been greatly diluted.

Against these new attitudes the Roman Catholic Church set its face as firmly as ever. In 1931, Pope Pius XI issued the encyclical *Casti conubii*, in which he restated the Church's historic position with great force. Marriage, the Pope declared, was a "perpetual and indissoluble bond which cannot be dissolved . . . by any civil law." [6] And, in 1958, the American bishops united in a statement defending the Church's right "to teach those moral principles which flow from the natural law and the positive law of God, and which are binding upon all men." The Church must uphold her own "concept of the holiness and inviolability of the marriage bond in a society which has legalized divorce and has advanced very far toward accepting it as a normal solution for marital problems of any kind." [7]

But to most Protestants the issue was not so simple. The Protestant Episcopal Church was sharply divided between those who wanted to follow the Catholics in condemning all divorce and those who wanted to acknowledge that divorce might be justifiable under certain circumstances. In 1916, the conservatives put up a strong fight for a canon prohibiting any remarriage of divorced persons during the lifetime of their former mates. This proposal passed the house of bishops and was defeated by a narrow margin in the house of deputies.[8] A decade later the pressure for change came from the opposite direction. Believing it unrealistic to permit remarriage only to the innocent parties in cases involving adultery, the liberals obtained the appointment of a commission to study the problem. In 1931, this group recommended that a divorced person's request to remarry should be submitted to an ecclesiastical court, which was to permit the new union if it decided "that the spiritual welfare of the applicant will be best served thereby." [9] But the conservatives strongly opposed this broad grant of discretion, and the general convention finally adopted a compromise permitting some relaxation of the old rule without surrendering the doctrine of indissoluble marriage. The new canon provided that any person whose former marriage had been dissolved by a civil court might apply to his bishop to have this former marriage declared null and void by reason of some one of nine historic impediments to marriage.[10]

Although this 1931 formula satisfied neither the conservatives nor the liberals, it remained the law of the Episcopal Church until 1946, when after another sharp debate a new compromise was hammered out. The revised canon still required the permission of the bishop for a divorced church member to marry again. This permission was to be granted only if in the earlier marriage certain impediments were found "to exist or to have existed which manifestly establish that no marriage bond as the same is recognized by this Church exists." The historic impediments were now broadened to include "such defects of personality as to make competent or free consent impossible." [11] Under this deliberately ambiguous formula the conservative bishops could refuse to invalidate first marriages except when some impediment could be proved to have existed from the beginning, while the liberal bishops could recognize latent "defects of personality" that had become dominant only in later married life.

Meanwhile, a somewhat similar struggle was in progress in the Methodist Church. Throughout the 1920's, successive general conferences retained the rule prohibiting ministers from marrying divorced persons except the innocent parties in cases involving adultery. This law was modified in 1932 to permit the remarriage of the innocent party in cases where "the true cause for divorce was adultery or other vicious conditions which through mental or physical cruelty or physical peril invalidated the marriage vow." [12] But the ministers became increasingly skeptical of basing the right of remarriage on the notoriously tricky concept of "innocence" in divorce actions. In 1960, this troublesome provision was dropped and each minister was enjoined to solemnize the marriage of a divorced person "only when he has satisfied himself by careful counseling that: (a) the divorced person is sufficiently aware of the factors leading to the failure of the previous marriage, (b) the divorced person is sincerely preparing to make the proposed marriage truly Christian, and (c) sufficient time has elapsed for adequate preparation and counseling." [13]

Until 1952, both the northern and southern branches of the Presbyterian Church continued to require that their ministers marry only those divorced persons who had been the innocent parties to dissolutions based on scriptural grounds—that is, adultery and willful desertion. But the northern church liberalized this rule in May, 1952, to permit ministers to marry divorced persons if they were satisfied that "there is penitence for past sin and failure and the intention to enter, with the help of God and through His church, into a marriage of love, honor, forbearance and loyalty, which will continue as long as both shall live." [14] In 1959, the Southern Presbyterians adopted a very similar rule. [15]

The United Lutheran Church of America also revised its policy toward divorce. Since 1930, its rule had been to limit the right of remarriage to the innocent party, but in 1956 it voted to permit a new marriage where there was evidence of repentance. Pastors and congregations were to base their decisions "on the particular circumstances in each case." [16]

Protestant acceptance of the idea that divorce might be justifiable in particular cases did not mean a complacent attitude toward problems of the family. On the contrary, Protestant ministers during the 1940's and 1950's undertook much more seriously than ever before their responsibility to counsel couples before and after marriage. Believing that divorce was the result, rather than the cause, of wrecked marriage, they sought the aid of doctors, psychologists, and social workers in getting at the real sources of family friction. With much of this new emphasis the Roman Catholic Church could agree. Like their Protestant counterparts, Catholic priests became increasingly involved in organizing classes for young people planning to marry and in counseling with husbands and wives involved in family quarrels.

During the 1920's, a number of writers called for divorce by mutual consent. The well known novelist and essayist, Katherine Fullerton Gerould, wrote in 1923: "So long as marriage is easy, divorce must be easy—ought, probably, to be easier than it is. . . . If you make it possible to marry at sight, you ought to make it possible to divorce on demand." [17] In 1928, Stephen Ewing made a similar plea, pointing with approval to experiments with divorce by mutual consent in the Scandinavian countries.[18] In 1927, Judge Ben B. Lindsey of the Denver Juvenile Court provoked heated controversy by advocating "companionate marriage," a plan whereby young couples could test their compatibility with the aid of legalized birth control and divorce by mutual consent.[19]

But other reformers were not prepared to go this far. The state, they argued, did have a legitimate interest in the preservation of marriages. This was so clear as to require little argument, where minor children were involved. It was not equally clear in the case of childless couples, but here too the community was injured when divorce set adrift untrained women unable to support themselves or when marriage dissolutions were followed by emotional disturbances and mental breakdowns. On the other hand, when marriages had finally and irretrievably failed, most authorities believed that it was healthier to have the union dissolved than to perpetuate it. Roswell H. Johnson, a professional marriage counselor, warned against what he called "suppressed divorces"—that is, divorces that did not take place despite the fact that they were needed to solve the personal problems of the parties. He called for divorce laws that would minimize such suppression while avoiding divorces that would be more harmful than beneficial. "A law should not have as its sole aim the reduction of the divorce rate," Johnson argued, "It should seek the wisest decision in each case as such, and let the divorce rate be so determined." [20] Morris Ernst, well known New York lawyer, called for "fewer but better" divorces. "It is in the interst of the state to maintain the home if possible, but also to dissolve the marriage with the least possible damage if the principals refuse to go on with it." [21]

To deny divorce or to greatly restrict it created more problems than it solved. This lesson, clearly to be drawn from the experience of New York State, was confirmed by developments in the District of Columbia and South Carolina.

Prior to 1901, the courts of the national capital had been authorized to grant divorces on four grounds: adultery, desertion, drunkenness, and cruelty. Since this law had been more liberal than that of neighboring Maryland and Virginia, Washington had become a minor divorce colony to the scandal of the reformers of the day. Many of the nation's religious leaders urged Congress to set a good example to the states, and the lawmakers responded by incorporating in the District of Columbia Code of 1901 stringent features copied from the New York law. Absolute divorce was to be granted only on the ground of adultery.[22]

But to follow the New York model was to invite the same kind of troubles that had long plagued that state. Inevitably the unhappily married of Washington sought divorces elsewhere, either by trekking out to Reno or by establishing residences in Arlington County, Virginia. These migratory divorces occasionally ran into trouble when their validity was challenged in the courts. Disallowing a Nevada divorce in 1934, the Court of Appeals conceded that a divorce law based only on adultery was probably "neither adequate or appropriate to the life of the community" and tended "to produce a train of perjury, bigamy and bastardy." [23] The remedy, the Court implied, lay with Congress.

In 1935, Congress liberalized the District law to permit divorce on four grounds: adultery, imprisonment for felony, desertion for two years, and voluntary separation without cohabitation for five years. In cases of cruelty, the only immediate remedy was judicial separation, but the decree might be enlarged to one of absolute divorce two years later upon application of the innocent party.[24] The statute's somewhat paradoxical character—liberal in permitting divorce after five years' voluntary separation, conservative in not recognizing insanity or alcoholism as causes—resulted from jockeying in Congress between those who wanted a thoroughly progressive statute and those who feared to have the District law too far out of line with that of Maryland and Virginia.[25]

An even more striking reversal of divorce policy was that adopted by South Carolina in 1948. Summarizing the state's record, a local scholar had once written: "There never has been a divorce in South Carolina—province, colony or State—except during the Reconstruction period after the war between the States, under the government of strangers, adventurers, and negroes, upheld by Federal bayonets." [26]

The brief earlier experience with divorce had come during the period of carpetbag rule. In 1868, a new state constitution had vested divorce jurisdiction in the courts of common pleas, and in 1872 the legislature had implemented this with a statute recognizing adultery and willful desertion as grounds. But the overthrow of the carpetbaggers had been followed by an immediate return to the older policy. In 1878, the legislature had repealed all laws relating to the granting of divorce, and in 1895 the revised state constitution had locked the door with the stern command: "Divorces from the bonds of matrimony shall not be allowed in this State." [27]

South Carolina's conservatism had its inevitable consequence in driving the unhappily married either to seek their freedom in other states, particularly in neighboring Georgia, or to defy convention by forming irregular alliances. Opponents of the no-divorce policy alleged that there were more people living in adultery or practicing bigamy in South Carolina than in any other state.[28] The local authorities tried to combat these abuses by sporadically prosecuting for adultery parties who had contracted second marriages after obtaining out-of-state divorces.[29]

During the 1940's, the South Carolina bar association spearheaded a drive to legalize divorce. By 1947, this demand had become so insistent that the legislature voted to submit to the citizenry a constitutional amendment that would permit divorce on four grounds: adultery, desertion, physical cruelty, or habitual drunkenness.

Realizing the importance of the issue, the Charleston County League of Women Voters undertook to encourage study and discussion of the proposed amendment. At a meeting on October 18,

1948, women favoring the change argued that when a married couple no longer accepted their mutual agreement no amount of legal force could keep them married. The failure of the state to provide a divorce law merely made the state "a party to any immorality or unhappiness which may result from the inability of the couple to get a divorce." [30] On the other hand, opponents contended that approval of the proposed constitutional amendment would lessen respect for marriage and increase the number of divorces.

The conservatives put up a resolute fight. The Fairfield Baptist Association, meeting in Columbia, resolved to oppose the amendment because it would "give divorce on grounds that the New Testament does not allow." [31] Several other religious groups took a similar stand. The *News & Courier* of Charleston based its opposition on racial grounds:

To this time, divorce has been unfashionable, or unknown, among South Carolina's negroes. Enactment of divorce laws would make it immediately popular among them and would yield handsome revenue to colored attorneys. . . .[32]

In later editorials the *News & Courier* reiterated this argument and also alluded to the disgraceful conditions alleged to abound in the states that permitted divorce. "Shall South Carolina also aid and abet in making the marriage contract a thing meaningless and contemptible?" [33]

When the ballots were counted on November 2, 1948, there were 57,000 votes in favor of the divorce amendment to 42,000 opposed. The proposal still required the approval of the state legislature, and here in March, 1949, the conservatives put up their last stand. Senator O. T. Wallace of Charleston claimed that the popular will had not been truly expressed, since many who had voted for President had ignored the divorce question. The prodivorce election victory had "been interpreted as a shout when it was really a whisper." In any case, Wallace argued, "the state cannot pass a law that is superior to the law of God." [34] But once again the conservatives failed, and on March 31, 1949, the legislature completed the ratification of the constitutional amendment.[35] Two weeks later,

the lawmakers quietly passed a bill authorizing the courts to grant
divorce on the four specified grounds and fixing a one-year residence
period.[36]

If some divorces are bad both for society and for the individuals
involved and others serve a necessary surgical purpose, how is the
good of divorce to be secured and the bad avoided? Although they
disagree on details, present-day authorities all emphasize the importance of improved court procedures. The tribunals that deal with
such cases ought to be dignified and unhurried. They should act
upon the basis of the fullest information about the parties themselves and their children. They ought to encourage reconciliation
where this is possible; where it is not, they should grant the divorce
under conditions that protect the interests of all parties concerned
and particularly those of the children.

Unfortunately, most divorce courts depart from this ideal model
at almost every point. The jurist hearing the case is rarely an expert; he is usually a judge from some court of more general jurisdiction assigned to divorce business as an unwelcome chore. Confronted with a crowded docket, he deals with each case as speedily
as possible. In less than 10 per cent of the actions is there any
genuine contest, in which one party is attempting to defend himself against the charges of the other. Instead of hearing the conflicting testimony of a variety of witnesses with vigorous cross-
examination, the divorce court judge usually hears only the plaintiff
and whatever corroborating witnesses are needed under state law.
The trial is not a genuine inquiry at all; it is only a perfunctory
ritual through which statutory requirements are met. An observer of
a Chicago divorce court was impressed by the monotonous repeti-
tion with which wives testified to their husband's "extreme cruelty."
Each had been slapped in the face exactly twice; once would not
have been enough, more than twice would have been redundant.[37]

Most shocking of all is the hurried and offhand way in which
the divorce court judge may decide such vitally important issues as
the custody of the children and the amount of support to be paid.
Usually the judge merely ratifies the separation agreement that has
been drawn up by the lawyers representing the husband and wife.
Yet these documents are rarely the products of sensible thinking;
usually they are mere treaties with provisions determined by the

relative bargaining power of the two sides. If the husband is the one more eager to gain his freedom, he may buy his wife's consent by surrendering the custody of the children or by promising to pay more alimony than he can really afford. If it is the wife who most wants the divorce, she may take less than she needs. In either case, the real welfare of the children is seldom the overriding consideration that it should be.

Standing in the way of a genuine inquiry are not only the divorce court judge's lack of time and staff but also certain antiquated legal doctrines. Originally erected as safeguards against easy divorce, these "defenses" are rooted in the premise that divorce is an adversary proceeding in which an "innocent" party attempts to prove his mate "guilty" of certain sins for which divorce is the proper punishment. Under this concept, when both parties are substantially at fault, no divorce can be granted. Yet this doctrine of "recrimination" is patently unrealistic. In most unhappy marriages husband and wife have both fallen short of perfection. Reconciliation can be achieved only if both recognize their faults and make a cooperative effort to repair the union. If such a reconciliation cannot be achieved, a rational divorce procedure would dissolve the union without attempting to brand one party innocent and the other guilty. Equally troublesome is the doctrine of "condonation." If the "innocent" party continues to live—or sleep—with the "guilty" party after he becomes aware of the latter's wrong behavior, this bars divorce. A more ingenious way of discouraging reconciliation could scarcely be devised. If a marriage counselor persuades a separated couple that they should try living together again, they may find it difficult to establish grounds for divorce in case the reconciliation fails. Similarly unrealistic is the doctrine that divorce must be refused if there is evidence of "collusion" between the parties. This principle hampers realistic marriage counseling by preserving the fiction that parties contemplating divorce can safely deal with each other only at arms' length.

In December, 1947, the *Atlantic Monthly* published an article entitled "Dishonest Divorce" by Reginald Heber Smith, widely respected Boston lawyer and father of the Legal Aid movement. The author pointed out the fallacies in the old premise of sin and punishment and called for the adoption of a new realistic premise

based upon the law's power to create, enforce, and dissolve contracts—a power that should be used to deal with family quarrels on
the basis of diagnosis and therapy. Ideal divorce procedure, in
Smith's view, would follow some such pattern as this. Persons seeking a divorce would petition the court where they resided. They
would present, not legal "causes," but the essential facts about themselves and their children. The judge would talk to husband and wife,
together or singly, or both. He would meet with them as long or as
many times as he thought beneficial. The case would then stand
over a period of six months, during which the judge would have
investigations made by specially trained personnel. At the end of
the waiting period, the judge would again talk with husband and
wife. "If, having used all the power and persuasiveness at his dis-
posal, he failed to effect a reconciliation, or a reconsideration, or
even a postponement, he would grant the divorce. Except in very rare
instances, there would be no fight in open court about 'causes.' " [38]
The judge would then take firm control of the welfare of the children,
determining their custody and means of support, and would keep this
control throughout the children's minority.

As chairman of the American Bar Association's delegation to the
White House Conference on Family Life in May, 1948, Smith presented an elaboration of the position that he had outlined in the
Atlantic Monthly article. So impressed was the Legal Section of
the conference that it unanimously recommended the creation of a
special commission to study the divorce problem from this point of
view. Two years later the Interprofessional Commission on Marriage
and Divorce Laws was created with a membership composed of lawyers, law teachers, judges, marriage counselors, psychiatrists, educa-
tors, sociologists, clergymen, and others. Under the chairmanship of
Judge Paul W. Alexander of Toledo, Ohio, the commission set for
itself the ambitious program of formulating new, realistic, and humane premises for the law of divorce, testing these hypotheses
through extensive research into the actual workings of the nation's
divorce courts, and reporting its findings to the National Conference of Commissioners on Uniform State Laws for preparation of a
model statute.[39] Although the American Bar Association and certain
foundations provided modest grants for the Interprofessional Commission's studies, these funds were inadequate for carrying out the

full program. Despite this handicap, the Commission made a number of valuable contributions. In 1951, it made a preliminary attempt to state the new premises to be tested:

1. Basing divorce on guilt and punishment has proven harmful to family stability.
2. The use of adversary procedures in divorce cases should be displaced.
3. The approach to the subject of divorce should be therapeutic with the interest of the family as the motivating factor.[40]

Among the several research projects sponsored by the Interprofessional Commission, the most ambitious was that of Maxine Virtue into the actual operation of the divorce courts in a number of American cities. Mrs. Virtue's book, *Family Cases in Court*, published in 1956, may be considered as the major report of the Interprofessional Commission.

Mrs. Virtue's findings strongly support the contention that the starting point for divorce law reform should be the establishment of unified family courts to put an end to the splintering of jurisdiction under which separate courts deal with divorce, custody of children, adoptions, bastardy, and juvenile delinquency. These family courts should handle these cases as problems in human relations. In 1945, Judge Alexander stated the idea with admirable clarity: "We took the children out of the adult criminal courts and put them into a socialized court, the juvenile court. . . . Since the problems in a divorce case are so much more social than legal, why isn't it logical to take the embattled spouses out of the antiquated old divorce mill with its creaking legalistic machinery and put them into a socialized court, as we have done with the juveniles?"[41]

The family court idea has made great progress in Ohio. The first tribunal to obtain most of the desired jurisdiction was the Division of Domestic Relations of the Court of Common Pleas in Cincinnati, over which Judge Charles W. Hoffman began to preside in 1914. The success of the Cincinnati experiment induced the Ohio legislature to extend the system to six other large counties, including all the major cities of the state except Cleveland. In 1938, the legislature gave the Ohio divorce courts discretionary power to make investigations into the character, family relations, past conduct, earning ability, and financial worth of the parties. In 1951, such investigations were made mandatory in all divorce cases where children under the age of fourteen were involved. The Ohio family courts used this authority to build up competent professional staffs.[42] "These Ohio family courts," Mrs. Virtue concluded, "probably exhibit at its most highly developed the therapeutic or humane handling of divorce cases." [43] Judge Alexander's own Toledo court was an outstanding example of this. Although Cleveland did not have a unified family court, it was a pioneer in linking divorce procedure with investigation of the parties, this being the function of the Cleveland Court of Common Pleas' department of domestic relations, established in 1920.[44]

Elsewhere in the country there were a number of other experiments with the family court idea. Tribunals either bearing this name or with similar functions were to be found in Milwaukee, St. Louis, Omaha, Des Moines, Portland (Oregon), and Washington, D.C. In 1949, the states of Washington and Texas initiated judicial reforms along this line.[45]

At least 40 per cent of American divorces have minor children involved, and it is in their protection that the family courts do their best work. But even in states with more conventional divorce courts, much may be done to put custody and support orders on a more intelligent basis. In 1918, the judges of the Wayne County Circuit Court in Detroit created the office of Friend of the Court. The next year the Michigan legislature extended the idea to require the appointment of a Friend of the Court in each county. The duty of this official was to make investigations in all cases involving alimony or the custody and support of children. In metropolitan counties like Wayne, the Friend of the Court employed a large professional staff for this purpose. In California, the San Francisco courts and some of the others have developed investigatory procedures to protect the interests of children involved in divorce cases.[46]

The divorce of their parents is not necessarily the worst thing that can happen to children. "I'll Take My Parents Separately," wrote "Gretchen" in Harper's in 1938, claiming that the children of divorced parents were freed from excessive attachment to home and learned how to avoid mistakes in their own marriages.[47] In 1960, Professor F. Ivan Nye of the State College of Washington announced findings based upon the study of a group of high school pupils: the children of divorced parents suffered less from psychomatic ailments, were less inclined toward delinquency, and had a better relationship with their parents than children whose parents quarreled perpetually.[48]

Nevertheless, the more conscientious divorce courts proceeded on the assumption that the children's best interests would be served if their parents could achieve a sound reconciliation. Therefore, in the Ohio family courts, in the Michigan Friend of the Court's office, and in other progressive jurisdictions attempts were made to establish procedures for conciliation.

Perhaps the most ambitious experiment along these lines was the Los Angeles Children's Court of Conciliation. This was established at the urging of Judge Ben B. Lindsey, who had moved to California after many controversial years as a juvenile court judge in Colorado. In 1939, the California legislature authorized the establishment of a children's court of conciliation in each county. The law provided that prior to the filing of any action for divorce, annulment, or separate maintenance, either spouse or both might petition the conciliation court for assistance in saving the marriage. The court was given jurisdiction to hear any family controversy where minor children were involved. No formal charges were to be made, proceedings were to be informal, and the judge was empowered to invoke the assistance of doctors, clergymen, and others. After either spouse had requested conciliation, there could be no petition for divorce for a period of thirty days. After this period, in cases that had been before it for conciliation, the special court was empowered to hear actions for divorce. Judge Lindsey was the first judge of the Los Angeles Children's Court of Conciliation, serving until his death in 1943.[49] The court claimed an impressive record of success. In 1959, Judge Louis H. Burke reported that over the preceding five years the conciliation court had been able to reconcile 43 per cent of the couples willing to listen to professional marriage counselors. He claimed that three-quarters of the reconciliations proved permanent.[50] This record would not have been possible, if the Los Angeles conciliation efforts had been postponed until the actual filing of the divorce petition with its specific charges—an embittering process likely to sweep a faltering marriage beyond the point of no return.

Despite the apparent success of the Los Angeles Children's Court of Conciliation, no other California county adopted the system. Many judges and lawyers regarded the experiment with suspicion as another example of Judge Lindsey's notorious lack of legal orthodoxy. They also disliked the Los Angeles court's heavy reliance on professional marriage counselors and social workers. They preferred to have efforts at conciliation carried on through more conventional channels.[51]

In Illinois a group of reformers made a long fight for new divorce procedures that would require waiting periods and efforts at conciliation. A 1947 act of the Illinois legislature was declared unconstitutional as special legislation applying only to Cook County (Chicago); a 1949 law was invalidated because it delegated legislative powers to the judiciary, tended to the establishment of religion by providing for the use of clergymen in reconciliation efforts, and violated due process of law in allowing investigatory reports to take the place of oral evidence; a 1953 law was declared unconstitutional because it deprived litigants of their prompt access to the courts. At long last, in 1955, the legislature succeeded in framing a statute that the Illinois Supreme Court would uphold. Under the new procedure, the plaintiff in a divorce case initiated the action by filing a so-called "praecipe" for summons. The defendant was thus put on notice that a divorce action was impending and was given thirty days to file his answer, but, except in unusual cases, no formal complaint was to be filed for a period of sixty days. Although the law did not require that this sixty-day "cooling-off" period should be used for conciliation efforts, it served this purpose in the hands of the more conscientious judges.[52]

The importance of making the conciliation effort before the filing of formal charges was illustrated by experience elsewhere. In 1957, the New Jersey Supreme Court tried the experiment in ten counties of requiring a conciliation effort in all divorce cases where minor children were involved or where one of the parties requested it. The Court terminated the program in 1960, announcing that reconciliation had been achieved in only 3 per cent of the cases. To be effective, the judges decided, marriage counseling must be available before marriage problems reached the divorce court.[53] After studying many court-connected counseling efforts, Mrs. Virtue's conclusions were not so negative. She believed that even when reconciliation was not achieved, professional counselors were able to ease the emotional tension suffered by the parties to divorce and to help the courts make a wise disposition of the cases.[54]

The lack of uniformity in American divorce law has long been a subject for lamentation. Earnest reformers have sought to remedy the situation by convincing the state legislatures that they should pass uniform statutes or by shifting the whole responsibility upon Congress through an amendment to the Federal Constitution. Yet something can be said on the other side. States and even counties have served as useful laboratories where hundreds of courts have been able to experiment with different methods of handling family problems. Out of this local trial and error much that is hopeful for the future has evolved. Unified family courts, staffs of trained investigators, safeguards for the interests of children, waiting periods, efforts at reconciliation, marriage counseling—any or all of these may help to prevent divorces that are unnecessary and to reduce the human damage from those that must be granted.

But better procedures are not enough. The Toledo family court is considered a model of its kind, yet its famous judge, Paul W. Alexander, writes: "Under presently subsisting law it appears that none of the handful of existing family courts has so far been able to achieve more than a fraction of its potential." The *ideal* family court, Judge Alexander continues, will require the fundamental changes in substantive law indicated by the first two assumptions of the Interprofessional Commission, "the substitution for guilt of a new and superior criterion and the consequent displacement of the conventional adversary procedures and the absurd and paradoxical 'defenses.' " [55] In such a reform, the old "grounds" for divorce would probably disappear except as symptoms of the sickness of a particular marriage. The test for divorce, writes Morris Ploscowe, should not be whether the "defendant" has committed adultery or cruelty or failed to support his wife or deserted, but "whether all life has gone out of the marriage." [56]

Notes

1. The Land of Make-Believe

[1] *Nevada State Journal* (Reno), May 9, 13, 1959.

[2] *New York Times*, May 13, 14, 1959.

[3] *Ibid.*, Sept. 27, 1955.

[4] Richard Booth, "Elizabeth Taylor: Aftermath of Scandal," *McCall's*, LXXXVI (Jan., 1960), 37 ff.

[5] *New York Times*, Sept. 11, 1958.

[6] *Ibid.*, Feb. 20, 1959.

[7] Justice Henry Clay Greenberg, "New York's Perjury Mills," *American Magazine*, CXLIV (Oct., 1947), 46 ff.

[8] Judge Charles S. Desmond, "The Annulment Problem," *New York State Bar Association Bulletin*, XX (April, 1948), 59-65.

[9] *World Almanac and Book of Facts, 1960* (New York: New York World-Telegram and The Sun, 1960), p. 317.

2. The Long Arm of the Past

[1] Edward Westermarck, *The History of Human Marriage* (5th ed., New York: Allerton Book Co., 1922), III, 318-323.

[2] Deuteronomy xxiv, 1-2.

[3] David W. Amran, *The Jewish Law of Divorce* (Philadelphia: Edward Stern & Co., 1896), pp. 32-35.

[4] Matthew xix, 4-9 (Revised Standard Version).

[5] See Mark ix, 2-9; Luke xvi, 18; and also Matthew v, 31-32.

[6] I Corinthians vii, 15.

[7] St. Augustine, *Treatises on Marriage and Other Subjects*, ed. by Roy J. Deferrari (New York: Fathers of the Church, Inc., 1955), p. 31.

[8] *Ibid.*, pp. 47-48.

[9] Ephesians v, 24-27, 31-32.

[10] I Corinthians vii, 8.

[11] St. Augustine, *Treatises on Marriage*, p. 22.

[12] *Ibid.*, p. 23.

[13] James Bryce, "Marriage and Divorce under Roman and English Law," *Studies in History and Jurisprudence* (New York: Oxford University Press, 1901), II, 803-805.

244

14 George E. Howard, *A History of Matrimonial Institutions* (Chicago: University of Chicago Press, 1904), II, 38, 44-45.

15 *Ibid.*, II, 53-54.

16 John Fulton, *The Laws of Marriage* (New York: E. & J. B. Young & Co., 1883), pp. 29-80; Charles E. Smith, *Papal Enforcement of Some Medieval Marriage Laws* (University, La.: Louisiana State University Press, 1940), pp. 5-53.

17 Howard, *History of Matrimonial Institutions*, II, 308-311.

18 Chilton L. Powell, *English Domestic Relations, 1487-1653* (New York: Columbia University Press, 1917), pp. 3-4.

19 *Ibid.*, pp. 6-7.

20 *Ibid.*, pp. 72-74.

21 G. G. Coulton, *Five Centuries of Religion* (Cambridge: Cambridge University Press, 1923-50), III, 695-696.

22 Ch. Petit-Dutaillis, *The Feudal Monarchy in France and England from the Tenth to the Thirteenth Century* (London: Kegan Paul, Trench, Trubner & Co., 1936), pp. 105-107. See also Smith, *Medieval Marriage Laws*, pp. 159-162.

23 Historical Manuscripts Commission, *Twelfth Report*, Appendix, Part VIII (London: H. M. Stationer's Office, 1891), p. 123.

24 Hist. Manuscripts Comm., Fourth Report (1874), Pt. I, p. 507.

25 Hist. Manuscripts Comm., *Reports*, Vol. XVII³ (1911), p. 120.

26 Fulton, *The Laws of Marriage*, p. 262.

27 *Ibid.*, p. 8.

28 *Ibid.*, pp. 79-80.

29 *Ibid.*, p. 63.

30 *Ibid.*, pp. 197-198.

3. Impact of the Protestant Revolt

1 "The Sermon on the Mount," *Luther's Works* (St. Louis: Concordia Publishing House, 1955-   ), XXI, 93.

2 Ewald M. Plass, comp., *What Luther Says: An Anthology* (St. Louis: Concordia Publishing House, 1959), II, 886.

3 *Luther's Works*, XXI, 93.

4 *Ibid.*, 94.

5 *What Luther Says*, II, 900-901.

6 Theodore Woolsey, "Divorce," *New Englander*, XXVII (Jan., 1868), 15.

7 *Ibid.*, 16, 20n.

8 *Ibid.*, 21-22.

9 Leviticus xviii; 16.

10 See depositions in *Letters and Papers Foreign and Domestic of the Reign of Henry VIII* (London, 1875-1920), IV, 2576-2582.

11 32 Henry VIII, cap. 38. *The Statutes at Large of England and Great Britain . . .* (London, 1811), II, 173-174.

12 George E. Howard, *History of Matrimonial Institutions* (Chicago: University of Chicago Press, 1904), II, 78.

13 *Ibid.*, II, 72.

14 *Ibid.*, II, 76.

15 *Ibid.*, II, 80.

16 *Ibid.*, II, 82.

17 Chilton L. Powell, *English Domestic Relations, 1487-1653* (New York: Columbia University Press, 1917), p. 78.

18 *Ibid.*, pp. 79-80.

19 *Ibid.*, pp. 68-70.

20 *Doctrine and Discipline of Divorce*, Bk. 1, ch. i, *The Prose Works of John Milton*, ed. by R. W. Griswold (Philadelphia: John W. Moore, 1847), I, 201.

21 *Doctrine and Discipline of Divorce*, Bk. 2, ch. xxi, *ibid.*, I, 250.

22 *Doctrine and Discipline of Divorce*, Bk. 1, ch. vi, *ibid.*, I, 208.

23 Powell, *English Domestic Relations*, pp. 225-230.

24 *Tetrachordon*, *Milton's Prose Works*, I, 321.

25 James P. Lichtenberger, *Divorce, A Study in Social Causation* (New York: Columbia University Press, 1909), p. 125.

26 James Bryce, "Marriage and Divorce," *Studies in History and Jurisprudence* (New York: Oxford University Press, 1901), II, 827.

27 "On the Scots Law of Divorce," *Blackwood's Edinburgh Magazine*, II (Nov., 1817), 184.

28 Howard, *History of Matrimonial Institutions*, I, 408-421.

29 John Cordy Jeaffreson, *Brides and Bridals* (London: Hurst and Blackett, 1872), II, 339.

30 Howard, *History of Matrimonial Institutions*, II, 83.

31 Jeaffreson, *Brides and Bridals*, II, 340.

32 John Macqueen, *A Practical Treatise on the Appellate Jurisdiction of the House of Lords & Privy Council* (London: A. Maxwell & Sons, 1842), p. 554.

33 *Ibid.*, pp. 562-574.

34 *Ibid.*, pp. 574-576.

35 Lord St. Helier, "Divorce," *Encyclopaedia Britannica* (11th ed., New York, 1910), VIII, 339.

36 Macqueen, *Practical Treatise*, pp. 496, 505-506.

37 *Ibid.*, pp. 474-482.

38 *Boswell's Life of Johnson*, ed. by G. B. Hill (New York: Harper & Bros., 1891), II, 63-64.

39 Howard, *History of Matrimonial Institutions*, II, 109-115.

4. DIVORCE IN THE AMERICAN COLONIES

1 William Bradford, *Of Plymouth Plantation, 1620-1647*, ed. by S. E. Morison (New York: Alfred A. Knopf, 1952), p. 86.

2 *Ibid.*, p. 274.

3 Howard, *History of Matrimonial Institutions* (Chicago: University of Chicago Press, 1904), II, 132.

4 *Ibid.*, II, 349-351.

5 *Winthrop's Journal "History of New England," 1630-1649*, ed. by J. K. Hosmer (New York: Charles Scribner's Sons, 1908), II, 330.

6 *Acts and Laws, Passed by the Great and General Court . . . of the Massachusetts Bay . . . Begun at Boston, the Eighth Day of June, 1692 . . .* (Boston: Benjamin Harris, 1692), p. 33.

7 William H. Whitmore, ed., *The Colonial Laws of Massachusetts . . .* (Boston: Rockwell & Churchill, 1889), p. 142. See also Charles Cowley, *Our Divorce Courts: Their Origin and History* (Lowell: Penhallow Printing Co., 1879), p. 12.

8 Cowley, *Our Divorce Courts*, pp. 28-31; Howard, *History of Matrimonial Institutions*, II, 332-340.

9 *Acts and Laws of Massachusetts Bay, 1692*, p. 33.

10 Cotton Mather, *Magnalia Christi Americana; or, The Ecclesiastical History of New-England* (Hartford: Silas Andrus & Son, 1853), II, 253-254.

11 *Acts and Laws, of His Majesties Province of the Massachusetts Bay, in New-England* (Boston: Green and Allen, 1699), p. 66.

12 *Ibid.*, p. 135.

13 Howard, II, 345-347.

14 *Ibid.*, II, 354.

15 *Acts and Laws of his Majesties Colony of Connecticut in New England* (New London, 1715), pp. 167-168.

16 J. Hammond Trumbull, comp., *The Public Records of the Colony of Connecticut* (Hartford: Brown & Parsons, 1856), I, 205, 301.

17 Howard, II, 357.

18 *Ibid.*, II, 358-359.

19 Benjamin Trumbull, *An Appeal to the Public, Especially to the Learned with Respect to the Unlawfulness of Divorces* (New Haven: J. Meiggs, 1788), p. 46.

[20] Cowley, *Our Divorce Courts,* p. 22; Howard, II, 360.

[21] Howard, II, 361, 363.

[22] *Ibid.,* II, 365.

[23] *Ibid.,* II, 348-349.

[24] *Ibid.,* II, 366-371.

[25] *Ibid.,* II, 371-376.

[26] Matteo Spalletta, "Divorce in Colonial New York," *New-York Historical Society Quarterly,* XXXIX (Oct., 1955), 422-423.

[27] *Records of the Colony of Rhode Island and Providence Plantation in New England* (Providence, 1856), II, 160-163.

[28] Spalletta, *New-York Historical Society Quarterly,* XXXIX, 423-424.

[29] *The Colonial Laws of New York from the Year 1664 to the Revolution* (Albany: James B. Lyon, 1894), I, 45.

[30] *Ibid.,* I, 78.

[31] Spalletta, *New-York Historical Society Quarterly,* XXXIX, 428.

[32] *Ibid.,* pp. 431-432.

[33] *Ibid.,* pp. 428-429.

[34] *Ibid.,* pp. 433-434.

[35] Jean Cast to Governor Hunter, March 27, 1711, *Documents Relative to the Colonial History of the State of New York,* ed. by E. B. O'Callaghan (New York: Weed, Parsons & Co., 1855-1883), V, 215.

[36] Cadwallader Colden to his son, 1759, Cadwallader Colden, "Letters on Smith's History of New York," *New-York Historical Society Collections,* I (1868), 187.

[37] William Nelson, "The Early Marriage Laws of New Jersey, and the Influences Bearing upon Their Formation," *Archives of the State of New Jersey,* 1st Series, XXII (1900), cxxiii.

[38] George J. Edwards, Jr., *Divorce: Its Development in Pennsylvania and the Present Law and Practice Therein* (New York: Clark Boardman Co., 1930), pp. 5-7.

[39] William R. Riddell, "Legislative Divorce in Colonial Pennsylvania," *Pennsylvania Magazine of History and Biography,* LVII (1933), 175-177.

[40] *Ibid.,* p. 178.

[41] *N.Y. Colonial Documents,* VIII, 402.

5. THE WINE OF INDEPENDENCE

[1] *An Essay on Marriage; or, The Lawfulness of Divorce in Certain Cases Considered* . . . (Philadelphia: Zachariah Poulson, 1788), p. 3.

[2] *Ibid.,* p. 16.

[3] *Ibid.,* p. 15.

[4] *Ibid.,* p. 25.

[5] George J. Edwards, Jr., *Divorce: Its Development in Pennsylvania and the Present Law and Practice Therein* (New York: Clark Boardman Co., 1930), p. 8.

[6] 9 *Minutes of General Assembly of Pennsylvania,* 127 (Feb. 9, 1785).

[7] 9 *Laws of Pennsylvania,* chap. ccxxxiv (Sept. 19, 1785).

[8] *Acts and Laws of Massachusetts, 1785-86,* chap. xxxi (March 16, 1786).

[9] Henry M. Dexter, *The Congregationalism of the Last Three Hundred Years* . . . (New York: Harper & Bros., 1880), p. 606.

[10] Howard, *History of Matrimonial Institutions* (Chicago: University of Chicago Press, 1904), III, 11.

[11] *Ibid.,* III, 15.

[12] *Ibid.,* III, 14.

[13] 19 *Acts of General Assembly of New Jersey,* chap. cxiv (Dec. 2, 1794).

[14] *Laws of Tennessee,* 1799, chap. xix (Oct. 26, 1799); *Laws of Kentucky,* 1808-1809, chap. xxxi (Jan. 31, 1809); Howard, *History of Matrimonial Institutions,* III, 113.

[15] Howard, III, 31-32.

[16] Feb. 23, 1827, *Annals of Cleveland,* X, 100.

[17] Howard, III, 35, 56.

[18] *Statutes at Large of Virginia,* III, Dec., 1803, Session, chap. vi.

[19] Ibid., III, Dec., 1806, Session, chap. lix.

[20] Richmond Enquirer, Dec. 22, 1808.

[21] Acts of Virginia, 1826-1827, chap. xxiii.

[22] Howard, History of Matrimonial Institutions, III, 51.

[23] Ibid., III, 43.

[24] Ibid., II, 375.

[25] Ibid., III, 44.

[26] Ibid., III, 45.

[27] Acts of the General Assembly of Georgia, 1831 Session, pp. 105-121.

[28] Head v. Head (1847), 2 Georgia Reports, 196.

[29] Ibid., 195.

[30] Ibid., 191-211.

[31] Howard, History of Matrimonial Institutions, III, 50.

[32] Ibid., III, 61-62.

[33] Laws of Kentucky, 1807-1808 Session, chap. xliii.

[34] Ibid., chaps. lxxxvi, xcvi, cix.

[35] Ibid., 1819-20 Session, chap. dx.

[36] Maryland, Virginia, Georgia, Alabama, and Mississippi all at one time or another combined judicial trial with legislative divorce.

[37] James Kent, Commentaries on American Law (2nd ed., New York: O. Halsted, 1832), II, 117.

[38] Messages and Proclamations of the Governors of Missouri (Columbia: 1922——), I, 260-263.

[39] Ibid., I, 265-266.

[40] Acts of Missouri, 1832-1833 Session, chaps. xcvii-cix.

[41] Jeffersonian Republican, Jefferson, Mo., May 9, 1835.

[42] Ibid., Jan. 12, 19, 1839.

[43] Henry Folsom Page, A View of the Law Relative to the Subject of Divorce in Ohio, Indiana and Michigan (Columbus: J. H. Riley & Co., 1850), p. v.

[44] Cf. Howard, History of Matrimonial Institutions, III, 31-50, 96-101; and Franklin B. Hough, comp., Constitution of the State of New York,

Adopted in 1846, With a Comparative Arrangement of the Constitutional Provisions of Other States (Albany: Weed, Parson & Co., 1867), pp. 22-23, 78.

[45] Howard, III, 100-101; National League for the Protection of the Family, Report for 1897, p. 11.

[46] Howard, III, 109.

[47] Zephaniah Swift, A System of the Laws of the State of Connecticut (Windham: John Byrne, 1795), I, 192.

[48] Acts and Laws Passed by General Assembly of Connecticut, Held May, 1797, p. 457.

[49] Benjamin Trumbull, An Appeal to the Public, Especially to the Learned with Respect to the Unlawfulness of Divorces . . . (New Haven: J. Meiggs, 1788), p. 36.

[50] Ibid., p. 31.

[51] Ibid., p. 32.

[52] Rev. H. Loomis, "Divorce Legislation in Connecticut," The New Englander, XXV (July, 1866), 440.

[53] Timothy Dwight, Theology: Explained and Defended in a Series of Sermons (5th ed., New York: Carvill, 1828), III, 427.

[54] Ibid., III, 433.

[55] Ibid., III, 434.

[56] Howard, History of Matrimonial Institutions, III, 13.

[57] Columbian Register, New Haven, Conn., June 16, 1849.

[58] Ibid., May 26, 1849.

[59] Idem.

[60] Ibid., June 9, 1849.

[61] Ibid., May 26, 1849.

[62] Idem.

[63] Howard, III, 13.

[64] Laws of Massachusetts, 1811, chap. cxix.

[65] Howard, III, 7-8.

[66] Ibid., 8-10.

[67] Idem.

[68] Massachusetts Senate Documents, No. 314 (June 8, 1870), p. 2.

[69] Howard, III, 113-115.

70 Jan. 18, 1834, *Annals of Cleveland*, XVIII, 170.

71 April 21, 1842, *ibid.*, XXV, 99.

72 Feb. 9, 1846, *ibid.*, XXIX, 62.

73 Page, *Divorce in Ohio, Indiana, and Michigan*, p. vii.

6. NEW YORK HOLDS BACK

1 10 *New York Assembly Journal*, 19 (Jan. 22, 1787).

2 *Ibid.*, 48 (Feb. 14, 1787).

3 10 *Laws of New York*, chap. 69 (March 30, 1787).

4 Minutes of the New York Council of Revision, March 19, 1787, microfilm copy of original mss. in Records of the States.

5 10 *Ass. Journ.*, 125 (March 28, 1787); 10 *Senate Journ.*, 70 (March 30, 1787).

6 102 *Laws of New York*, chap. 321 (May 19, 1879).

7 36 *Senate Journ.*, 89 (Feb. 4, 1813), 93 (Feb. 5, 1813).

8 36 *Ass. Journ.*, 460-461 (March 26, 1813).

9 *Ibid.*, 531-536 (April 5, 1813).

10 *Ibid.*, 562 (April 7, 1813), 569 (April 8, 1813).

11 36 *Laws of New York*, chap. 102 (April 13, 1813).

12 47 *ibid.*, chap. 205 (April 10, 1824).

13 *Albany Argus and Daily City Gazette*, Nov. 24, 1827.

14 *Revised Statutes of the State of New York, Passed during the Years 1827 and 1828.* part 2, chap. 8, "Of the Domestic Relations."

15 Petition of Henry Steward, March 12, 1802, New York Assembly Papers, 6:51, New York State Library.

16 24 *Ass. Journ.*, 21 (Feb. 1, 1811).

17 32 *Private Laws of New York*, chap. 92 (March 24, 1809).

18 34 *Laws of New York*, chap. 212 (April 9, 1811).

19 34 *Ass. Journ.*, 101-102 (Feb. 18, 1811).

20 *Ibid.*, 151, 158, 167-168 (Feb. 25, 26, 28, 1811).

21 *Ibid.*, 354 (March 30, 1811); 34 *Senate Journ.*, 205-206 (April 8, 1811).

22 34 *Laws of New York*, chap. 212 (April 9, 1811).

23 [Richard McNemar], *The Other Side of the Question* (Cincinnati, 1819), p. 24.

24 *Ibid.*, pp. 22-28; Eunice Chapman, *No. 2, Being an Additional Account of the Shakers* (Albany, 1818), pp. 7-24.

25 38 *Ass. Journ.*, 168-169, 481, 558 (Feb. 7, March 28, April 8, 1815).

26 38 *Laws of New York*, chap. 221 (April 17, 1815).

27 39 *Senate Journ.*, 41 (Feb. 21, 1816).

28 *Ibid.*, 265-266 (April 12, 1816).

29 40 *Senate Journ.*, 226-227 (March 22, 1817).

30 *Ibid.*, 247, 282 (March 27, April 7, 1817).

31 41 *Senate Journ.*, 31 (Jan. 29, 1818).

32 *Albany Gazette and Daily Advertiser*, Jan. 29, 1818.

33 41 *Senate Journ.*, 31 (Jan. 29, 1818).

34 *Ibid.*, 37 (Feb. 2, 1818).

35 *Ibid.*, 98-101 (Feb. 27, 1818).

36 *Ibid.*, 111-112 (March 4, 1818).

37 *Albany Gazette*, March 12, 1818.

38 *Ibid.*, March 14, 1818.

39 *Ibid.*, March 13, 1818.

40 *Ibid.*, March 14, 1818.

41 *Ibid.*, March 23, 1818.

42 41 *Laws of New York*, chap. 47 (March 14, 1818).

43 See Nelson M. Blake, "Eunice Against the Shakers," *New York History*, XLI (October, 1960), 374-377.

44 56 *Assembly Documents*, No. 97 (Jan. 23, 1833).

45 59 *Ibid.*, No. 328 (May 26, 1836).

[46] 63 *Ibid.*, No. 323 (April 2, 1840).

[47] 63 *Ibid.*, No. 324 (April 18, 1840).

[48] 64 *Ibid.*, No. 202 (March 16, 1841).

[49] 68 *Ibid.*, No. 139 (March 4, 1845).

[50] 68 *Ass. Journ.*, 962 (April 26, 1845); 68 *Senate Journ.*, 578-579 (May 2, 1845).

[51] Article 1, Section 10.

[52] 89 *Laws of New York*, ch. 621 (April 16, 1866). See also 71 *ibid.*, ch. 87 (March 13, 1848) and 75 *ibid.*, ch. 23 (Feb. 16, 1852).

[53] 63 *Ass. Doc.*, No. 324 (April 18, 1840).

[54] 72 *Ibid.*, No. 66 (Jan. 30, 1849).

[55] *Albany Argus*, Feb. 28, March 5, 10, 14, 1849; *New York Tribune*, March 5, 8, 14, 16, 1849.

[56] 72 *Ass. Journ.*, 764 (March 9, 1849).

[57] *Ibid.*, 829 (March 13, 1849).

[58] 73 *Ass. Doc.*, No. 72 (Feb. 13, 1850).

[59] 75 *Ibid.*, No. 73 (March 2, 1852).

[60] 75 *Ass. Journ.*, 978 (April 9, 1852).

[61] 78 *Ass. Doc.*, No. 119 (March 26, 1855).

[62] 79 *Senate Doc.*, No. 49 (Feb. 27, 1856).

[63] 83 *Senate Journ.*, 68, 101, 193, 242, 279, 282, 303, 398 (Jan 13, 23; Feb. 7, 14, 25, 27, 28; March 10, 1860). See also *Albany Atlas and Argus*, Feb. 7, 15, 28, March 12.

[64] *New York Tribune*, March 12, 1860.

[65] *Albany Evening Journal*, Feb. 10, 1860.

[66] *Ibid.*, Feb. 14, 1860.

[67] *New York Tribune*, March 1, 1860.

[68] 83 *Senate Journ.*, 525 (March 23, 1860).

[69] 84 *Ibid.*, 184 (Feb. 15, 1861).

7. DIVORCE DEBATED

[1] *Niles' Register*, XXVIII (June 11, 1825), 229.

[2] Joel P. Bishop, *Commentaries on the Law of Marriage and Divorce* (6th ed., Boston: Little, Brown & Co., 1881), I, 22 fn.

[3] *Ibid.*, I, 30.

[4] *Ibid.*, I, 24.

[5] *Ibid.*, I, 26.

[6] *New York Tribune*, Sept. 18, 1852.

[7] *New York Observer*, XXX (Nov. 11, 1852), 366.

[8] *New York Tribune*, Nov. 16, 1852.

[9] *Ibid.*, Dec. 1, 1852. See also *ibid.*, Dec. 16, 1852.

[10] *Ibid.*, Dec. 18, 1852.

[11] *Idem.*

[12] *Ibid.*, Dec. 24, 1852.

[13] *Idem.*

[14] *Ibid.*, Jan. 28, 1853.

[15] *Idem.*

[16] *Love, Marriage, and Divorce and the Sovereignty of the Individual: A Discussion Between Henry James, Horace Greeley, and Stephen Pearl Andrews . . .* (Boston: Benj. R. Tucker, 1889), p. 72.

[17] *Ibid.*, p. 78.

[18] *New York Tribune*, Dec. 28, 1852.

[19] *Ibid.*, Dec. 31, 1852.

[20] *Ibid.*, Feb. 4, 1853.

[21] Undated clipping in Elizabeth Cady Stanton Papers, Library of Congress.

[22] Mrs. Stanton to Temperance Convention at Albany, Jan. 28, 1852, Stanton Papers.

[23] Elizabeth Cady Stanton, Susan B. Anthony, and Mathilda J. Gage, *History of Woman Suffrage* (New York: Fowler & Wells, 1881), I, 483.

[24] Mrs. Stanton to Miss Anthony, March 1 [1853?], Stanton Papers.

[25] Mrs. Stanton, "Address to the Legislature of New York, Adopted by

the State Woman's Rights Convention Held at Albany . . . February 14 and 15, 1854," *ibid.*

26 Lucy Stone to Mrs. Stanton, Aug. 14, 1853, *ibid.*

27 Lucy Stone to Mrs. Stanton, Oct. 22, 1855, *ibid.*

28 Lucy Stone to Mrs. Stanton, Sept. 17 [1856?], *ibid.*

29 Lucy Stone to Mrs. Stanton, March 16 [1859?], *ibid.*

30 *New York Tribune*, March 1, 1860. The entire Greeley-Owen correspondence is reprinted in Horace Greeley, *Recollections of a Busy Life* (New York: J. B. Ford & Co., 1869), pp. 570-618.

31 *New York Tribune*, March 5, 1860.

32 *Ibid.*, March 5, 1860.

33 *Ibid.*, March 12, 1860.

34 *Ibid.*, March 17, 1860.

35 *Ibid.*, March 28, 1860.

36 *Ibid.*, April 7, 1860. For later letters, see *ibid.*, April 21, 31, 1860.

37 Stanton and others, *History of Woman Suffrage*, I, 717.

38 *Ibid.*, I, 720.

39 *Ibid.*, I, 722.

40 *Ibid.*, I, 727.

41 *Ibid.*, I, 731.

42 *Ibid.*, I, 732.

43 *Ibid.*, I, 733-734.

44 *Ibid.*, I, 735.

45 *New York Tribune*, May 14, 1860.

46 *Ibid.*, May 30, 1860.

47 *Address of Elizabeth Cady Stanton on the Divorce Bill, Before the Judiciary Committee of the New York Senate in the Assembly Chamber, Feb. 8, 1861* (Albany: Weed, Parsons & Co., 1861).

8. THE SHOALS OF FREE LOVE

1 *New York Times*, Aug. 17, 1855.

2 *Ibid.*, Oct. 10, 1855.

3 *Ibid.*, Oct. 19, 1855.

4 *Ibid.*, Sept. 21, 1861.

5 E. C. Stanton to Emily Howland, Sept. 1, 1867, Theodore Stanton and Harriot S. Blatch, *Elizabeth Cady Stanton: As Revealed in Her Letters, Diary and Reminiscences* (New York: Harper's, 1922), II, 117.

6 Alma Lutz, *Created Equal: A Biography of Elizabeth Cady Stanton* (New York: John Day Co., 1940), pp. 151-154.

7 *Ibid.*, pp. 157-158.

8 *The Revolution*, I (June 18, 1868), 381-382.

9 *Ibid.*, II (July 23, 1868), 36.

10 *Ibid.*, II (Oct. 15, 1868), 233-234.

11 *Ibid.*, III (April 8, 1869), 217-218.

12 *New York Times*, May 14, 1869.

13 Alice Stone Blackwell, *Lucy Stone, Pioneer of Woman's Rights* (Boston: Little, Brown & Co., 1930), p. 213.

14 *New York Tribune*, May 11, 1870.

15 *Ibid.*, Nov. 26, Dec. 1, 3, 1869.

16 *New York Times*, Dec. 4, 1869.

17 *Revolution*, IV (Dec. 23, 1869), 385.

18 *The Richardson-McFarland Tragedy* (Philadelphia: Barclay & Co., 1870), pp. 89-90.

19 *Idem.*

20 *Revolution*, V (May 19, 1870), 307.

21 *Ibid.*, V (May 26, 1870), 329-330.

22 *The Independent*, XXII (May 12, 1870), 4.

23 *Ibid.*, XXII (May 19, 1870), 4.

24 *Woman's Journal*, I (June 4, 1870), 173.

25 Mss. in Elizabeth Cady Stanton Papers, Library of Congress.

26 E. C. Stanton to S. B. Anthony, June 27, 1870, Stanton and Blatch, *Stanton*, II, 127.

27 E. C. Stanton to Mrs. Griffing, Dec. 1, 1870, E. C. Stanton Papers.

28 Library of Congress.
29 *Revolution*, VI (July 7, 1870), 1.
30 *Ibid.*, VI (July 21, 1870), 43.
31 *Ibid.*, VI (Aug. 18, 1870), 104.
32 Quoted in *Woman's Journal*, I (Oct. 22, 1870), 332.
33 *Idem.*
34 *Ibid.*, I (Nov. 5, 1870), 348.
35 *Ibid.*, I (Oct. 22, 1870), 329.
36 *Revolution*, VI (Oct. 27, 1870), 264.
37 *Ibid.*, VI (Dec. 1, 1870), 344.
38 *New York Tribune*, May 12, 1871.
39 *Ibid.*, June 17, 1871.
40 *Ibid.*, July 20, 1871.
41 *Idem.*
42 *Ibid.*, Aug. 1, 1871.
43 Robert Shapen, *Free Love and Heavenly Sinners: The Story of the Great Henry Ward Beecher Scandal* (New York: Knopf, 1954), pp. 3, 65-67.
44 *Independent*, XXII (Dec. 1, 1870), 6.
45 *Golden Age*, I (April 22, 1871), 4.
46 *Ibid.*, I (June 24, 1871), 4.
47 *Ibid.*, I (Aug. 5, 1871), 4.
48 *New York Tribune*, Aug. 9, 1871.
49 *Golden Age*, I (Aug. 19, 1871), 4.
50 *Ibid.*, I (Aug. 26, 1871), 4.
51 *Ibid.*, I (Oct. 7, 1871), 3.
52 *Ibid.*, II (May 11, 1872), 4, and subsequent issues.
53 *Ibid.*, I (Aug. 12, 1871), 5.
54 *New York Tribune*, Aug. 9, 1871.
55 *Ibid.*, Nov. 21, 1871.
56 Lutz, *Created Equal*, p. 226.

9. RISE OF THE DIVORCE COLONIES

1 *New York Times*, Dec. 9, 1869.
2 *Ibid.*, Dec. 5, 1869.
3 *The McFarland-Richardson Tragedy* (Philadelphia: Barclay & Co., 1870), p. 108.
4 James Kent, *Commentaries on American Law* (2nd ed., New York: O. Halsted, 1832), II, 98.
5 63 *New York Assembly Documents*, no. 324 (April 18, 1840), p. 12.
6 Anne Fréchette, "A Banner Divorce County," *Century Magazine*, LIX (Feb., 1900), 639.
7 *Cleveland Leader*, Feb. 24, 1871, quoted in *Annals of Cleveland*, LIV, 179.
8 *Revolution*, I (June 4, 1868), 342.
9 *New York Times*, Dec. 27, 1868.
10 *Ibid.*, Aug. 28, 1870.
11 *New York Herald*, Sept. 18, 1870. For other examples, see Donald N. Koster, *The Theme of Divorce in American Drama, 1871-1939* (Philadelphia: University of Pennsylvania, 1949), p. 117.
12 Quoted in *New York Times*, June 9, 1867.
13 *Ibid.*, Nov. 13, 1870.
14 Val Nolan, Jr., "Indiana: Birthplace of Migratory Divorce," *Indiana Law Journal*, XXVI (Summer, 1951), 517-520.
15 *Indianapolis Daily Journal*, Dec. 3, 1858, quoted in Nolan, *Indiana Law Journ.*, XXVI, 522.
16 *New York Tribune*, March 1, 1860.
17 March 9, 1860, quoted in Nolan, *Indiana Law Journ.*, XXVI, 520.
18 Dec. 11, 1858, quoted in Nolan, p. 522.
19 40 *Laws of Indiana*, ch. 60 (March 4, 1859).
20 Nolan, *Indiana Law Journ.*, XXVI, 523-524.
21 *Ibid.*, p. 526.
22 *Indiana Daily Sentinel*, Feb. 12, 1873.
23 48 *Laws of Indiana*, ch. 43 (March 10, 1873).
24 Nolan, *Indiana Law Journ.*, XXVI, 526-527.
25 *Ibid.*, XXVI, 515-516.
26 *Cleveland Leader*, May 28, 1864, quoted in *Annals of Cleveland*, XLII, 54.

27 Howard, *History of Matrimonial Institutions*, III, 136-143.

28 *Ibid.*, III, 131-133.

29 *New York Tribune*, July 28, 1879.

30 "Divorce as a State Industry," *Nation*, XXV (May 5, 1892), 334.

31 *Argus-Leader* (Sioux Falls, S.D.), Jan. 10, 1893.

32 National Divorce Reform League, *Report for 1891*, p. 12.

33 *Argus-Leader*, Jan. 26, 1893.

34 James Realf, Jr., "The Sioux Falls Divorce Colony and Some Noted Colonists," *Arena*, IV (Nov., 1891), 696-703.

35 *Argus-Leader*, Jan. 26, 1893.

36 *Nation*, XXV (May 5, 1892), 334.

37 *Argus-Leader*, Jan. 26, 1893.

38 M. A. De Wolfe Howe, *The Life and Labors of Bishop Hare, Apostle to the Sioux* (New York: Sturgis & Walton Co., 1911), p. 356.

39 *Ibid.*, pp. 356-357.

40 *Argus-Leader*, Jan. 2, 1893.

41 Howe, *Bishop Hare*, p. 357-358.

42 *Argus-Leader*, Jan. 14, 1893.

43 Howe, *Bishop Hare*, p. 358.

44 *Argus-Leader*, Jan. 13, 1893.

45 *Ibid.*, Jan. 16, 24, 1893.

46 *Ibid.*, Feb. 15, 1893.

47 3 *Laws of South Dakota*, chap. 75 (March 1, 1893).

48 *Argus-Leader*, Feb. 9, 1895; Howe, *Bishop Hare*, pp. 371-372.

49 *Argus-Leader*, Feb. 25, 1895.

50 *Ibid.*, March 2, 1895.

51 Howard, *History of Matrimonial Institutions*, III, 157.

52 10 *Laws of South Dakota*, chap. 132 (March 8, 1907).

53 *Argus-Leader*, March 8, 1907.

54 Howe, *Bishop Hare*, pp. 374-375.

55 *The Foreign Divorce Traffic in South Dakota: The Legislature of 1907 and the Referendum* (Sioux Falls: Will A. Beach Printing Co., 1908), p. 7.

56 *Argus-Leader*, Nov. 12, 1908.

57 Howe, *Bishop Hare*, p. 377.

58 *New York Tribune*, Feb. 20, 1894.

59 *New York Times*, Aug. 2, 1895.

60 *U.S. Statutes at Large*, XXIX, 136 (May 25, 1896).

61 *New York Tribune*, Aug. 26, 1899.

62 Howard, *History of Matrimonial Institutions*, III, 157.

10. The Conservative Reaction

1 Rev. H. Loomis, "Divorce Legislation in Connecticut," *New Englander*, XXV (July, 1866), 442.

2 Theodore Woolsey, "Divorce," *ibid.*, XXVI (Jan., 1867), 113.

3 Nathan Allen, "Divorces in New England," *North American Review*, CXXX (June, 1880), 560.

4 National Divorce Reform League, *An Abstract of Its Annual Reports, October, 1885* (Montpelier, Vt., 1885), pp. 1-2.

5 National League for the Protection of the Family, *Annual Report for 1897*, p. 5.

6 National Divorce Reform League, *Abstract of Annual Reports*, pp. 5-6.

7 National Divorce Reform League, *Report for 1887*, p. 7.

8 *New York Times*, Dec. 9, 1869.

9 *New York Tribune*, July 28, 1879.

10 Carroll D. Wright, ed., *A Report of Marriage and Divorce in the United States, 1867-1886* . . . (Rev. Ed., Washington: Government Printing Office, 1891), p. 10.

11 National Divorce Reform League, *Abstract of Annual Reports*, p. 6.

12 Wright, *Report on Marriage and Divorce, 1867-1886*, pp. 12-13.

13 *Ibid.*, pp. 13-15.

14 *Ibid.*, pp. 17-18.

15 *Ibid.*, p. 18.

16 *Ibid.*, pp. 139-140.

17 *Ibid.*, p. 148.

18 *Ibid.*, pp. 150-157.

254

19 *Ibid.*, p. 197.

20 Walter F. Willcox, *The Divorce Problem* (Columbia College, *Studies in History, Economics and Public Law*, vol. I, no. 1, New York, 1891), p. 45.

21 *Ibid.*, p. 72.

22 National Divorce Reform League, *Report for 1889*, p. 15.

23 Charles Z. Lincoln, ed. *Messages from the Governors* (Albany: J. B. Lyon Co., 1909), VIII, 689.

24 *Ibid.*, VIII, 929.

25 113 *Laws of New York*, ch. 205 (April 28, 1890).

26 National Divorce Reform League, *Report for 1891*, p. 9; *Report for 1892*, p. 11; National League for the Protection of the Family, *Annual Report for 1898*, p. 10.

27 National Divorce Reform League, *Report for 1892*, pp. 12-15.

28 Wilbur Larremore, "American Divorce Law," *North American Review*, CLXXXIII (July, 1906), 74.

29 National League for the Protection of the Family, *Report for 1897*, p. 9.

30 National League for the Protection of the Family, *Report for 1899*, pp. 8-10.

31 *New York Tribune*, Nov. 27, 1899.

32 *Handbook of the National Conference of Commissioners on Uniform State Laws . . .* , 1959, p. 294.

33 *Marriage and Divorce: Bulletin of the Association for the Sanctity of Marriage*, X (Oct., 1927), 4.

34 *New York Tribune*, May 10, 1899.

35 James P. Lichtenberger, *Divorce, A Study in Social Causation* (New York: Columbia University Press, 1909), pp. 123-124.

36 *New York Times*, Nov. 15, 1904.

37 Lichtenberger, *Divorce*, p. 126.

38 *Ibid.*, p. 127.

39 *Ibid.*, p. 129.

40 *New York Times*, May 25, 1904.

41 Lichtenberger, *Divorce*, pp. 123, 138-141.

42 *New York Tribune*, May 24, 25, 1904.

43 *Ibid.*, Jan. 27, 1905.

44 *Ibid.*, Jan. 31, 1905.

45 *U.S. Statutes at Large*, XXXIII, 1282 (Feb. 9, 1905).

46 *New York Tribune*, Aug. 4, 1905.

47 *Ibid.*, Aug. 14, 1905.

48 *Proceedings of the National Congress on Uniform Divorce Laws, Held at Washington, D. C., February 19, 1906* (Harrisburg: Harrisburg Publishing Co., 1906), pp. 4-8.

49 *Ibid.*, pp. 57-58.

50 *Ibid.*, pp. 20-21.

51 *Ibid.*, p. 126.

52 *Ibid.*, p. 128.

53 *Ibid.*, p. 132.

54 *Ibid.*, p. 133.

55 *Ibid.*, p. 139.

56 *Ibid.*, p. 71.

57 *Ibid.*, p. 81.

58 *Ibid.*, p. 79.

59 *Ibid.*, pp. 75-76.

60 *Ibid.*, p. 93.

61 *Idem.*

62 *Ibid.*, p. 94.

63 *Ibid.*, p. 121.

64 *Proceedings of the Adjourned Meeting of the National Congress on Uniform Divorce Laws, Held at Philadelphia, Pa., November 13, 1906* (Harrisburg: Harrisburg Publishing Co., 1907), p. 131.

65 *New York Tribune*, Nov. 21, 1906; National League for the Protection of the Family, *Annual Report for 1906*, p. 7.

66 *New York Tribune*, Nov. 16, 1906.

67 *Handbook of the National Conference of Commissioners on Uniform State Laws*, 1959, p. 294.

68 American Bar Association, *Reports*, XXI (1907), 1191.

69 *Cong. Rec.*, XV, 279 (Jan. 8, 1884).

70 *Ibid.*, XIX, 165-170 (Dec. 22, 1887).

71 *Ibid.*, XXII, 790-793 (Feb. 3,

1892); XXVIII, 219 (Dec. 17, 1895).

72 "Marriage and Divorce," 52 Cong. 1 Sess., *House Reports*, No. 1290 (May 5, 1892), pp. 1-8.

73 *New York Tribune*, June 18, 1897.

74 "Annual Message of the President . . . December 3, 1906," 59 Cong., 2 Sess., *House Documents*, No. 1, p. xxxv.

75 134 *New York Senate Journal*, 2485 (Sept. 18, 1911).

76 F. D. Roosevelt to Mrs. F. D. Roosevelt [Sept. 19, 1911], Elliott Roosevelt, ed., *F.D.R.: His Personal Letters* (New York: Duell, Sloan & Pearce, 1947-1948) II, 172. Dated erroneously Sept. 12.

77 *New York Times*, Sept. 8, 1911.

78 *Uniform Laws as to Marriage and Divorce.* Hearing before the Committee on the Judiciary, House of Representatives, 65 Cong., 2 Sess., on H.J. Res. 187 (October 2, 1918), pp. 3-4, 12.

79 *Ibid.*, pp. 38-40, 59-62.

80 See *Cong. Rec.*, L, 2719; LI, 2863; LIII, 2097, 7214; LVIII, 381, 885, 1013.

81 *Marriage and Divorce—Amendment of the Constitution of the United States.* Hearing before a Subcommittee of the Committee on the Judiciary, Senate, 67 Cong., 1 Sess. on S.J. Res. 31 (Nov. 1, 1921), p. 5.

82 *Constitutional Amendment Grant-ing Congress Power to Establish Uniform Laws Relating to Marriage and Divorce.* Hearing before the Committee on the Judiciary, 67 Cong., 2 Sess. on H.J. Res. 83 (Jan. 26, 1922), pp. 3-11.

83 General Federation of Women's Clubs, *Sixteenth Biennial Convention, 1922, Report*, pp. 655-656.

84 *Marriage and Divorce (Amendment to the Constitution).* Hearing before a Subcommittee of the Committee on the Judiciary, Senate, 68 Cong., 1 Sess., on S.J. Res. 5 (Jan. 11, 1924), pp. 2, 14.

85 *Ibid.*, p. 1.

86 *Ibid.*, pp. 5, 15-16.

87 *Marriage and Divorce: Bulletin of the Association for the Sanctity of Marriage*, VIII (Sept., 1923), 6.

88 *Cong. Rec.*, LXIX, 1064-1066 (May 26, 1928).

89 *Ibid.*, XCIII, 334 (Jan. 15, 1947).

90 *Ibid.*, XCIII, Appendix, 1498-1499.

91 *Statistical Abstract of the United States, 1949*, p. 80.

92 Robert G. Ingersoll, "Is Divorce Wrong?" *North American Review*, CXLIX (Nov., 1889), 533.

93 Clipping from Geneva, N.Y., *Advertiser-Gazette*, Nov. 18, 1902, in Elizabeth Cady Stanton Papers.

94 William E. Carson, *The Marriage Revolt: A Study of Marriage and Divorce* (New York: Hearst's International Library Co., 1915), p. 461.

11. DIVORCE AND THE TOURIST TRADE

1 Leslie Curtis, *Reno Reveries: Impressions of Local Life* (Reno: Chas. E. Weck, 1912), p. 93.

2 F. W. Ingraham and G. A. Ballard, "The Busines of Migratory Divorce in Nevada," *Law and Contemporary Problems*, II (June, 1935), 304.

3 George A. Bartlett, *Men, Women and Conflict* (New York: G. P. Putnam's Sons, 1931), p. 11.

4 *In re* Schnitzer, 33 *Nevada*, 581 (1911), 112 *Pacific Reporter*, 848-852.

5 Curtis, *Reno Reveries*, p. 18.

6 *Ibid.*, p. 60.

7 *Nevada State Journal*, Feb. 1, 1913.

8 *Ibid.*, Feb. 1-4, 1913.

9 *Ibid.*, Feb. 8, 18, 1913.

10 *Ibid.*, Nov. 5, 1914.

11 *Ibid.*, Jan. 30, Feb. 4, 1915.

12 *Ibid.*, Feb. 12, 13, 16, 18, 1915.

13 *Ibid.*, Feb. 24, 1915.
14 *Ibid.*, Nov. 10, 1922.
15 *Ibid.*, March 19, 1927.
16 *Ibid.*, Feb. 25, 1931.
17 *Ibid.*, March 7, 17, 20, 1931.
18 *Ibid.*, March 9, 1931.
19 Ingraham and Ballard, *Law and Contemporary Problems*, II, 307-309.
20 Paul H. Jacobson, *American Marriage and Divorce* (New York: Rinehart & Co., 1959), pp. 103, 104, 171.
21 *Ibid.*, p. 104.
22 Lindell T. Bates, "The Divorce of Americans in France," *Law and Contemporary Problems*, II (June, 1935), 322-328.
23 *New York Times*, Feb. 17, 1924.
24 Gould v. Gould (1923), 235 *New York Reports*, 14.
25 *New York Times*, July 25, 1923.
26 *Ibid.*, Feb. 7, 1924.
27 *Ibid.*, Oct. 23, 1927; Bates, *Law and Contemporary Problems*, II, 328.
28 Bates, II, 328.
29 *New York Times*, March 1, 1928.
30 *Ibid.*, March 14, 1928; Bates, *Law and Contemporary Problems*, II, 328.
31 Lionel M. Sumners, "The Divorce Laws of Mexico," *Law and Contemporary Problems*, II (June, 1935), 311.
32 *New York Times*, Feb. 19, 1928.
33 Gregory Mason, "Mexico's Cash-and-Carry Divorce for Americans," *Scribner's Magazine*, LXXXVIII (Oct., 1930), 360-367.
34 *New York Daily Mirror*, March 15, 1935.
35 Rollo Bergeson, "The Divorce Mill Advertises," *Law and Contemporary Problems*, II (June, 1935), 351.
36 "Prohibit the Use of the Mails for the Solicitation of the Procurement of Divorces in Foreign Countries," 74 Cong., 1 Sess., *House Reports*, No. 1643 (July 24, 1935), p. 2.
37 "Prohibiting the Use of the Mails for the Solicitation of the Procurement

of Divorces in Foreign Countries," 76 Cong., 1 Sess., *Senate Reports*, No. 683 (June 27, 1939), pp. 1-2.
38 53 *U.S. Statutes at Large*, 1341, ch. 638 (Aug. 10, 1939).
39 Sumners, *Law and Contemporary Problems*, II, 319; Javier Alvarez, "The Divorce Laws of Mexico," *Divorce in the "Liberal" Jurisdictions* (New York: Federal Legal Publications, Inc., 1955), pp. 25-28.
40 Jacobson, *American Marriage and Divorce*, p. 108.
41 *Ibid.*, p. 407.
42 *Idaho Daily Statesman* (Boise), Feb. 21, 22, 1931.
43 *Ibid.*, Feb. 26, 1931.
44 *Ibid.*, Feb. 27, 1931.
45 *Ibid.*, March 1, 1931.
46 *Ibid.*, March 4, 1931.
47 *New York Times*, March 7, 1937.
48 U.S. Bureau of the Census, *Statistical Abstract of the United States: 1958* (Washington: Government Printing Office, 1958), p. 72.
49 *Arkansas Democrat* (Little Rock), Feb. 12, 1931.
50 *Idem.*
51 *Ibid.*, Feb. 20, 27, 1931.
52 *Statistical Abstract of U.S.: 1949*, p. 81; *Statistical Abstract of U.S.: 1958*, p. 72.
53 *New York Times*, Feb. 24, 1935.
54 *Statistical Abstract of U.S.: 1958*, p. 72.
55 *Florida Times-Union* (Jacksonville), May 11, 1935.
56 *Ibid.*, May 1, 1935.
57 *Idem.*
58 *Ibid.*, May 7, 1935.
59 *Ibid.*, May 11, 1935.
60 W. Cecil Grant, "The Divorce Laws of Florida," *Divorce in the "Liberal" Jurisdictions*, p. 19.
61 *Ibid.*, p. 20.
62 *Statistical Abstract of U.S.: 1949*, p. 81.
63 *Statistical Abstract of U.S.: 1958*, p. 72.
64 *Florida Times-Union*, April 3, 4, 1957.

[65] *Ibid.*, April 9, May 16, 1957.
[66] *Ibid.*, April 25, 1957.
[67] Jacobson, *American Marriage and Divorce*, p. 105; Eugene V. Dench, "The Divorce Laws of the Virgin Islands," *Divorce in the "Liberal" Jurisdictions*, pp. 42-44.
[68] Jacobson, p. 105; J. H. Berman, "The Divorce Laws of Alabama," *Divorce in the "Liberal" Jurisdictions*, pp. 9-11.
[69] *New York Times*, July 16, 1960.
[70] Frankfurter's dissent in *Sherrer* v. *Sherrer*, 334 *U.S.*, 369-370 (June 7, 1948).

[71] Jacobson, p. 109. In 1932, it was estimated that migratory divorce accounted for no more than 3 per cent of the national total. See Alfred Cahen, *Statistical Analysis of American Divorce* (New York: Columbia University Press, 1932), p. 78.
[72] Ingraham and Ballard, *Law and Contemporary Problems*, II, 305.
[73] *Statistical Abstract of U.S.: 1960*, p. 69.
[74] Jacobson, p. 116.
[75] Frankfurter's dissent, *Sherrer* v. *Sherrer*, 344 *U.S.*, 370, f.n. 18.

12. "FULL FAITH AND CREDIT"

[1] *United States Statutes at Large*, I, 122 (May 26, 1790).
[2] *Pennoyer* v. *Neff* (1878), 95 *U.S.*, 714.
[3] *Borden* v. *Fitch* (1818), 15 *Johnson's New York Reports*, 121.
[4] *Vischer* v. *Vischer* (1851), 12 *Barbour's New York Reports*, 640.
[5] *Kerr* v. *Kerr* (1869), 41 *New York Reports*, 272.
[6] *New York Times*, Dec. 10, 1869.
[7] *Harding* v. *Alden* (1832), 9 Maine *Reports*, 140.
[8] *Ditson* v. *Ditson* (1856), 4 *Rhode Island Reports*, 87.
[9] *Burlen* v. *Shannon* (1874), 115 *Massachusetts Reports*, 438.
[10] Dissent by Justice Brown in *Haddock* v. *Haddock* (1906), 201 *U.S.*, 624.
[11] *Atherton* v. *Atherton* (1901), 181 *U.S.*, 155.
[12] *Bell* v. *Bell* (1901), 181 *U.S.*, 175.
[13] *Streitwolf* v. *Streitwolf* (1901), 181 *U.S.*, 179.
[14] *New York Tribune*, April 17, 1901.
[15] *Andrews* v. *Andrews* (1903), 188 *U.S.*, 14.
[16] *Haddock* v. *Haddock* (1906), 201 *U.S.*, 562.
[17] 201 *U.S.*, 629.

[18] 201 *U.S.*, 628.
[19] *Davis* v. *Davis* (1938), 305 *U.S.*, 32.
[20] *State* v. *Williams* (1941), 17 *Southeastern Reporter*, 2d Series, 769.
[21] *New York Times*, December 22, 1942.
[22] *Williams* v. *North Carolina* (1942), 317 *U.S.*, 269, 302.
[23] 317 *U.S.*, 312.
[24] 317 *U.S.*, 311.
[25] *State* v. *Williams* (1944), 29 *Southeastern Reporter*, 2d Series, 744.
[26] *Williams* v. *North Carolina* (1945), 325 *U.S.*, 226.
[27] 325 *U.S.*, 262, 278.
[28] *Sherrer* v. *Sherrer* (1948), 344 *U.S.*, 343; *Coe* v. *Coe* (1948), 334 *U.S.*, 378.
[29] 334 *U.S.*, 351, 356.
[30] 334 *U.S.*, 377.
[31] *Essenwein* v. *Penn.* (1945), 325 *U.S.*, 279.
[32] *Estin* v. *Estin* (1948), 334 *U.S.*, 541.
[33] 334 *U.S.*, 549.
[34] 334 *U.S.*, 554.
[35] *Rice* v. *Rice* (1949), 336 *U.S.*, 674.
[36] *Anderson* v. *Anderson* (1953), 345 *U.S.*, 528.
[37] *Vanderbilt* v. *Vanderbilt* (1957), 354 *U.S.*, 416.

[38] 336 *U.S.*, 680.

[39] 354 *U.S.*, 420.

[40] *Handbook of the National Conference of Commissioners on Uniform State Laws* . . . , 1947, pp. 177-184. Up to 1959, the uniform divorce recognition act had been adopted by the following states: California, Louisiana, Nebraska, New Hampshire, North Dakota, Rhode Island, South Carolina, Washington, Wisconsin. *Ibid.*, 1959, pp. 294-295.

[41] "Marriage and Divorce," 52 Cong. 1 Sess., *House Reports*, No. 1290 (May 5, 1892), p. 2.

[42] *Cong. Rec.*, XCIX, 4575 (May 6, 1953).

[43] Senate Judiciary Committee, "Implementing the Full Faith and Credit Clause of the Constitution," 82 Cong., 2d Sess., *Senate Reports*, No. 1156 (Feb. 4, 1952), p. 8.

[44] *Cong. Rec.*, XCIX, 4575 (May 6, 1953).

[45] *Ibid.*, XCVIII, 7775 (June 21, 1952); XCIX, 4575 (May 6, 1953).

[46] 334 *U.S.*, 553.

13. NEW YORK'S TWISTING PATH

[1] [James G. Power], *Marriage and Divorce* (New York: American News Co., 1870), pp. 111-112.

[2] Wilbur Larremore, "American Divorce Law," *North American Review*, CLXXXIII (July, 1906), 73-74.

[3] *New York Sun*, July 1, 1882.

[4] *New York Times*, Oct. 10, 1869.

[5] *Ibid.*, Nov. 13, 1870.

[6] *Ibid.*, Oct. 20, 1870.

[7] *New York Tribune*, Feb 12, 1884.

[8] *New York Times*, Nov. 26, 1890.

[9] *New York Tribune*, Dec. 27, 1890.

[10] *Ibid.*, Nov. 13, 1900.

[11] *New York Mirror*, Sunday Magazine, Feb. 18, 25, March 4, 1934.

[12] *Annotated Consolidated Laws of the State of New York* . . . (New York: Banks Law Publishing Co., 1909), I, 1021; *Keyes* v. *Keyes* (1893), 26 *New York Supplement*, 910; *King* v. *Brewer* (1894), 29 *N.Y. Suppl.*, 1114.

[13] Of the *essentialia* doctrine, an authority writes: "The case law has come to make the meaning of this concept rather specific. Concealed pregnancy by another man (at least in the absence of premarital intercourse with the plaintiff), concealment of venereal disease, or of sterility, and a concealed intent not to permit normal intercourse or to maintain a normal home—these represent, for practical purposes, the limits of essential fraud. False claims of pregnancy, concealment of previous bad character, or of ill-health, lack of love and affection—these, except in rare and extreme instances, will afford no ground for relief." Robert Kingsley, "What Are the Proper Grounds for Granting Annulments," reprinted from a symposium, *Divorce—A Re-examination of Basic Concepts*, Vol. 18, p. 47, by permission from *Law and Contemporary Problems*, published by the Duke University School of Law, Durham, N.C. Copyright, 1953, by Duke University.

[14] *Fisk* v. *Fisk* (1896), 6 *New York Appellate Division of Supreme Court Reports*, 432.

[15] *Shandry* v. *Logan* (1896), 40 *New York Supplement*, 1010.

[16] *Di Lorenzo* v. *di Lorenzo* (1903), 174 *New York Reports*, 467.

[17] *Shonfeld* v. *Shonfeld* (1933), 260 *New York Reports*, 477.

[18] *Dromschke* v. *Dromschke* (1910), 122 *New York Supplement*, 892.

[19] *Waff* v. *Waff* (1947), 71 *New York Supplement*, 2d Series, 775.

[20] *Miller* v. *Miller* (1928), 132 *New York Miscellaneous Reports*, 121.

[21] *Coppo* v. *Coppo* (1937), 297 *N.Y. Suppl.*, 744.

[22] *Fundaro* v. *Fundaro* (1947), 70 *N.Y. Suppl.*, 2d, 510.

23 *Schulman* v. *Schulman* (1943), 46 N.Y. *Suppl.*, 2d, 158.

24 Joseph R. Clevenger, *Annulments of Marriage, Being a Treatise Covering New York Law and Practice with Composite Forms* (New York: Fallon Law Book Co., 1946), p. 27.

25 *Ibid.*, pp. 25-26.

26 Milton L. Grossman, "How Can We Make Divorce Realistic?" *New York State Bar Bulletin*, XXIII (Oct., 1951), 351.

27 Charles Desmond, "The Annulment Problem," *New York State Bar Bulletin*, XX (April, 1948), 61.

28 "Annulments for Fraud—New York's Answer to Reno?" *Columbia Law Review*, XLVIII (Sept., 1948), 904-905.

29 24 *Laws of New York*, ch. 58 (March 21, 1801); *Revised Statutes of New York, 1829*, pt. II, chap. 8, par. 5; In the Matter of Deming (1813), 10 *Johnson's Reports*, 232.

30 *Revised Statutes of New York, 1829*, pt. II, ch. 8, par. 6.

31 145 *Laws of New York*, ch. 279 (March 25, 1922).

32 *New York Times*, April 22, 1922.

33 151 *Laws of New York*, ch. 589 (March 26, 1928).

34 100 *Ibid.*, ch. 168 (April 20, 1877).

35 122 *Ibid.*, ch. 661 (May 25, 1899).

36 125 *Ibid.*, chs. 203, 364 (March 21, April 3, 1902).

37 *Van Voorhis et al.* v. *Brintall et al.* (1881), 86 *New York Reports*, 18.

38 101 *New York Assembly Journal*, 1188 (May 10, 1878).

39 *New York Tribune*, May 8, 10, 1878; March 10, 1884.

40 102 *Laws of New York*, ch. 164 (April 16, 1879).

41 102 *Senate Journ.*, 102, 216, 750, 759 (Feb. 6, 28, May 7, 8, 1879).

42 102 *Laws of New York*, ch. 321 (May 19, 1879).

43 120 *Ibid.*, ch. 452 (May 17, 1897); 142 *ibid.*, ch. 265 (May 3, 1919).

44 142 *Ass. Journ.*, 1143 (March 26, 1919).

45 154 *Ibid.*, 907, 1514 (March 11, 24, 1931).

46 155 *Ibid.*, 59 (Jan. 19, 1932); 156 *ibid.*, 62 (Jan. 17, 1932).

47 Paul H. Jacobson, *American Marriage and Divorce* (New York: Rinehart & Co., 1959), p. 117.

14. Politics and the New York Divorce Law

1 Author's interview with I. A. Ross in New York City, September 24, 1959.

2 Assembly Bill Int. 824 was to amend Section 1150 of the Civil Practices Act dealing with proof in actions for divorce. Int. 825 was to amend Sec. 1147 dealing with actions for absolute divorce.

3 157 *New York Assembly Journal*, 521 (Feb. 28, 1934).

4 Interview with Ross, Sept. 24, 1959; *New York Times* March 7, 1934.

5 Numerous comments in Material on Divorce Bill in 1934 Legislature in possession of I. A. Ross, New York City, hereafter cited as Ross Papers.

6 Ross Papers.

7 List of endorsements in Ross Papers.

8 S. S. Goldstein to Ross, April 4, 1934; L. F. Ward to Ross, March 24, 1934; H. E. Fosdick to Ross, March 27, 1934, Ross Papers.

9 *New York Times*, March 29, 1934.

10 Memorandum in Ross Papers.

11 Mimeographed letter signed by James J. Landers, Secretary of Brooklyn Catholic Action Council, March 31, 1934, Ross Papers.

12 *Memorandum in re Assemblyman Ross' Bill Allowing Desertion for Three Years as an Additional Ground for Divorce in This State*, April 9, 1934, pp. 2-3, 8.

13 *New York Times*, April 11, 1934.

14 157 *Ass. Journ.*, 1660, 2285 (April 10, 18, 1934).

15 Interview with Ross, Sept. 24, 1959.

16 *Idem*; see also *New York Times*, Oct. 16, 26, Nov. 8, 1934.

17 *New York Times*, Oct. 28, 1934.

18 *Ibid.*, Jan. 19, 1936; *Binghamton Press*, March 14, 1936.

19 *New York Times*, March 5, 1936.

20 *Albany Evening News*, March 14, 1936.

21 159 *Ass. Journ.*, 1416 (March 18, 1936).

22 159 *Senate Journ.*, 1555 (March 29, 1936). The division was strictly on party lines: all the affirmative votes were from Republicans; all the negative votes were from Democrats.

23 *New York Times*, April 1, 1936.

24 Author's interview with Miss Todd, Oct. 1, 1959.

25 159 *Ass. Journ.*, 2097 (March 31, 1936).

26 *New York Times*, April 5, 1936.

27 Author's interview with Miss Todd, Oct. 1, 1959.

28 Henry C. Greenberg, "New York's Perjury Mills," *American Magazine*, CXIV (Oct., 1947), 46.

29 Charles Desmond, "The Annulment Problem," *New York State Bar Association Bulletin*, XX (April, 1948), 61.

30 Richard H. Wels, "New York: The Poor Man's Reno," *Cornell Law Quarterly*, XXXV (Winter, 1950), 304.

31 *Ibid.*, p. 322; *New York Times*, Feb. 24, 1948.

32 *New York Times*, Aug. 25, 1948.

33 Wels, *Cornell Law Quart.*, XXXV, 321.

34 171 *Ass. Journ.*, 924 (Feb. 20, 1948).

35 *New York Journal-American*, Nov. 30, Dec. 1, 2, 3, 1948; *New York Times*, Jan. 25, 1949.

36 Citizens Committee for the Improvement of Family Laws, *Failure of a Law* (March 3, 1953), p. 3.

37 *New York Times*, Dec. 4, 1948.

38 *Ibid.*, Dec. 5, 1948.

39 *Ibid.*, Jan. 23, 1949.

40 *Ibid.*, Dec. 11, 1948.

41 *Ibid.*, Jan. 21, 1949.

42 *Ibid.*, Jan. 22, 1949.

43 *Ibid.*, Feb. 8, 1949; also mimeographed press release in Papers of Janet Hill Gordon, Norwich, N.Y., hereafter cited as Gordon Papers.

44 *New York Red Book*, 67th ed., 1958-1959, p. 191; *New York Times*, Jan. 25, 1956; author's interview with Mrs. Gordon, December 8, 1959.

45 *New York Times*, March 25, 1949.

46 Mrs. Gordon to Charles H. Doerr, March 28, 1950, Gordon Papers.

47 *New York Times*, Feb. 16, 1951.

48 *Failure of a Law*, p. 3.

49 *New York Journal-American*, Jan. 9, 12, 1951; *New York Times*, March 5, 1951.

50 *New York Herald Tribune*, March 8, 1951.

51 *Binghamton Press*, March 5, 1951.

52 *New York Times*, Jan. 5, 1932.

53 *Ibid.*, Jan. 30, Feb. 18, 1952.

54 *Ibid.*, Feb. 17, 1953.

55 William Philo Clark to R. G. Wels, Feb. 19, 1953, Gordon Papers.

56 Bishop Walter Higley to Mrs. Gordon, March 10, 1953, *ibid.*

57 Public Hearing of Assembly Ways and Means Committee on Gordon-Peterson Bills, held . . . March 5, 1953, mimeographed transcript in Gordon Papers, *passim.*

58 *Ibid.*, pp. 4-5.

59 *Ibid.*, p. 38.

60 Mrs. Gordon to David E. Lee, Sr., March 6, 1953, Gordon Papers.

61 *New York Times*, March 21, 1953.

62 176 *Ass. Journ.*, 2795 (March 21, 1953).

63 *New York Times*, Jan. 22, 1954.

64 Outline of Comments and Suggestions of Orrin Judd Esquire on December 2, 1954 . . . , mimeographed memorandum in Gordon Papers.

65 Public Hearing of Assembly Ways

and Means Committee on Gordon-Peterson Bill, held . . . February 24, 1955, mimeographed transcript in Gordon Papers, p. 3.

66 *Ibid.*, pp. 86-87.

67 *Ibid.*, p. 16.

68 *Ibid.*, p. 80.

69 *Ibid.*, p. 116.

70 Translation of article "Renew Battle Against New York Divorce Laws" by Jean Jaffe in *Day-Jewish Journal*, New York, Feb. 23, 1955, in Gordon Papers.

71 Author's interview with Mrs. Gordon, Dec. 8, 1959.

72 *New York Times*, March 30, 1955.

73 R. H. Wels to Mrs. Gordon, June 14, 1955, *ibid.*

74 178 *Laws of New York*, chap. 257 (April 13, 1955).

75 Mrs. Gordon to Oswald D. Heck, April 6, 1955, Gordon Papers.

76 Heck to Mrs. Gordon, April 12, 1955, *ibid.*

77 Mrs. Gordon to Rev. Leland B. Henry, Nov. 9, 1955, *ibid.*

78 Author's interview with Mrs. Gordon, Dec. 8, 1959.

79 *Report of the Joint Legislative Committee on Matrimonial and Family Laws, 1957* (New York Legislative Document, 1957, no. 32), pp. 63-64.

80 179 *Ass. Journ.*, 3288 (March 22, 1956); 179 *Senate Journ.*, 2464 (March 22, 1956).

81 *Report of the Joint Legislative Committee on Matrimonial and Family Laws, 1957*, pp. 73-103; *Report of the Joint Legislative Committee on Matrimonial and Family Laws, 1958* (New York Legislative Document, 1958, no. 26), pp. 106-128; *Report of the Joint Legislative Committee on Matrimonial and Family Laws, 1959* (New York Legislative Document, 1959, no. 44), pp. 10-11, 65-72.

82 182 *Laws of New York*, ch. 423 (April 15, 1959); 181 *Laws of New York*, ch. 804 (April 16, 1958).

83 181 *Ass. Journ.*, 2897 (March 18, 1958).

84 Author's interview with Mrs. Gordon, Dec. 8, 1959.

15. The Path of Reason

1 Paul H. Jacobson, *American Marriage and Divorce* (New York: Rinehart & Co., 1959), p. 90; *New York Times*, May 13, 1960.

2 *Statistical Abstract of the United States, 1960*, p. 69.

3 James P. Lichtenberger, *Divorce, A Social Interpretation* (New York: McGraw-Hill, 1931), p. 257.

4 Kimball Young, *Personality and Problems of Adjustment* (New York: F. S. Crofts & Co., 1940), pp. 544-546.

5 Meyer F. Nimkoff, *Marriage and the Family* (Boston: Houghton Mifflin, 1947), pp. 629-639.

6 *New York Times*, Jan. 9, 1931.

7 *Ibid.*, Nov. 16, 1958.

8 *Ibid.*, Oct. 15, 1916.

9 *Ibid.*, Sept. 20, 1931.

10 *Ibid.*, Sept. 30, 1931.

11 *Constitution and Canons for the Government of the Protestant Episcopal Church in the United States* (1946), pp. 45-47.

12 *New York Times*, May 25, 1932.

13 *Doctrines and Disciplines of the Methodist Church* (1960), p. 143.

14 *New York Times*, May 24, 1952.

15 *Ibid.*, April 25, 1959.

16 *Ibid.*, Oct. 17, 1956.

17 Katherine F. Gerould, "Divorce," *Atlantic Monthly*, CXXXII (Oct., 1923), 466.

18 Stephen Ewing, "The Mockery of American Divorce," *Harper's Magazine*, CLVII (July, 1928), 153-164.

19 Ben B. Lindsey and Wainwright Evans, *The Companionate Marriage* (New York: Boni & Liveright, 1927), *passim*.

20 Roswell H. Johnson, "Suppressed,

Delayed, Damaging and Avoided Divorces," *Law and Contemporary Problems*, XVIII (Winter, 1953), 72.

21 Morris L. Ernst and David Loth, *For Better or Worse: A New Approach to Marriage and Divorce* (New York: Harper & Bros., 1952), p. 244.

22 *U.S. Statutes at Large*, XXXI, 1345 (March 3, 1901).

23 Quoted in *Cong. Rec.*, LXXIX, 11588 (July 22, 1935).

24 *U.S. Statutes at Large*, XLIX, 539 (August 7, 1935).

25 *Cong. Rec.*, LXXIX, 11587 (July 22, 1935).

26 Edward McCrady, *The History of South Carolina under the Proprietary Government, 1670-1919* (New York: Macmillan, 1901), p. 11.

27 J. Nelson Frierson, "Divorce in South Carolina," *North Carolina Law Review*, IX (Feb., 1931), 265. See also *Brown v. Brown* (1949), 56 *Southeastern Reporter*, 2d Series, 332.

28 Jacobson, *American Marriage and Divorce*, p. 111.

29 Frierson, *North Carolina Law Review*, IX, 281.

30 *News & Courier* (Charleston), Oct. 19, 1948.

31 *Ibid.*, Oct. 20, 1948.

32 *Ibid.*, Oct. 19, 1948.

33 *Ibid.*, Oct. 26, 1948.

34 *Ibid.*, March 17, 1949.

35 *Ibid.*, April 1, 1949.

36 46 *South Carolina Statutes at Large*, p. 216 (April 15, 1949).

37 Maxine Boord Virtue, *Family Cases in Court: A Group of Four Court Studies Dealing with Judicial Administration* (Durham, N.C.: Duke University Press, 1956), p. 90.

38 Reginald Heber Smith, "Dishonest Divorce," *Atlantic Monthly*, CLXXX (Dec., 1947), 44.

39 *Reports of the American Bar Association*, LXXXI (1956), 326.

40 Paul W. Alexander, Introduction to Virtue, *Family Cases in Court*, pp. xxx-xxxi.

41 P. W. Alexander, "Is There a Divorce Evil?" *Ohio Magazine*, April, 1945, reprinted in *Cong. Rec.*, XCI, A 1222.

42 Charles L. Chute, "Divorce and the Family Court," *Law and Contemporary Problems*, XVIII (Winter, 1953), 51-54.

43 Virtue, *Family Cases in Court*, p. 176.

44 Chute, *Law and Contemporary Problems*, XVIII, 54.

45 *Ibid.*, XVIII, 55-65.

46 *Ibid.*, XVIII, 54-55.

47 "Gretchen," "I'll Take my Parents Separately," *Harper's Magazine* CLXXVI (April, 1938), 441-444.

48 *New York Times*, March 29, 1960.

49 Chute, *Law and Contemporary Problems*, XVIII, 58-59.

50 *New York Times*, Nov. 24, 1959.

51 Virtue, *Family Cases in Court*, pp. 8-9.

52 Julius H. Miner, "An Illinois Innovation: The 'Cooling-Off' Divorce Law," *American Bar Association Journal*, XLII (Dec., 1956), 1131-1134.

53 *New York Times*, July 2, 1960.

54 Virtue, *Family Cases in Court*, pp. 226-227.

55 *Ibid.*, p. xxxv.

56 Morris Ploscowe, *The Truth About Divorce* (New York: Hawthorn Books, Inc., 1955), p. 258.

Index

Adultery, 5-7, 10-12, 15, 24; in England, 31-33; in New York, 42, 192-194, 200, 211-212, 216-217; Protestant teachings, 138-140; in South Carolina, 234
Adversary proceedings, 236-239, 243
Advertising, divorce, 123, 128, 153-154, 163, 190; prohibited, 164, 200
Affiliated Young Democrats of New York State, 212-213
Affinity, 15, 20
Alabama, 8, 169-170, 226
Alcoholism, 4, 7, 54, 56, 59, 233; and woman's rights movement, 88; Owen on, 90; Capper Bill on, 150
Alexander, Judge Paul W., 238-240, 243
Alimony, 40, 184-185
Alterman, Meyer, 202
American Bar Association, 143, 148, 238
American Woman Suffrage Association, 100, 108
Andrews, Rev. J. L., 126
Andrews, Stephen Pearl, 83-86, 97, 113
Andrews, William T., 212
Andrews v. *Andrews*, 177-178
Annulment, 53, 141; in Roman Catholic Church, 14-21; in New York, 6-7, 66-67, 194-200, 219, 222
Anthony, Susan B., 87-88, 94; publishes *The Revolution*, 98-100; defends divorce, 108; and V. Woodhull, 112-113
Arizona, 226
Arkansas, 8, 166-167, 170
Association of the Bar of the City of New York, 212-214, 216, 218
Association for the Sanctity of Marriage, 149
Athens, 9

Atherton v. *Atherton*, 176
Augustine, Saint, 12-13
Austin, Bernard, 213

Baker, Conrad, 121
Balzer, Fred B., 157
Baptist Home Mission Society, 139
Barthou, Louis, 161
Beach, Lewis, 145
Beecher, Henry Ward, 98, 100; and McFarland-Richardson case, 101-102, 116; and Elizabeth Tilton, 110-115
Bell v. *Bell*, 176-177
Bible, 10-12, 82
Bishop, Joel Prentiss, 81-82
Black, Justice Hugo, 183
Blackwell, Rev. Antoinette, 93-94
Blackwell, Henry, 100, 104
Bloomer, Amelia, 88
Boardman, William W., 60
Borden v. *Fitch*, 174
Boyle, Emmet D., 156
Brown, Justice Henry, 179-180
Brown, Sadie, 4-8
Bucer, Martin, 27
Bullard, Laura Curtis, 106
Bullinger, Henry, 26
Bungard, Maurice C., 201-203
Burke, Judge Louis H., 241

California, 3, 122, 147, 165, 241-242
Calvin, John, 24
Cambridge Association, 37
Canon law, 14-22, 26
Capper, Arthur, 148-150
Carranza, Venustiano, 161
Carson, William E., 151
Cartwright, Thomas, 28
Cast, Jean, 44
Castle, Irene, 160
Catherine of Aragon, 25

263